The Visions Of

Therese Neumann

by

Johannes Steiner

INTRODUCTION

Father Joseph Naber was Therese Neumann's spiritual advisor from 1909 until her death on September 18, 1962. He has left us the following expression of his life-long attitude towards this famous mystic: "My point of view, from the beginning, was this: I must make a very careful observation of these extraordinary experiences to see if there is anything to offend against the teaching or morality of the church. If there is, then I must take a stand against them, mercilessly; if there is not, then I can let affairs take their own course, lest man, in what he falsely thinks to be his wisdom, should meddle dangerously in the plans of God."

Leopold Witt, pastor of the neighboring parish at München-reuth, who was the first to record a thorough account of the events that occurred during Konnersreuth's first years, as early as 1928, writes:

"The most incorrect procedure of all is to be found in the case of those learned scholars who approach Therese with a certain prejudice, already strongly formed, and think that Therese's case must be just exactly the same as that of many other people, whom they equally fail to comprehend. Genuine mysticism, however, must always be more or less original. This special garden of God, made up of human souls, must be just as varied as the gardens we see in the world of nature. Father Naber refuses to intrude upon the individual freedom of his spiritual charge; he does not want to stick her into a prearranged pigeonhole. But this spiritual charge of his herself would surely prove too difficult a substance for him to model simply at will.

'A man can only try to do what he thinks is right in his own conscience,' says Therese herself. 'And I neither could nor would want to be anything but what God wants me to be.' "

The learned historian and state archivist, Dr. Fritz Gerlich, at that time (1926) chief editor of the *Münchener Neueste Nachrichten*, was struck by a report written by a colleague, Erwein Baron of Aretin, in the *Einkehr*, a supplementary publication of his paper. He considered the report impossible, undeserving of belief, and prejudicial to the reputation of his paper. Accordingly, he decided to visit Konnersreuth himself and conduct a most thorough investigation into the possibility of any illusion or deception. The position taken by the article in question simply could not be brought into harmony with his own personal attitudes. In 1929 (vol. I, p. XIII) he writes the following:

"I came to Konnersreuth as a man of almost forty-five. Since my twenties I had been actively engaged in the intellectual life of my country, had formulated many thoughts about nature as it surrounds us and incorporates us into its scheme, about the meaning and purpose of our life, with the result that one must certainly admit that I had achieved a personal philosophy of life. In this philosophy of life many of the things that I experienced or investigated in the case of Therese Neumann had no place at all. This was only one more reason for making the most thorough and painstaking investigation possible. The following is my report of these investigations. How all this managed to harmonize with my philosophy of life is not the question here. The question here is simply the facts of Therese Neumann's life. Scientific investigation—so-called objective or neutral scientific investigation—has, in my opinion, to be guided by one single thought, and that goal, for any individual philosophy of life, is one and the same: 'Thou shalt not bear false witness.' "

His vigorous championing of the truth he came to know drove him to take up the battle against the growing power of the "Third Reich," and in this undertaking he was further encouraged by ecstatic pronouncements from Konnersreuth. He pursued this battle in the pages of his weekly journal, *Der gerade*

Weg (founded by him together with Erich, prince of Waldburg-Zeil), without sparing even himself.

On March 9, 1933, he was to pay for this courageous stand with "protective custody" and on June 30, 1934, he was murdered at Dachau. These are historical facts that our contemporary generation is too little acquainted with, and that is why the Author of this book, at one time Gerlich's colleague in the publication of his paper, is concerned to reestablish his memory and his honor.

This is the atmosphere of reverence and critical objectivity which the present Author has continued in the more than thirty years of his own close personal attachment with Therese Neumann and her family, and the members of the so-called "Konnersreuth Circle" to whom he has earlier devoted a book (published in 1946), *Gerlich-Naab, Prophetien wider das Dritte Reich*.[1]

And this is the very same spirit that animates this present book, which now follows, after an interval of ten years, his earlier effort, *Therese Neumann, A Portrait Based on Authentic Accounts, Journals, and Documents*.

The present book is not another biography: the reader must refer to the previous study, now translated into several languages. Its primary area of concern will be Therese's visions, even though some biographical data and explanations have also been inserted.

Today, ten years after Therese's death, when an author[2] and his interpreters and devotees who, like the author himself, have never been to Konnersreuth—even though, to judge from their ages, they had more than thirty years' opportunity to do so—while Therese Neumann was alive and thus cannot pretend to any eye-witness authority, when these people base their arguments on a few carefully selected archives and ancient, long since refuted attacks to represent Therese Neumann herself and her parents and immediate family and that pious soul Father Naber, now in his grave, as conspirators in deceit, then perhaps this present book of mine might make some contribution to the task of rediscovering the truth about Konnersreuth and gratefully accepting the grace of Therese's divine mission, given to her by God as a first line of defense against the insidious encroachments of a modern sense of rationalism that does away with all religion and forces us to sheer materialism. This, at least, is the opinion and heartfelt wish of the Author.

Waldsassen, Christmas 1972

Johannes Steiner

1. Gerlich–Naab: prophets against the Third Reich.

2. Haneur, Josef. **Konnersreuth als Testfall** (Konnersreuth as Test Case), Munich, 1972.

C O N T E N T S

The Visions Of
Therese Neumann

CHAPTER ONE

VISIONS

Visions are optical sense impressions which the visionary receives in an ecstatic state. Generally his physical eyes and bodily motions work as if he were attempting to adapt to the course of the activities he sees in the vision, although his optic nerves really could not relay to his brain anything other than the physical surroundings that actually confront his eyes. It is in this respect that the vision is distinguished from the dream, which is a visual sense perception occurring in a state of sleep, in which the physical eyes are, as a rule, closed, and thus cannot be directed to any object which might influence the optic nerves.

Hallucinations, which can evoke impressions that are just as vivid as visions, are distinguished, once again, from the vision in that they are artificially evoked, either by reason of a pathological physical disposition (such as a brain disease) or by the introduction of certain stimulants into the body—by either assimilation, inhalation, embrocation, or injection—whereas we can speak of a vision only when the phenomenon was present without any activity whatsoever on the part of the recipient and, by virtue of its character, can obviously be traced back to illumination. In many cases the vision is enhanced by audition (from the Latin word *audire*—to hear), a phenomenon in which the recipient also perceives sounds, especially words or conversations, which accompany the activities presented in his visions, whether it is he himself to whom words are addressed or whether he hears various persons in conversation with each other or speaking to a group. Frequently—and this is important for the case of Therese Neumann—the other senses also share in the visions, such as the sense of smell, when, for example, the ointment was poured out, or the sense of touch for warm and cold, when, for example, her visions led her into an area of bright sunshine, or also physical contact with the person seen in a vision (for example, in the case of Anthony of Padua, who, in his vision, was privileged to take the Christ child into his arms and feel his physical features and warmth.)

Visions are of different quality and different intensity. The present author has neither the intention nor the inclination to embark upon the current exchange of theoretical opinions regarding the various forms of visions. He will, instead, present simply an historical account of the concrete case of "visions at Konnersreuth," in an attempt to fit these events properly into the forms of this phenomenon thus far officially recognized or extend our knowledge in this domain by appealing to precedent. For the non-professional reader, however, a few basic principles of distinction must be presented.

Following the example of Augustine and Thomas Aquinas, Tanquerey divided visions into three groups:

1. Visiones Corporales, physical visions, in which the object of the vision is physically present and, as a rule, is visible to all present.

2. Visiones Imaginativae, imaginary visions—which is not to say "made up," or hallucinatory—in which the visionary sees or hears persons or activities. He can then pass on his mystic experience to others, either orally or in writing.

3. Visiones Intellectuales, purely intellectual visions, which provide spiritual insights or illuminate unclear areas of knowledge.

The whole problematic of distinctions, particularly in the first and second group, as well as the many perils of deception, physical disturbance, and the possibility of natural explanation, are lucidly discussed by Karl Rahner, with many enlightening examples, in his book, *Visions and Prophecies,* in which he arrives at the following conclusion: "As a matter of principle, very likely we do not have to contest the fact that there can be physical visions (even quite apart from the "apparitions" of the

Risen Christ to the Apostles); but, in individual cases, it is difficult to actually document such an occurrence. In general, in the
case of genuine visions, we are dealing with imaginary visions. . . ."

On the other hand, we must also consider the question of
whether a vision of Christ, which does not involve a new appearance of Christ upon earth, is, on the basis of this reasoning
alone, to be considered simply as an imaginary vision. It would
seem that the above-mentioned experience of St. Anthony would
contradict this. It is recorded also of Elizabeth of Schönau, that
she claimed to be able to see the reality itself in her visions. In
the case of Therese Neumann—and we shall experience this in
the description of the individual visions—she can personally "see
the Savior quite well" and, in addition, receives the stigmata.
Moreover, by personal contact with the Blessed Virgin during a
vision (the Assumption of the Blessed Virgin) she was suddenly
completely healed of the consequences of a stroke. Are these
physical or imaginary visions?

In the Sacred Scriptures of the Old Testament there are
many accounts of visions. Beginning with the Books of Moses (the
burning bush out of which God proclaims his name), and running through the prophets up to John the Baptist, the chain of
visions extends into the New Testament with the apparition of
the Angel Gabriel at the Annunciation of the Virgin Mary
(both audition and confirmation of the genuinity of his words by
his reference to Elizabeth), from the good news proclaimed to
the shepherds down to the conversion of St. Paul, which, by
virtue of the combination of his vision (which had involved all
his senses) with that of Ananias (Ac 9), became one of the most
important experiences of the early Church, second only to the
miracle of Pentecost.

Even the winning of the pagans for Christianity was made
possible only through the cooperative activity, so movingly described in the Book of Acts, of the visions enjoyed by the god-
fearing pagan Cornelius and Peter, the prince of the Apostles.
Peter appeals to this event in the Apostolic Council when the
question arises as to whether the pagans who are to be received
into the Christian community must first be submitted to the

Jewish ritual of circumcision, and opposes the position taken by some Pharisees who had embraced the Faith by observing that God himself has made no distinction between us and them (Ac 15). Finally, the Holy Scripture concludes with the magnificent visions of the Apocalypse of St. John. The Christian centuries that followed display numerous accounts of visions enjoyed by a number of mystics.

Karl Rahner has this point to make: "Since such phenomena occurred at the establishment of the revealed religion of both the Old Testament and the Christian era, then we cannot a priori and on principle contest the possibility of their occurrence in the post-Christian era as well. Since the final and definitive revelation and self-disclosure of God occurs in the person of Christ, such post-Christian revelations of God must have— theologically if not also psychologically—an essentially different character; but that is no grounds for maintaining that such revelations on the part of God can no longer occur at all. They make their appearance even in the Church of the Apostolic era where they are considered to be essentially bound up with the abiding prerogative of the Church, the possession of the Spirit. . . ."

Insofar as these visions and auditions, operating on what is obviously a supernatural level, afford the recipient with religious thoughts or explanations that go beyond the common fund of revelation set down in Sacred Scripture, they are called "private revelations."

The Church is particularly cautious and deliberate in judging these visions and auditions, particularly because so many "apparitions" can occur in circumstances where there is no question of anything supernatural. We have already referred to the possibility of intoxication by narcosis, or we might think of persons with an extremely labile psychic equilibrium as ideal sources for accounts of visions or prophecies they have received. The genuine vision, on the other hand, is completely independent of the will and thus certainly the manipulation of the recipient, and from any suggestion arising from his surroundings. It begins, generally, quite without warning, with a so-called rapture, that is, a sudden ecstatic seizure, in the midst of work or conversation with someone about an entirely different matter. The immediate result is a complete block of all ability to observe what was going on all about, or to respond to any conversation or questioning; the receptivity of the visionary is concentrated solely on the impressions which form the vision.

Because of the great difficulty of distinguishing genuine from alleged or even deliberately counterfeit visions, the Church insists on examining first of all whether the visionary maintains a high ethical level of conduct, far surpassing the average, and has distinguished himself by a superior, heroic degree in the imitation of Christ. It also determines as precisely as possible whether there is visible evidence substantiating the accounts of third parties with respect to other extraordinary gifts enjoyed by the visionary which, as a rule, occur together with the gift of visions. This testimony must be based not on one individual, but rather a number of trustworthy persons. These special gifts of faith, or gifts of the Holy Spirit, called charismata or charismatic gifts, from the Greek, include the following, not all of which generally occur in one and the same case:

1. Stigmatization: The imprint of the wounds of Christ, in temporary or permanent form, as incurable and deeply set wounds, generally on the hands and feet and in the region of the heart.

2. Lack of Nutrition: Freedom from the normal physical need for food and drink, without damage to the maintenance of life, for a long period of time.

3. Hierognosis: The mystic recognizes or senses whether relics placed before him are genuine or false, whether a person or object has received a consecration, whether someone whom he cannot see is giving him a blessing or not.

4. Kardiognosis: The mystic is able to penetrate the inner conscience of the person who is speaking or writing to him. He knows their thoughts and intentions before they are put into words.

5. *Bilocation*: While the mystic remains at one specific place, he appears to a person or an entire group at a different location, often far away.

6. *Elevation, also called Levitation*: The mystic is released from the power of gravity, in prayer or in vision or in spiritual conversations, and hovers freely above the floor in a visionary ecstatic state.

7. *Mystical Experiences* with the Eucharist, with angels, with the Poor Souls.

Many of these charismata will be encountered by the reader if he finds opportunity to examine the life stories of famous mystics. I shall name only a few: Polycarp of Smyrna, Benedict of Nurtia, Francis of Assisi, Hildegard of Bingen, Gertrude the Great, Margaret Ebner (Maria-Medigen), Angela of Foligno, Catherine of Siena, Theresa of Avila, John of the Cross, Nicolas of Flue, Marguerite Marie Alacoque, Anna Maria Lindmayr (Munich), Anna Katherina Emmerich, Therese of Lisieux, Gemma Galgani of Lucca, Anna Schäfer (Mindelstetten), Jean Vianney of Ars, Padre Pio (Giovanni Rotondo).

One of the basic sources for this material is and continues to be the standard work by Joseph von Görres, *Die Christliche Mystik* (Regensburg, 1837). Another fundamental text, based upon the more recent investigation of our own era, is the book by Ernest Benz, *Die Vision Erfahrungsformen und Bilderwelt,* (Stuttgart, 1969). The beauty of his presentation prompts me to cite the following paragraph from Walter Nigg, *Grosse Heilige,* (Zurich, 1952), p. 255: "John of the Cross was once conversing with Theresa of Jesus on the subject of the Trinity. In the midst of this conversation he felt as though his soul were being overpowered by a divine rapture. He quickly tried to hold himself tightly in his chair, but the power of the ecstasy was too strong and he began to hover in the air, together with his chair. At the same time, Theresa was seized by the ecstasy and began to hover in the air while kneeling inside the grating. A nun who was passing by witnessed the entire incident, which can only be described as the most extraordinary encounter between two people in the whole of Christian literature. Such a fantastic story makes us automatically shake our heads in disbelief: it demands too much of the modern spectator. What kind of a man was that. . . ?"

Therese Neumann is only one in a long series of Christian mystics. She was born in Konnersreuth, on the night of Good Friday, 1898, the first of eleven children in the family of the tailor Ferdinand Neumann and his wife Anna. She grew up in the most impoverished circumstances and, although she would have preferred to be a missionary sister, she was forced to take employment as a children's maidservant after the beginnings of the First World War. While helping to put out a fire in March, 1918, she had a serious accident; she dislocated her spine. This resulted in an impaired sense of balance, lameness, and, one year after the accident, total blindness. All this she bore with the greatest patience—as did her parents—and it contributed to her interior maturity.

From her father, when he returned from the war, she had received a small picture of the Carmelite Therese of the Child Jesus, and soon developed great sympathy and veneration for this remarkable soul. On April 29, 1923, the day on which the Little Flower was beatified, she was suddenly healed of her blindness. On the feast of the Saint's canonization, two years later, May 17, 1925, during the course of a vision, she was also suddenly healed of her lameness. On March 4, 1926, the visions of the Passion began, in the course of which she received the wounds of Christ: first the stigma of the wound in the heart, which she kept secret, and then, on the next two Fridays, stigmata in the hands and feet as well. These visions continued even after Lent.

Beginning with the vision of Mt. Tabor (Feast of the Transfiguration of Christ, August 6, 1926), we can date the beginning of her period without nourishment, which lasted until the end of her life, on September 18, 1962. There are dozens of depositions, taken under oath, and kept in Regensburg, to substantiate these facts. In addition to the audio-visions, which she experienced, in which the senses of smell and touch were also involved, Therese also experienced many of the above-mentioned physical experiences of which those connected with the Eucharist are the most fundamental for her whole story, since it was only through her daily reception of Holy Communion, a practice which she cultivated throughout her entire life, that her vital powers were maintained. This short description of her life and activity must suffice.

The purpose of this book is to describe her visions. Still, a proper understanding of these phenomena and visions requires a brief word or two on the subject of Therese Neumann's states of consciousness.

Her general state was that of any intelligent person, specifically characterized, in her case, by a religious attitude that had become a customary practice since early youth, pious in the good sense, not entirely free of human weaknesses—which she continually fought against—particularly a somewhat abrupt manner which frequently offended especially insistent visitors, but which was compensated for, on the other hand, by a great sense of compassion and willingness to be of help wherever she saw real need. The ecstatic state had various forms:

1. The state of visionary contemplation, which always began as rapture, coincides with what has been described above in general terms (complete spiritual and mental detachment from the actual place and location, and insensitivity to everything happening all around).

2. In the state of "elevated calm," which occurred after almost every reception of Holy Communion, but also appeared between the visions of suffering, to give her strength to endure she would get the impression that she was already joined to Christ in full beatitude. In this state it was possible to speak with her and receive answers to questions. Father Naber, the local pastor, often asked her questions designed to enlarge upon what she had seen in her visions, and which she could not possibly have been able to answer in a normal state from her own knowledge. We shall encounter this very frequently.

3. The state of "prayer of quiet," a state in which the soul, united with God, loses all conception of time. This state was manifest during the octave of Christmas and Easter, during Mass, from the Consecration to the Communion. During this time Therese had a vision of the Savior as a small child or as the risen Christ, and during these blessed visions she would remain almost motionless at her prie-dieu, her eyes closed.

4. The state of "rapture" over the grandeur and power of God would come over her from time to time whenever she saw any particularly overpowering beauty of nature, for example, a particularly magnificent sunset, or when she would listen to a sermon on the love and goodness of Our Savior. In this state she would sit or stand quietly, smiling happily, her hands crossed over her breast. On such occasions, as Father Naber reports, she would say that she "could no longer think, she could only feel the greatness and power of God."

One very special, we might say "half-ecstatic" state, but one very important for the description of our visions, was that of "childlike prepossession," which occurred during or between visions. In this state she could be asked about the content and details of what she saw, whereas in her normal state she did not like to discuss these matters. In this state, however, her normal concepts and ideas would fail her. She would have to grope for expressions and would then give very telling characterizations, describing the persons she had seen in her visions on the basis of their activities and conduct. She would recognize the same persons and places in her later, different visions, and give the same characterizations which she had first used to describe them. All of the visions dealt with here are based on her descriptions given during this state, only occasionally enlarged upon by questions asked in her state of elevated calm, or in her normal state.

As a matter of procedure, we must still raise the question of the possibility of a representation of the past in visions. This reproduction of what has gone before is possible only within a theistic frame of reference. For atheistic materialism, whose whole point must necessarily be to explain every mystical phenomenon in a natural way and exclude the possibility of every miracle in order to demonstrate its basic justification, there can be no objective support from any factual certitude. If a person maintained that thought is formed by the spiral revolutions of the brain atoms, instead of accepting the fact that, conversely, it is rather thought that determines the brain cells to a corresponding action, it is "unthinkable" to reproduce past events without any stimulus from a higher being, that is, without any illumination, unless we are simply to revel in a world of fantasy or to retrieve accumulated data from the "computer" brain.

The man who is theologically aware, however, comes to this conclusion: the past exists only for our fragmented earthly existence, in which time plays a role as a fourth dimension. In the great breadth of the universe, on the other hand, everything is hovering somewhere in space as a living present. Stars which are two thousand light years distant from us are still well within the outer confines of the cosmos. Since light from them requires two thousand years to reach us, we see, insofar as we can see or distinguish anything with instruments that are admittedly weak with reference to such immense distances, only the processes that have gone on there some two thousand years ago. And from the vantage point of those stars, events that have transpired two thousand years ago on earth would still be visible as present. For God, who in his infinite perfection or perfect infinity is subject neither to temporal nor spatial boundaries or limits, and whose perceptual ability requires the medium of no instrumentation, in order to grasp everything perfectly, there is certainly not the least difficulty in observing this past, this today, as present time. Thomas Aquinas teaches that God does not live in any world of time and that, accordingly, all of human history and, moreover, the history of the entire universe is seen by him as a present phenomenon. Everything that we regard as past or future he sees as present (I 14, 13).

Let us now attempt to introduce this rather formidable concept into terms of human capacity and experience. Let us suppose that God were occupying a position in the cosmos which was some one hundred light years distant from us—and this he could easily do without any sacrifice of time. From there he would see, with the eyes of his spirit that require the aid of no instrumentation, the Franco-Prussian War, occurring as a present reality.

If he then, "in the next moment," moved to a star that was one thousand light years distant, he "sees" the beginning of the Holy Roman Empire of the German Nation, under Emperor Otto the Great, and permits the visionary Roswitta of Gandersheim some glimpses of the past and future.

And if, finally, he removed himself to a distance of two thousand light years, he would be seeing the death and Resurrection of his Incarnate Son and, going back even further in time, the hour of his birth at Bethlehem. Now, since for God everything exists in the present, and incomprehensibly more perfect than we could possibly understand, that is, God sees everything all at once and without any circumscription in space or time, he can, if he so desires, always reproduce these events by spiritually transferring them through the medium of visions to chosen creatures for the edification of their fellow men. It depends upon the individual capacity of the "seer" to grasp the substance of his vision, to organize, appreciate, and reproduce it for others.

This line of thought, of course, gives only a vague and approximate explanation of God's ability to review the whole past. Our mental capacity and our powers of imagination are insufficient, and the lack of measurable quantities prevents us from explaining God's knowledge of the whole future. In this respect, it is only the theological concept of the infinite perfection of God that can save us. God, an eternal and infinite spiritual being, for whom space and time do not exist, knows, on the basis of this infinite and unbounded perfection, the past as well as the future; for, in his plan of creation, when he spoke his initial *fiat,* he saw everything in advance, from the beginning to the end of time.

Thomas Aquinas formulates this capacity of God's Knowledge in the following words: *"In seipsis quidem futura cognosci non possunt nisi a Deo, cui etiam sunt praesentia, dum in cursu rerum sunt futura, inquantum eius aeternus intuitus simul fertur supra totum temporis cursum* (I 86, 4). "In itself the future (for creatures) is not knowable, but only for God, for whom everything which, in the course of history, is still future already exists as present, because his eternal intelligence extends, at one and the same time, over the entire course of time."

Drawing upon this knowledge, God does, from time to time, allow one or another of his favorite souls to participate in visions, always in a carefully circumscribed compass, and, in order not to encroach too strongly upon the individual freedom of decision that is an essential part of his rational creatures, in visions that are not particularly clear. He even gives enlightenment in circumstances in which the details announced never actually take place, because they were only meant to stimulate a change of heart. For example, the prophet Jonas, who feels he has made a fool of himself since although God had informed the prophet of his firm resolution to destroy the city of Nineveh, he did not execute this threat because of the conversion and repentance of its inhabitants. In our own days we might think of the threats and warnings of Fatima.

The conclusion from this attempt to make the eternal present of God, his "I am," easier to understand must not be the supposition that the Author explains historical visions as some sort of retrogression into past time on the part of the visionary. Quite the contrary, he sees them as the seer's being intimately bound up into the timeless eternity of God. The seer enjoys the privilege of being elevated into the near vicinity of God himself.

These remarks are not meant to conclude anything with respect to the reliability or unreliability of visions, or with respect to their historical fidelity or fulness. For, if we begin to examine the visionary reproduction of certain definite themes, we are immediately struck by the fact that visions on the same theme do not always agree with each other in every detail, in the case of one mystic to another. We might then be too readily inclined either to reject visions out of hand as unreliable proof of any historical event or to credit one visionary with historical reliability on the basis of some grounds or other that would seem to justify his superiority, and to reject the others. Neither of these reactions is proper. A more profound examination would prompt us to take into account a variety of factors regarding one and the same theme in comparing the different visions, factors which would suggest caution indeed, but certainly not rejection.

The first and most important factor is this: in visions God is not bound to reproduce the historical course of events exactly, in full detail. In most cases, he grants these visions only for the personal edification of the visionary, although he may indeed have the ulterior motive of strengthening and deepening the faith of others as well. He does not let these visions range very far beyond the seer's capacity or the current state of investigation. Accordingly, the fact that legendary events are frequently the subject of visions should not lead us to the immediate conclusion that they are not of divine origin. Stigmatization, as it occurs in different subjects, also displays remarkable differences in form and areas of the body affected.

The second factor is a scholastic principle: everything that comes from God is received by the seer or the recipient of the inspiration *"per modum recipientis"* (with the modality of the receiver) and reproduced in proportion to his kind and capacity for expression. It is also conceivable that various elements of consciousness which have been recorded in the memory of the recipient or which perhaps are a residue from an inherited fund of concepts can also blend together with what has been received in the vision. Investigation in the realm of so-called depth-psychology is of considerable importance here.

The perceptions received in the vision thus pass through what we might describe as a subjective sieve. We can understand this easiest perhaps by thinking of the great discrepancy that often exists between the testimony of two different eye-witnesses to one and the same event, for example, an automobile accident. The descriptions are often quite different in many details. These discrepancies are to be explained not only in terms of the different positions occupied by the various witnesses, but even more so by the individual witnesses' abilities to receive and reproduce impressions, even though there is absolutely no doubt with respect to their earnest desire to tell the truth.

A third factor, and one which frequently carries considerable weight, is the fact that the narrator of the vision does not hold himself to a complete factual reproduction of what he has seen, either because of his carelessness, or because of his inability, or by reason of the fact that he has had opportunity to record what he has seen and heard only some time after the vision and thus introduces slight changes of fact into his account. For Fritz Gerlich, for example, it was a matter of some concern that the visions of Anna Katherina Emmerich as described by Brentano did not agree with those of Therese Neumann in many points. Brentano was a poet and his language and form of expression clearly reveal the fact that many of his ideas were presented subjectively and put into poetic form for the edification of his readers.

Gerlich was intensively occupied with the prospect of a synthesis between Emmerich and Konnersreuth and was always faced with the questions of whether a given vision is the work of Anna Katherina Emmerich or—in the very best sense of the word—ornamental detail from Brentano. This concern of his succeeded in sharpening a sense of historical precision for those of us who were then his young collaborators. With a sense of responsibility developed through these experiences and study, I have made every effort to achieve the greatest possible fidelity to the original and respect for the truth in my description of the visions that follow, and in my reproduction of any other accounts. Thus I have excluded at least the third of the above-mentioned factors, to the best of my ability.

One further remark in the special case of Therese Neumann: Therese Neumann, a simple peasant girl, had not read very much at the time her visions first commenced. From the Stations of the Cross in the parish church she had a completely different conception of the surroundings, clothing, and conduct of the persons involved in each scene, than what she later recounted in the description of her visions. These descriptions were, insofar as they could objectively be controlled, for example, in the scenes in Jerusalem, in the clothing of that era, in household furnishings, etc., so striking as to introduce a correspondingly higher degree of probability into her description of the course of events itself.

There is the added consideration that Therese had these visions not only once, but, as mentioned above, every year, and the vision of the Passion almost every week, and that always, throughout her entire life, the course of action was the same. After having just called attention to certain factors of unreliability in the case of visions, we might point to these facts in the special case of Therese Neumann as justifying our presupposition of the historical fidelity of many of her visions. If exegetical investigation, on one point or another, should come to some certain knowledge which is different, the deviations from the truth are not owing to the fault of the Author who has made it a matter of conscience to reproduce everything precisely as it occurs in his sources.

Dr. Carl Sträter, S.J., the Bishop's representative for the investigation of Therese Neumann's life, describes her situation as follows: "Since God in his eternity sees all that happens as present, we cannot consider it impossible for God to allow a human being to share in this divine knowledge in some special way, for example, by allowing this person to have a vision of the sufferings of Christ in their actuality, and not simply in pictures, and to experience them along with Christ. I consider the visions of Therese Neumann as essentially supernatural and, accordingly, I am of the opinion that it is not possible to offer any positive proof of the possibility of such a vision; it is sufficient to point up the fact that no one can demonstrate the impossibility.

"But since Therese, at the time she began to enjoy these visions, had already accumulated a fund of thoughts, representations, and impressions, it is certainly very possible that these subjective elements have a role to play in the visions themselves. Thus it is not always possible to separate the subjective elements easily from the objective; but neither is this necessary. Gifts of grace like this are never given simply to provoke historical research.

"We might further ask whether these considerations might serve as explanation of the fact that some visions make a much more strongly objective impression than others. Perhaps we might answer that the subjective elements recede into the background in proportion as the divine activity is stronger. And the divine influence was at its strongest when Resl was taken over wholly into the central mystery of our redemption, the Passion of Christ."

CHAPTER TWO

SOURCES

Accuracy and reliability, both of which are primary objectives of this book, require that sources be identified for every vision. In order to reduce the compass of this documentation, some form of abbreviation must be employed. The simple key to this system is explained below.

1. The original and primary source of every text is Therese Neumann herself, whose descriptions, in a state of elevated calm, in a state of prepossession, or in her ordinary waking state, have been faithfully recorded and preserved. In addition to all the Konnersreuth literature and the descriptions recorded in journals, there is a whole series of conversations and interrogations recorded immediately after the visions by her brother, Ferdinand Neumann, on wax matrices and later recorded onto tape. Since the content of all these visions goes back directly to the accounts of Therese Neumann herself, there is no need to list her as the source of each individual vision. I have considered it essential to my research to determine that everything recorded in these sources represents the immediate description of Therese herself, and have, as a matter of principle, rigidly excluded all accounts given by a third party.

2. After Therese herself, the most important source is her confessor, Father Naber, who kept a copy of the content of her visions for the years 1928-1932, as described to him upon questioning, in two journals. He graciously made them available to the Author in October, 1962, with permission to make photocopies. Before his death they were returned to him. They have as yet not been published, although the Author has provided

them with page numbers. They are, accordingly, referred to in visions that follow as N 1 (p. 1), N 2 etc. Before this time, Father Naber had recorded the visions on individual sheets of paper and these were presumably destroyed in the fire that occurred at the shelling of Konnersreuth towards the end of the war. Dr. Gerlich had, however, opportunity to examine them and use them in his biography, so that their content has survived.

3. As we have frequently mentioned, the most important source prior to 1929 is the two-volume work of Dr. Fritz Gerlich, *Die Stigmatisierte Therese Neumann von Konnersreuth,* published by Kösel in Munich. Gerlich had reserved the copyright to this book for himself, and, after the war, when the original publisher declared that he did not intend to republish the book, the copyright was made over to the Author by Mrs. Sophie Gerlich. The present Author is thus in a position to quote from the book without reservation. The abbreviation is G 1 and G 2.

4. Somewhat earlier, Angerer in Waldsassen published the work of Leopold Witt, also in parts: *Konnersreuth im Lichte der Religion und Wisenschaft.* This book too contains many accounts of the visions. As a rule, however, the descriptions are only very general. Where there are details, the details have been carefully examined by this Author to determine whether or not they are in harmony with the above-mentioned sources. The letter W is used as reference to the Witt document (W 1, W 2).

5. Dr. Franz X. Mayr, professor of chemistry, biology, and geology at the philosophical and theological high school at Eichstätt, also witnessed a series of visions, and left a written record of the events. He has graciously allowed the Author the use of this document for his book. This record contains accounts of some visions that are not to be found either in Naber or in Gerlich. When descriptions from this record are used or when they served to complete and expand descriptions from other books, the name Mayr is used as documentation.

6. For the period after 1930, Anni Spiegl published a very personal little book, in 1963, *Leben und Sterben der Therese Neumann von Konnersreuth.* This book contains accounts of

visions which enlarge upon many details or call attention to points which had been passed over without sufficient notice.

7. Every other description of the visions which is to be found in the rich Konnersreuth literature is, with very few exceptions, third-hand, that is, derived from one of the above sources and thus not an original source of its own. Among the exceptions I would include—expressly restricted to the realm of visions—those people who witnessed Therese's visions in Konnersreuth themselves and left some kind of record behind. These would include Erwein von Aretin, Munich; Cardinal Kaspar, Prague; Chaplain Fahsel, Berlin; Dr. (med.) Hynek, Prague; P. Odo Staudinger, Salzburg; Archbishop Teodorowicz, Lemberg; Archbishop Waitz, Salzburg. When quotations are made from these sources, they are documented by reference to the author's full name, as in sources 5 and 6.

8. An outstanding source of the very first caliber, as we have already mentioned above, are the conversations recorded by Ferdinand Neumann immediately after the visions. These conversations generally took place between Therese Neumann and Father Naber, occasionally including other persons who happened to be present. The conversations established the content and detail of the visions with painstaking exactitude. It was my duty as author to seize upon each important new fact that could be derived from these often hour-long interrogations which delved into every conceivable point of interest. Resl herself always wanted to speak only of the Savior and the persons standing in his immediate company, regarding everything else as purely secondary. My task was made all the more difficult by the fact that these conversations were recorded on easily damaged wax discs with a sadly insufficient recording mechanism. The mechanical noises of the machine as it operated frequently distort or drown out the spoken words. Further difficulty arises from the fact that the conversations were conducted in the Egerländer dialect, a particularly uncouth variant of the Oberpalzer dialect, and are thus practically incomprehensible for anyone not native to the dialect. Since I grew up in that part of the Oberpfalz, where it begins to mingle with Upper and Lower

Bavaria, this fact did not present any particular difficulties for me. In those instances in which the conversations recorded originally on wax discs and later rerecorded on tapes have been used in the account, they are referred to by the word *tape*.

9. In the first years of my involvement with Konnersreuth I myself witnessed a considerable number of Therese's visions and made careful records of them or, where the records were already available in Gerlich, have enlarged upon them with marginal notes immediately after seeing them or after conversing about them with Therese Neumann. In such cases the abbreviation is the letter A—Author.

10. Christian dogma has its roots in Sacred Scripture. All later pronouncements, if they are to bear the stamp of divinity and be regarded as revelation, must be in perfect harmony with Scripture. On this ground I would not only recommend, but regard it as absolutely essential, for the appreciation of this book, that the reader have available a good copy of the New Testament and that he consult the corresponding sections for every vision discussed. The appropriate citation from Scripture is always given at the beginning of each vision. Only thus will he be in a position to really understand and appreciate the references to conversations taking place between the persons in the vision, or the changing expressions and actions of the visionary herself.

In proofreading the manuscript for factual accuracy, I was greatly helped by several above-mentioned fellow-witnesses of many visions, Msgr. Franz X. Mayr, Miss Anni Spiegl, and Therese's brother, Ferdinand Neumann, to whom I am once again indebted for a large portion of the material of this book. I should like to express the most heartfelt gratitude to Professor Carl Sträter, S.J. and Father Ulrich Veh, O.F.M. Cap. for their work in proofreading the entire text, word by word, together with the corrections.

CHAPTER THREE

VISIONS OF CHILDHOOD, HEALING, AND STIGMATIZATION

The First Vision

Therese experienced her first vision already as a child, without realizing that this was an extraordinary event. She told no one in her family about the vision, and none of her biographers—although perhaps she mentioned it once to Father Naber apropos of a vision of purgatory, and he kept it silent. Perhaps the vision never would have come to light, except for the fact that she was asked to give an account of her entire life by the Church authorities, under oath. The story behind the vision is as follows. Upon the request of the Bishop's office at Regensburg in July, 1927, Therese submitted to fifteen days of intensive physical observation on the subject of her lack of nourishment-intake. She lay under strict observation, day and night. On this occasion the stigmata were also examined and even photographed. A further examination and evaluation by the Church authorities was announced, but never took place.

Cardinal Faulhaber, when I visited him in 1949 and brought up the subject of Konnersreuth (cf. Steiner, *Therese Neumann*, p. 67), expressed his concern that one day historians would find fault with the Bavarian Bishop's office for not having sufficiently clarified the question of Konnersreuth. He admitted being concerned. As we can now see from the acta, however, this fear was partially ungrounded. In Eichstätt, which had become Therese Neumann's second home, two bishops had prudently undertaken a full ecclesiastical investigation.

In 1942 Bishop Michael Rackl empowered a commission to record a deposition, taken under oath, from Ottilie Neumann, who was then employed as housekeeper for Professor F. X. Wutz, on the subject of events she had witnessed and experienced in the company of her sister Therese. The commission drew up an official protocol, which is still on record. And in January, 1953, when Therese Neumann was once again in Eichstätt for a lengthy Christmas visit, the Bishop Joseph Schröffer, after first advising Therese Neumann, empowered a commission of two university professors (members of a religious congregation) to invite her to an official deposition under strict oath.

The two professors first administered to each other the official canonical form of the oath for a faithful and conscientious execution of their mandate and then heard Therese Neumann's oath in the usual form for ecclesiastical depositions, before a crucifix and two lighted candles, promising to give truthful answers to the questions that would be put to her. I mention these details in order to demonstrate the great earnestness of the full proceedings and the significance with which we must thus regard any statements made by such a strongly believing and religious person as Therese Neumann.

Among the questions, not previously known to Therese, which were put to her under oath is one which led to her revelation of the first vision she had ever experienced. The following is the exact transcript of the question and answer insofar as the vision is concerned.

Question: Did you experience any extraordinary apparitions already in your youth? What kind?

Answer: "At my First Communion, when the priest (Father Ebel) was distributing the Sacred Host to me, I saw not the Host, not the priest, but the glorified child Jesus; I saw this, however, at that time, not as something extraordinary; I thought that this was what everyone experienced on this occasion. Father Ebel, who had noted my behavior during Holy Communion, interpreted this as a distraction on my part and he remonstrated me the following day and punished me before all the children. Since my First Communion (spring, 1909), I experienced a growing love for the Savior in the Blessed Sacrament and a desire for frequent Communion.

"Since this desire, in keeping with the rather strict practice of those days, could not be satisfied—Father Ebel allowed us children to receive Communion only four times a year—we children would only visit Our Savior in the Blessed Sacrament, and practice spiritual communion. On the occasion of such visits when I was kneeling at the communion rail, two or three times, or perhaps more often, it happened that the Sacred Host would float out of the tabernacle over to me and, when I opened my mouth, I could feel and taste it lying on my tongue, and I would swallow the sacred species. Once a girlhood friend of mine, Therese Döhla, was witness to the entire procedure; I described the entire thing to her when she asked me about it. She wondered why she did not have the same experience. When in September, 1909, Father Naber became Pastor, we children were allowed to receive Communion more often. I note that I observed the above-mentioned events with a clear and sober mind."

This is the first part of Therese's answer to the question stated above. She goes on to recount a further experience in her early years which left a strong impression on her. It does not indeed fall into the realm of visions, but it does recall experiences with animals such as are well known in the life of the saints, for instance, St. Francis or St. Anthony. The story should not be kept from the reader. Therese recounts this second remarkable experience of her childhood.

"Another remarkable experience happened to me during my seventh year in school, when I was keeping the cattle at Fockenfeld's for hire. During the noon period while I was working, I was praying the rosary, when one of the workmen attacked me. He gagged me with his filthy handkerchief so that I almost threw up, tied my hands with his apronstring, and, while I lay helpless on the ground, had already managed to pull up my skirt. At this very moment the bull from the herd came charging up and chased the man away with his horns. The bull came back to me, but, despite my fear, did me no harm. He simply waited until I had laboriously freed myself from my bonds and the gag, and then lowered his head to the ground and, when I trembling laid hold of his horn, gently pulled me up to a standing position; then he allowed me to lean against him until I had recovered from my terrible ordeal."

Originally I had not included the account of this experience in the manuscript of my book, because Therese begged me, at the conclusion of my three days recording with her, not to include anything that "would be ticklish or painful or anything that could make anyone ashamed." Meantime, however, another author (Hanauer, p. 374) recorded this moving experience of Therese's childhood. This author, however, had, as I have already pointed out, no experience in Konnersreuth, but prefers to believe that everything that happened there is simply deception and accuses all the eyewitnesses and authors of written records, insofar as they reach any positive conclusions, of being guilty of insufficient powers of observation and lack of critical judgment, so that 1 have felt obligated to make public the word-for-word description of the events taken from the official protocol.

The Light Visions at Therese's Cure

Therese Neumann, born on Good Friday, 1898, just prior to the midnight before Holy Saturday, was a strong and healthy peasant child in her youth. As she grew up she was hired out in order to assist in the support of the twelve persons, parents and children, in the family of the not well-to-do tailor. This was the era of the First World War. There was a shortage of men, and she had to help with the heavy field work. On March 10, 1918, a fire broke out in the neighborhood. Therese was brought in to help with the job of putting the fire out. Standing on a bale of hay, it was her duty to take the buckets of water that were brought to her and swing them up sideways over her head through an opening onto the barn floor. After two hours of this very strenuous activity she suddenly felt a stabbing sensation in her backbone. The bucket fell from her hand and one foot lost its power to support her. Subsequent examination revealed that she had wrenched the second and third lumbar vertebrae which enclose the central nerve fiber of the backbone, the cauda. As a result of this impairment of her equilibrium, she experienced several falls in the weeks that followed, and eventually became bed-ridden.

In March, 1919, she also became blind. Fully reconciled to her own misfortune, she was willing to accept the sufferings thus thrust upon her; but she was very disturbed by the fact that instead of helping her parents she had now become a further claim upon their care. This condition lasted for four years. Suddenly everything changed. It is at this point that her visions begin. On the occasion of the initial cure, the mystical power did not as yet manifest itself as an apparition; only on the basis of the date is it possible to realize the connection. Still, it is important to the description of this sudden cure of Therese's blindness. It is Sunday, April 29, 1923.

Blindness Cured

Gerlich (G 1, 76ff.) records the event as follows: "It seemed in her sleep as if something were being done to her pillow, 'as if something were scratching.' She awoke—it was about six-thirty in the morning—and saw her hands, her black mittens, and her white bedjacket, as well as the upper parts of the bed with its decoration of small flowers. Amazed, she looked around the room. Then she knocked on the floor with the cane in her right hand, trying to call her mother. Instead of her mother, Therese's sister Crescentia came into the room. At first Therese did not recognize her. In the more than four years since she had lost her sight, Crescentia had really grown up. Crescentia came to ask Therese if she needed anything. 'Yes, I want mother to come, right away,' Therese answered. Her sister summoned her mother at once. Therese recognized her mother immediately, since she had not changed at all, and greeted her by exclaiming: 'Mother, I've got something! Mother, I can't tell you.' At first her mother thought that her daughter had once again had an accident in bed, and was ashamed to tell her about it. So she asked her very quietly: 'Resl, what is it?' Whereupon she answered: 'Mother, I can see just fine.' Her mother could not believe the good news. She called her daughter Crescentia and told her to run over to Martin Neumann's inn and get another sister, perhaps Ottilie. But she was to say nothing to Martin Neumann, so that he would not tell anybody else, in case it were not really true that Therese could see. While Crescentia was rushing off to her sisters, Therese's mother, with trembling hand, took some flowers with white blossoms which stood on the windowsill and held them before her daughter's eyes. Therese reached for the flowers. Then her mother took a flower with red blossoms and showed them to her daughter. Therese reached for the red flower and said that the blossoms would look very fine in church."

Then her mother awakened the youngest child, little Hansel, who was sleeping in the room. "Hansel! Just think, Resl can see." Hansel jumped out of his bed still wearing his nightshirt, took another flower from the window, and held it out to Therese. At this point Therese could not control her inclination to laugh and jest: "Hansel," she said making a joke on his white shirt, "Did you just come from Church? Are you an altar boy?" Meantime her sister Ottilia came from Martin Neumann's establishment. Therese had heard her mother give the order to call Ottilia and thus she asked immediately: "Ottilia, is that you? —Yes it is; my, but you certainly have grown since I last saw you!" Then the sisters wept together for sheer joy.

The next morning her mother sat down beside her daughter's bed and read from the journal *Rosenhain* which is dedicated to the veneration of Therese of the Child Jesus who was later canonized as the Little Flower. Therese Neumann looked at the magazine together with her mother, and read along with her in a murmur. Her mother was very much surprised; she had not yet got used to the idea that her daughter would now be able to read. But actually from that time on, Therese was able to read even very small writing and print, like the print in the prayer book, without any difficulty.

On the day of Therese Neumann's cure from blindness (April 29, 1923) Therese of the Child Jesus, the Carmelite from the monastery of Lisieux, was beatified. Therese Neumann was extremely interested in the Little Flower because of her childlike piety. In the year 1914, when her father had to join the army, he gave Therese a small picture of the Little Flower which he had bought the day before in Waldsassen. A small picture of this Carmelite saint, who was honored by Therese Neumann as a venerable servant of God, later hung above her bed. On the back of the picture is a prayer for the beatification of the Little Flower, a prayer which Therese Neumann used to pray every Sunday, and later every day. Therese knew that the Carmelite saint was going to be beatified on that day. For that reason she had wanted to hold a novena to prepare for the event, but was unable to complete the nine day's devotion because she was prevented by a great fatigue, caused primarily by a severe stomach disorder.

This novena was intended to honor the beatification of the Little Flower, and not because of Therese's desire to be cured herself. As she herself later explained, at the beginning of the illness she very much wanted to be cured, but later, after she had become totally blind, she gave less and less thought to the prospect of ever praying for her health to be restored. The only thing she asked for herself in this novena was to share in the childlike spirit of the Little Flower.

Cure of The Wrenched Vertebrae

Resl was thus finally able to see again, and in her great happiness she wrote the good news to her close friends. But her lameness remained and kept her for many more years in her bed. I quote once again from Gerlich (G 1, 84ff., excerpts):

On the afternoon of May 17, 1925, during the May devotions, Therese Neumann's parents were at home in their living-work room. They had left the doors leading to the upstairs open in order to hear their daughter if she should call for them. Therese lay alone in her room on the second floor, praying her rosary silently. Because of her crippled condition, she was unable to take part in the May devotions at church. Then occurred an experience which Therese describes in the following words: When she came to the second phrase added to the Hail Mary, "Jesus, who ascended into heaven," she could not help thinking of the following Thursday which would be the Feast of Christ's Ascension. "How they must have felt when the Savior suddenly left. They must have thought that they certainly needed to have him very much." Then, as she recounted later, a white light suddenly appeared before her eyes, hovering over the bed. At first she was frightened at the light, but she was raised up by an invisible hand and, as her parents recount, uttered two small exclamations, "Oh, Oh," which they heard. Her parents quickly rushed to the scene, her father taking the lead, and there in the room on the second story they found their daughter staring fixedly at something in front of her. Her father cried aloud in consternation at his daughter's condition and offered her something to drink, thinking she was suffering from a spasm. She said nothing to either of them and later claimed that she was not aware of their presence. Her face began to change its hue, from the pallor of the sickroom, which had marked her features before, to a fresh, ruddy complexion.

Meantime Sister Regintrudis, a Mallersdorf Sister who was working as a nursing sister at Arzberg and used to visit Therese Neumann frequently, came into the room. It was about 2:30 in the afternoon. Father Witt has recorded the account written by this sister (Witt 1, p. 90ff.), from whom I [Gerlich] cite the following: Therese's mother and father were standing by the bed. They received no answer to their greeting to Therese. Then Therese, with wide open eyes, began to stare fixedly in front of her, looking upwards and to the right, but, more towards the wall and not into the room where everyone was standing. Her expression was more "friendly and loving" than they had ever seen in their earlier visits. The expression "radiant joy" is an inadequate description. Their repeated questions remained then, without answer. The sister took her pulse, which was perfectly normal. Her respiration, too, was relaxed and regular. There was no indication of excitement, fright, or anxiety. Everyone present had the impression that Therese was engaged in a lively conversation with some invisible person.

She moved her lips as if speaking, nodded her head from time to time in affirmation or shook it in disagreement. Her hands made simple gestures, like those made by a person who is speaking with someone or trying to explain something. Her expressions changed frequently, but for the most part she displayed "a loving expression of supreme joy," and then again an expression of deepest earnestness. The words could not be understood. They got the impression that she was engaged, not in an interior meditation or vision, nor for that matter a monologue or even a prayer, but rather a direct conversation. Therese Neumann "acted as if she were speaking to a person visibly present before her," someone who meant more to her than "we and all the rest of the world."

Shortly after the nursing sister had entered the room, Therese cried out "Father" (referring to the priest). Her mother states that she asked Therese: "Do you want him?" But Therese gave no answer. The parents then sent their daughter Anna to Father Naber. The Mallersdorfer nursing sister recounts that all present were seized with the greatest astonishment when they saw how Therese suddenly raised herself to a sitting position in her bed without help. "She did, however, make a very painful expression. Involuntarily she grasped the sore spot in her back with both hands." After Therese's first attempt to sit up, her mother, amazed at the fact that Therese was able to sit, raised the covers a little at the foot of the bed and saw that Therese's left foot was lying at the end of the bed frame. This left foot, which had been drawn up tightly against her right thigh as a result of muscular contraction, was once again normally extended and in its natural position.

Meantime the good news had been told to Father Naber as he returned from the afternoon devotions in the parish church. "Father, could you please come immediately; we do not know what is wrong with Resl." Father Naber thought that perhaps St. Therese—this was the day of her canonization—had come to take Therese Neumann home, and accordingly then brought the blessed oils and his stole with him. When he came into the room he was prepared to comfort Resl's father who came to meet him. But when he saw Therese, he exclaimed: "Therese is not going to die; we can let her rest quietly."

Father Naber explained in the local paper for April 15, 1926 that he found Therese with her eyes staring fixedly at something in front of her, her hands reaching out after it, her face beaming with joy. She was moving her head and shaking it as if she were speaking with someone; suddenly she sat upright, after six and a half years of immobility, although she experienced great pain in her back at this activity. At her second attempt to sit up, Therese Neumann once again felt a sharp stab of pain in the sore spot on her spinal column, but not nearly so marked as before, accompanied by "a crack, as when something snaps in two." The light disappeared and she was once again aware of being in her room in bed. She began to cry in her disappointment that the light had disappeared. Physically she was in perfect condition; her back had ceased to give her pain. She took no notice of those present. While she was crying she thought of her mother and took the stick with which she was accustomed to pound on the floor in order to let her mother or whoever else was there in the workroom immediately below know that she needed attention. When she reached for the stick, the pastor spoke to her: "Resl, where have you been?" She looked up and saw in her room the pastor, her parents, the Mallersdorf sister, the aspirant, and her sister Anna standing around the bed, all of them crying, with the exception of the priest.

But instead of answering him, Therese Neumann suddenly exclaimed with astonished certitude: "What's wrong with you? I can sit up now and even walk." Her mother considered this absolutely impossible in view of the six years of immobility, particularly because of the crippled left foot, and examined it once again. But the left foot, as she had noticed at her first examination, once again lay normally beside the right foot, a fact which all present convinced themselves to be true. The Mallersdorf sister found Therese Neumann's claim absolutely incomprehensible. She decided to attempt a little test and told her: "Resl, try to sit up a little bit higher." Therese supported herself with both hands on the bed and easily raised herself. The pastor was considering that she might try standing up, but Therese suddenly cried aloud: "Quick. Bring me a dress." Her mother immediately brought her a dress. While her father, as he later recalled the incident, was thinking that it would be impossible for Therese to stand up, that she would collapse, they heard Therese Neumann's determined words: "Then let's try it in the name of God," and saw her suddenly get out of bed and stand on both feet. Her parents were so excited that they were incapable of moving. Father Naber, who had remained calmest of all, was concerned that she might fall and called to everyone to help her. He and the sister grasped her under the arms. Responding to the pastor's call, her father came up and held her under the arms while the pastor stepped back. Supported by her father and the sister, Therese Neumann walked half-way across the room and back again.

Then some other neighbors suggested that this was enough, and Therese Neumann was put back onto the bed, supporting herself with both arms on the back of the chair. Her father explained that they had not needed to support her with any great strength, only to lead her, and that she was able to walk alone. Since everyone felt she was still too weak to be allowed up for a lengthy period of time, the pastor told her to go back to her bed. When she was back in bed, he repeated his question, asking her once again where she had been, and that she must tell him. She said she was willing to do so, but only to him.

This was her story: From the midst of the wonderful bright light she heard a beautiful friendly voice asking her: "Resl, wouldn't you like to be well again?" And she answered: "Everything is allright with me: living and dying, being well or sick, whatever my dear God wills, he knows what is best." The voice asked her again: "Wouldn't you like to be able to get up this very day and be able to walk and take care of yourself again?" She answered: "I want anything and everything that comes from God. I am happy with all the flowers and birds, or with any other suffering he sends. And what I like most of all is our dear Savior himself." Then the voice told her: "Today you may have a little joy. You can sit up; try it once, I'll help you."

At these words she felt herself lifted up by her right hand, and she "tried to get up herself," as she recounts. "Something cold touched me." She experienced an extremely painful tearing and wrenching in the section of her vertebrae that had been crippled, more painful than ever before, as if something were being torn backwards and to the left. During all this, someone invisible to her had taken her by the hand. She describes her feelings in the following words: she felt as if "two bones were being rubbed together. Oh that hurts!" She felt as if she were being "twisted forward to the left, towards the wall," and "just exactly as if something that had been twisted out of place was twisted back and snapping into place."

The voice then addressed her once again with these words: "You still have very much and very long to suffer, and no doctor can help you, either. Only through suffering can you best work out your desire and your vocation to be a victim, and thereby help the work of the priests. Through suffering you will gain more souls than through the most brilliant sermons. I have already described it before." Who this person was the voice did not say; but it added these words: "You can walk, too."

The witnesses to this miraculous cure were waiting outside the door of the bedroom during this conversation between the pastor and Therese. When the pastor called them back into the room after a short time, Therese explained to them that her back no longer caused her any pain and asked them to look and see if there were not some change there. The nursing sister quickly examined her back. When she saw the formerly crippled spot, she was astounded: "Jesus, Mary, and Joseph! The back is healed too." "Yes, I can feel it myself," answered Therese. But only a short time before the wounds were still there. The fresh gown that her mother, with the help of her sister Crescentia, had dressed her in just the day before was drenched with blood and pus.

The words "I have described it all before" prompted Father Naber and another priest to whom he related the whole incident to look in written records. Since they already supposed that St. Therese of Lisieux was the authoress, since it was on this day, May 17, 1925, that she was canonized, they did not experience too much difficulty. They found the passage about more souls being saved through suffering than through brilliant sermons in her own autobiography, in the sixth letter to the missionaries.

Vision and Cure of September 30, 1925

Toward the end of September Therese Neumann began a novena to achieve someone's conversion. On September 30, the anniversary of the death of St. Therese of the Child Jesus, about 12:30 at night, she was lying awake in bed, reading the litany in honor of this saint by the light of the electric lamp. Suddenly she was confronted by the same light as had appeared to her when her vertebrae were cured and the same voice spoke to her again: "Resl! God wants every visible part of your suffering to disappear. You can now walk without any help. The suffering which strikes the eye will diminish. But in its place something worse will come. Encourage your people to have confidence in God." "But," Therese answered, "I don't know myself whether I am really on the right path." Then the voice answered: "Follow your father confessor in blind obedience and trust everything to him. You must die more and more to your own ego. Always remain childlike in your simplicity."

Then the voice was silent and the light disappeared. Once again Therese Neumann saw her familiar room. Only the prayerbook which she had been holding in her hand now lay on the floor. As soon as she realized what the voice had actually told her, she immediately stood up and was able to walk without any support. In her great joy she walked back and forth in her room for a good quarter of an hour. Then she lay down in bed, but could not get to sleep, and could barely wait for daylight. When the Angelus sounded from the church tower next morning, she got up and went into her parents' room on the ground floor. Her mother was astonished and asked her if she needed some help. She answered simply that she was on her way to church, and did not need any assistance. When her father asked her if something had happened, she answered simply: "Yes! I am going to church now." As she said this there were tears of joy in her eyes. As she made her way out into the fresh morning air and began walking slowly away, she shivered. Even though she tried to hurry her steps, it still took her a few minutes for the short stretch of about 300 feet before she stood at the foot of the stone steps which led from the market place up to the church. These she mounted with difficulty, but was able to enter the church, without assistance and without a cane.

From the church she went around to the priests' house which, approached from this side, was not further away from the church than her parents' house. She was received by the housekeeper, Anna Forster, who was amazed to find Therese standing alone. She gave Therese some roses from the parish garden and Therese brought them happily into the church where she decorated the crucifix and the picture of the Holy Family behind the altar. This picture had previously been donated by Therese herself, paid for from her modest savings (G 1, 93-94).

Appendicitis Cured

Around the Feast of All Souls in 1925 Therese Neumann contracted a severe cold as a result of her long vigil in the cold church. Once again she was forced to take to her bed. A increasing agony of pain soon set in, accompanied by a high fever. Doctor Seidl, who was finally summoned on November 13, diagnosed her condition as acute appendicitis and ordered her to be transferred immediately to the Waldsassen hospital for an operation. The distraught mother refused to let her daughter out of the house. She complained loudly of the inadvisibility of operating upon such a weakened patient. Therese's father, too, was unwilling to follow the doctor's advice. He remembered the statement that no doctor could help her. He already had visions of their bringing her home as a corpse the next morning. Doctor Seidl spoke to him in the most serious tone, urging him to be reasonable and look for some kind of transportation; there was hardly a minute to spare.

Both parents turned to the priest, asking whether it would not be better under these circumstances simply to leave Therese at home. After discussing it briefly with the doctor, the priest told them that in his opinion they ought to see the doctor's judgment as the will of God and follow it. At that, Therese's father ran off to borrow horses and a carriage from Mr. Schiml the innkeeper, while her mother, crying all the while, hurried to prepare some sort of bed so that her daughter could be laid comfortably in the wagon, and to find the necessary articles of clothing. Therese herself was perfectly resigned to whatever was going to happen. The inconsolable sorrow of her mother struck her deeply, and made her feel that it would not be wrong, in this most extreme necessity, to turn once again to St. Therese the Little Flower who had promised that she would help in the future. She had already told the doctor that she was quite certain that the Little Flower would help her if she asked her to. The doctor, who saw this as tempting God, had answered, "Yes, St. Therese has always got to work some miracles for you." Therese then asked the pastor if her prayer would really amount to tempting God. The priest had no objection to her praying to the Little Flower, asking her to help without any operation at all, if it was God's will.

Therese Neumann had a relic from the Little Flower, a hair that the Carmelite Father Seraphim of Reisach had given her. This relic was contained in a small capsule which had been sewn into a small cloth bag. She generally wore it over her dress, hanging from her neck on a string. This relic was now applied by the parish housekeeper, Anna Forster, to the part of her body that was causing her such pain, while all present began to pray to the Little Flower. Therese was in too great pain to join the others in prayer. She only said: "You know, Little Therese, that you could help me. You have helped me many times before. It makes no difference to me; but you can hear how mother is carrying on." Then, as the pastor recounts the story, her great pain forced her to squirm about in bed like a worm.

All of a sudden Therese sat up somewhat, opened her eyes, and her face was transfigured. She raised her hands and held them up towards someone standing before her, and said "Yes" a few times, and then sat all the way up. The whole activity took place remarkably fast, so that those in the room saw Therese suddenly come out of her visionary state and with the exclamation "Really?" suddenly grasp the part of her body that had been so painful. Therese later explained that she meant this word "Really?" in the sense of "Is it possible?" For suddenly, she said, she no longer experienced any pain, and felt herself transformed. Father Naber then asked her if perhaps the Little Flower had been with her again, and helped her. She answered: "Yes, and she told me I should go right over to the church and thank God. Mother, bring me something to wear."

The Little Flower herself had not personally appeared to Therese, but she had seen the very same light as before, when she was cured from her crippled condition, and the very same voice had spoken to her. Father Naber reports, that according to Therese, these were the words she heard: "Your perfect resignation and joy in suffering pleases us. And so that the world will know that there is a higher plan at work, you will not need to be cut open now. Get up and go right to church and thank God, right now." The voice continued: "You will still have a lot to suffer and you will be able to cooperate in saving many souls. Your own self you will have to constantly keep dying to, more and more. And keep your childlike simplicity, always." Therese said that, together with the appearance of the light, a hand had reached towards her, a hand which she had tried to grasp, but she could not reach it. It was a slim, white hand.

Therese had concluded her answer to the pastor's first question with the words: "Mother, bring me something to wear." Mrs. Neumann's motherly concern for her daughter's health caused her to hesitate, pointing out how dark and cold the evening was. But since the voice had not only ordered Therese to get up and go to church, but told her to do so immediately, Therese insisted on obeying, despite her mother's protests. She took her clothing, got herself dressed, and accompanied by all present, some ten persons, made her way to church. She remained there for twenty minutes. She had enough strength to make two genuflections before the high altar; during her prayers she was kneeling. The whole series of events, from the arrival of the doctor to her return from the church, took place in the hour between six and seven P.M.

About 11:30, as Therese recalls, she felt "noise in her stomach" followed by a discharge: at first pus, then blood mixed with pus, and finally a slender, viscous object some four inches in length, yellow-gray, highly inflamed.

The next day Father Naber and Therese took the bus around noon to Waldsassen to Dr. Seidl's sanitarium. He was amazed to receive their visit. He explained that it did occasionally happen, but only very rarely, that the infection of appendicitis empties out naturally through the intestines. But even then the cure of such a patient required more time than normal operations and recovery (Sources: N; G 1, 96ff., abridged).

The Stigmata Visions

The investigation of the Bishop's commission, the story of which had already been told in the chapter entitled "The First Vision," also made a thorough investigation of Therese Neumann's stigmatization. On this occasion, she also described the visions she experienced during the stigmatization. These visions of the Passion, which are here presented only in outline form, the way in which she first experienced them, were constantly repeated for the rest of her life, on every Friday, with the exception of festive seasons in the church calendar or Holy Days which fell on a Friday, and with the addition of several particulars. They are reproduced later in this book, in fuller form, where they fit in more properly with the course of Christ's life.

In the paragraphs that follow I reproduce the questions asked by the commission and Therese Neumann's answers exactly according to the record of the protocol.

Eichstätt, January 13, 1953

Catalogue of questions, division Specialia: Chapter Three, Stigmatization

Question 1. Have you ever wished for the wound marks of Christ?

Answer: I have never wished for the marks of Christ's wounds; what is more, I didn't even know what such special graces were all about.

Question 2. Have you ever done anything yourself to bring them about?

Answer: Naturally I have never done anything to bring them about. Nothing was further from my mind.

Questions 3. and 4. What was going on in your mind when wound marks made their appearance?

What did you do after you received them?

Answer: During Lent of 1936, one Thursday night, I was busy with my prayers, without being particularly conscious of the Passion of Christ, when, for the first time, I saw the Savior and as a grown man, in fact, I saw him in the Garden of Olives, sweating blood, and heard him pray the words: Te sebud ach (after his third prayer). Then the Savior looked at me with a loving expression; at that very moment I felt as if someone had pierced me from my right side to the left side through the heart with a sharp object, and then withdrawn it. At the same time I noticed that warm blood was flowing (when I later examined it, it had already clotted); then I no longer saw the Savior in the Garden of Olives, nor did I know that I was in bed. However, I was not unconscious—I kept feeling this stabbing pain in my heart, a pain which, with the exception of Easter week, has never since completely left me. It's just that I didn't know where I was and wasn't thinking about what I had seen or experienced.

I asked an old friend, who was then working as the pastor's housekeeper, a lady who often used to visit me and who had been supplying me with bandages for my sores all the years that I was sick, if she could find something for this wound in my heart. The meaning of this wound in my heart, that is, the fact that it would remain with me, was something I did not understand for a long time; I still had visions of being a missionary sister. Whether my old friend understood what it was all about, I do not know. I did think, from time to time, of what the Little Flower had told me would happen, that I would have a lot to suffer for a long time, and that no doctor could help me.

The deposition was continued January 15, 1953. After a short prayer and reminder of the obligation to tell the truth and maintain secrecy, about 3:00 P.M., Therese Neumann continued her answer to questions 3 and 4:

On the next Friday, I saw Christ's sufferings in the Garden of Olives, and for the rest of that night, as far as the scourging inclusive; on the third Friday, I saw the sufferings as far as the crowning with thorns; on the fourth, which was Friday in Passion Week, I saw the entire Way of the Cross, up to the point where the Savior was thrown into an empty tomb to await the time of his own crucifixion; on the fourth Friday, which was Good Friday, I saw the entire Passion of Christ, down to the sealing of the tomb. During the nailing to the cross, the Savior looked at me with great love again (exactly as when I had, received the wound to the heart) and at this moment I experienced a dull pressure of pain in my hands, at the very spot where ever since I have had the marks of wounds (these wound marks, however, were only on the backs of my hands at that time, in a round and sharply outlined form, as if they had been cut out. Only later, on another Friday in that same year, did the wounds go through my entire hand; the precise date I no longer know. On another Good Friday, in 1927, I think, they took on the square form they now have). At the nailing of the feet, the Savior looked at me in the same way, and at that very moment, at the place where I have the wounds in my feet today, I felt the same dull sensation of pain, but this time even stronger. The wounds in my feet underwent the same change as those in my hands, and at precisely the same time.

I had my sister Crescentia bandage these wound marks but demanded that she speak of it to no one, and I did everything I could to conceal the wound marks. I simply presumed that the wound marks would disappear again. That is why both I and my mother used various home remedies (chopped begonia and geranium leaves; boracic salve, marigold salve, all prepared by my mother). Naturally, as time went on, I was unable to prevent my mother, who slept in the same room with me, from noticing the wound marks, and from telling the pastor, my father, and the rest of the family.

Question 5. Have you ever done anything in order to keep the wound marks from healing or from changing?

Answer: I have done just the opposite. Dr. Seidl, our family doctor, also tried various means of curing the wounds, thereby causing me great pain and swelling on my whole hand and foot. When there was nothing more that I could do to help, on the night after the application of the doctor's salve and his bandaging of the wounds, I stormed the Little Flower, whom I had especially venerated since 1917, begging her to help me heal the wounds or at least to give me some relief and advice. You see, the doctor had forbidden us to change the bandages, although my family were urging me to do so.

The saint did bring me relief. The swelling subsided and the formerly moist wounded areas, as we noticed when we took off the now pliable bandages, were now covered with a thin transparent coating of skin.

Question 6. What do you yourself think about the wound marks?

Answer: In receiving these wound marks I had recognized the will of God and thus I bear them the way I do everything that God sends, primarily in the spirit of propitiation for others and in order to bring souls closer to the Savior; every year the Little Flower admonishes me to do this (on May 17 and October 3). I recall, too, that in the same year (1926), in addition to the wounds already mentioned, I also received a permanent wound in the head, which came the same way as all the others (the Savior looked at me during the crowning with thorns).

There are also wounds that are not permanent, a wound in the (right) shoulder (during Lent) and the wounds from the scourging (on Good Friday); these wounds came, once again, in the same way as the others (the Savior looked at me when he picked up the cross at Pilate's house, or when he was being scourged).

Author's note: Therese Neumann mentioned that the Little Flower admonishes her every year, on May 17 and October 3. May 17 is the date of the Little Flower's canonization (1925), the day on which, as we have seen, Therese Neumann was cured of her wrenched vertebrae. The Little Flower's date of death is September 30 (1897) and on the anniversary of this date, 1925, Therese experienced her third cure. But what about October 3? In March, 1928, Pope Pius XI, who made the Little Flower St. Therese patroness of all missionaries and missions (together with St. Francis Xavier)—and here again there is a certain connection with Therese who wanted very much to be a missionary sister—composed a proper mass formula in honor of the Little Flower and proclaimed October 3 as her feast day. From 1928 on, the Little Flower's admonition to Therese Neumann was changed to October 3, an example of the very close connection between her visions and the liturgy of the Church. We shall see many others.

Therese Neumann after receiving the stigmata; in the parish garden, 1926.

CHAPTER FOUR

VISIONS OF LIGHT AFTER THE STIGMATIZATION

(Source G 1, 15ff., abridged)

May 17, 1926, first anniversary of the canonization of the Little Flower: Therese was bedridden during this time, for only a few weeks previously, without knowing what it was and what it meant, she had received the stigmata of Christ. Both she and her doctor were busily engaged in their attempt to cure these wounds, and Therese was still very weak. Father Naber had come to visit her about 12:30 and they were speaking about a picture which had been given her by some visitor, a picture of an unclothed Christ child which went against her sensitivities. The conversation turned to clothing and she said she would have preferred to have very common looking clothing, but that her father likes to see bright clothes. "Just look, God has created the world with all sorts of colors, red, yellow, blue, and the goldfinch there with his beautiful little red body . . . ." She pointed to her bird cage—and then suddenly she was carried off into a vision. Once again she saw the light which had appeared to her often before, and heard the voice speaking: "Have patience and do not be annoyed. Today you will experience some little relief. But you will still have very much to suffer. I have helped you up till now and have always told you: 'You needn't fear anything! Remain humble and do not lose your childlike spirit.' "

After the vision was over, and he had discussed it briefly with Therese, Father Naber went back to the rectory, and it was not long before he heard a knock on the door. Therese was standing there. When he had left the Neumann house, Therese immediately got up. She felt strong enough to go directly to church, to thank God for curing her from her thirty weeks' illness. Then she stopped at the rectory.

On the anniversary of the death of the Little Flower, September 30, 1926, around 8 o'clock P.M., the light appeared to her once again and the voice spoke to her. Her parents record the event (W 1, 242 and G, 1, 117): The apparition lasted for about five minutes. Resl's face was radiant. We heard her speak the word "Yes" a few times, barely audible. For the rest she was whispering quietly. All of a sudden it was gone. Her face was no longer joyfully excited and ruddy; it had a somewhat sad expression. None of us said anything. Then Resl said: "It is very, very gloomy." We all felt that it was light in the room, because the electric lamp and two candles were burning. "Ah," Resl went on, "I am really here. This is no longer really beautiful, but now I will be happy to suffer again," and she smiled joyfully again because she was able to see once more how beautiful this life is. The voice from out of the light, speaking in friendly tones with Resl, had told her, among other things, that she would have to suffer many things.

Thus far the story recorded by her parents.

On November 16, 1926, a Tuesday, Therese was attacked by a bronchial catarrh, and lung infection, which had grown so serious by Thursday that she fainted during confession. In addition, she had such a high fever that she no longer recognized her closest friends and family. Early Friday morning, the pastor, who feared the worst, anointed her with the oils of the sick. On the night between Thursday and Friday, November 18-19, she had her regular historical visions of the Passion of Christ from the Garden of Olives to his death on the cross.

During the vision of the crowning with thorns, for the first time those present in the room noticed blood oozing through three places on her white headcloth. As they watched, they noticed that the hair on these three places was drenched with blood. The pain in her head was excruciating until the vision of the "light" that evening. In the intervals between the individual visions she was extremely weak.

Father Witt considers the following point worth noting: "Whenever it happened that she had just begun to cough and suddenly a vision came along, then the coughing immediately subsided. But when the ecstasy had passed, Therese began coughing again."

After the vision of the crucifixion, the phlegm obstruction of her air passages became so severe that she was seized by fits of choking and unconsciousness. From 2:00 P.M. on, she no longer gave any indication of understanding what was said to her. Her heart, too, seemed to have weakened considerably. From just about 3:00 on she began to suffer attacks of pulmonary fatigue. The pastor returned to the rectory and then to the church, and did not return until after 5:00.

Therese, meantime, had grown so weak that her sister had to continuously hold up her head so that she could still get some air. The color of her face had turned ashen, like a dying person's. Her lips were all swollen, her chin was somewhat protruding, and her eyes were dull. She kept them half-open, and looking upwards. Her face began to sink, and her nose looked peaked. Her hands and feet were cold and stiff. Her father tried to massage her back and, from time to time, stuck his fingers into her neck, in order to induce an attack of coughing which would clear the accumulated phlegm from her throat. At the same time, her two sisters kept moving her arms. But Therese only sank into unconsciousness. Her breathing grew slower and slower.

All present—several friends of Therese had also gathered—encouraged by Father Naber's advice, began to beg the Little Flower, who had so often helped her before, to assist her now. But even Father Naber, who had always kept hoping she would be saved, finally gave up all hope. He had them put the lighted candle in her hand which was supported by one of the sisters; and he himself put the crucifix in her other hand. The bells of the Konnersreuth church were just ringing the Angelus when the pastor began to recite the prayers for the dying. As soon as the last stroke of the smaller bell, the one dedicated to St. Therese of the Child Jesus, had faded away—in the prayers for the dying they had reached the passage which says: "May today see your arrival at the place of peace in holy Zion"—it seemed to those present that Therese had breathed her last.

Then suddenly the prostrate patient was carried off into a vision. She began to breathe again, displayed a lively set of facial expressions, and then sank back quietly on her pillows, as she usually did after a vision. Her expression was normal, and her limbs were warm again. After a short time the pastor who, as she began her vision, had both cried and laughed at the same time in his great joy at her being saved, began a conversation with her. She was in the state of prepossession; and thus it was difficult to get out of her just what happened. The conversation went something like this:

Therese: "I got so cold and so upset. But I don't know what from. Then suddenly the light came and from the light something spoke. Something went through me there (pointing to her breast) but didn't stick me. I began to breathe again." Then the pastor asked her about the words which the voice had directed to her. Therese informed him that the voice had said: "Dear child, your resignation pleases the Savior. In order to show the world that there is a higher plan at work you are to be able to get up again. You are not allowed to die yet. You must suffer more and work together with the priests for the salvation of souls."

Therese always reproduced the words spoken by the voice in High German, whereas she commonly speaks in the Oberpfalz dialect. In her state of prepossession she often speaks pure dialect. This explains the following remark which she made after repeating the words spoken by the voice: "I wonder if they all speak that way in heaven? Well now, the Savior will have to teach me. But he will have his work cut out for him."

Towards morning she returned to her normal state. Her pain had disappeared. She had a fit of coughing and coughed up the phlegm that was blocking her upper air passages. Next day she was able to get up and walk about.

It has already been pointed out that three stigma marks now appeared on her head. In the course of the next Friday visions of the Passion, their number increased to eight.

Christmas, 1926 (W1, 261ff. Abridged)

In 1926 Christmas fell on Friday. On the previous night, and in the forenoon, Therese experienced the vision of Christ's Passion as she had on every Friday since Lent. She was therefore in no way prepared for the Christmas holiday and could not be put into the proper mood, neither by her mother, who watched her that afternoon, nor by Father Naber. In the evening, while the family were gathered downstairs to exchange their Christmas presents, Therese lay quietly resting in her bed, as if she were asleep. The family went to church for the Christmas Mass. Only Therese's father remained home to keep the house and take care of his daughter.

While the Mass was going on in the church, he was reading the Christmas Gospel. From the church nearby he could hear the bells ringing at the time of consecration. When he rose from his knees after hearing them ring for the second time, he suddenly heard his daughter give a loud cry. Frightened, he looked in on her. He saw her lying there with a smile, her eyes open, her face turned to one side, as if she were listening attentively to something in the distance. Soon she raised her head from the pillow with the most intense attention. Then she turned her face completely in the direction from which the sound seemed to be coming. Her expression was much more lively, she looked radiant and began to smile joyfully; but once or twice her face also took a more serious expression. At the same time she stretched out her arms towards some invisible thing and raised herself completely from the bed.

Meantime the family, together with one of her father's married sisters who was there as a guest, had returned from church and now assembled around Therese. The youngest son was sent off to the pastor who came immediately to the scene. The vision had lasted some ten minutes more after the arrival of the family, but now her eyes were fixed immovably in one definite direction. Then she sank back on her pillows, closing her eyes. After about two minutes she opened her eyes, looked strangely at the group gathered silently about her, and spoke very softly: "Now I could gladly die." She had completely returned to herself; she clutched her hands over her face to hide the tears.

Father Naber asked her why she was crying. She answered that since it was never beautiful here she would like to leave. She would like to die. Everything here was so gloomy. The pastor let her continue in this vein for a few minutes, and then he spoke to her again. "Resl, we have just come from the Mass." Then Therese, who seemed not to have paid attention to his words, asked him what time it was. The pastor answered: "One o'clock." "No, no," answered Therese, "that is not what I mean." Then the pastor said: "It is Christmas; it is Christmas Eve." But once again Therese did not seem to hear what she had missed. Then he told her: "The Christ child has come." These words suddenly found a ready ear in Therese. Now, she suddenly understood and exclaimed happily: "Yes, that must certainly have been the Christ child."

At the pastor's insistence she then told him what she had experienced. She had been awakened from her sleep by song and music. But it was a singing and a music that was much more beautiful than human voices could possibly produce. Throughout the entire vision the same words were sung over and over. When the pastor asked her what words had been sung, she answered that she had already heard it but could not reproduce it. At first the song had resounded through the darkness. Suddenly that same light that had often appeared to her came before her eyes. At the same time the voice again spoke to her: "You may also rejoice together with him. But always keep resigned and childlike."

Suddenly the brilliance of this light was outshone by a much more radiant brilliance in which she saw a beautiful child elevated on a white cloud standing before her. She saw the child in the middle of the light. Dressed in a white shirt, he had fine red cheeks, "not bright red, just a little," and beautiful little feet. The child's fine hair was blond and it framed the radiant face with gentle locks. With brilliant blue eyes the child—which had stretched its arms out towards Therese—smiled gently upon her. It seemed to her that the child was trying to reach her and when the pastor asked her if she had not wanted to go to the child, she answered that she would have liked to, but didn't trust herself to do it.

VISIONS FROM THE LIFE OF JESUS AND MARY

Father Naber prefaced the beginning of his second journal with these words: "The recorded content of these visions has been expanded by questioning during the elevated state of calm." The elevated state of calm is the ecstatic state which regularly made its appearance after each Holy Communion—and, occasionally, under other circumstances as well.

The Life of the Virgin Before Jesus

The story of the life of Jesus and Mary begins with the conception of Mary. There is no historical vision by Therese on this subject known to me. Still, on this feast day, which can be traced back in the Greek Church as far as the sixth century and has also been taken over in our western tradition (in 1854, being incorporated as the Feast of the Immaculate Conception, a holy day of obligation celebrated on December 8), she always used to see a magnificent picture of the Immaculate Conception, similar to what the evangelist John saw and described as the "great sign in the heavens" (Rv 12:1).

The Life of the Blessed Virgin: September 8
(Sources: N 1, 38; G 1, 263ff.)

Under date of September 8, 1928, Father Naber makes the following brief entry: Therese sees the birth of the Blessed Virgin in three tableaux; first the preparation which consists of prayer on the part of her mother Anne and a few other women who are present; then the midwife placing the newly born child into its

mother's arms, the child bathed in a heavenly ray of light, opening its eyes and smiling; the child in the arms of the grateful
father.

Gerlich has these further details to add: I was able to record
the following explicit account of these visions, drawing primarily
upon direct interrogation of Therese herself in her state of prepossession in her normal state.

First Vision: Therese saw herself transported to a great house
lying outside Nazareth. Joachim and Anne, the parents of the
Blessed Virgin, owned both a smaller house in Nazareth itself
and this larger house standing isolated outside the city. In one
small room with a door, beside which Therese was standing, and
a window situated high in the opposite wall, were Anne and
the three women. In a singing tone they were praying, reading
from small scrolls. They were standing by the window, looking
out. There were no pictures in the room. After the prayers, two
maids brought in a table and at the same time showed another
woman into the room, who seemed to be a visitor. She was carrying fruit and a flat loaf of bread, about an inch high, baked with
grooves on the top. The women broke the bread along the
grooved marks and all shared in the meal.

Second vision: Therese saw herself transported into a rather
long room which was not very large and provided with a window
high in the wall and a door, near which she was standing. Across
from the window, on the floor, a bed had been prepared. The bed
itself consisted of a mattress which had been rolled up several
times towards the head, thus making a somewhat elevated pillow.
The blankets had been spread over the mattress. On the bed lay
a woman, Anne, covered with blankets. Another woman, a nurse,
was wrapping the obviously just-born child in a material which
seemed to be made of natural colored wool. Then she gave the
child to its mother, who was lying on the bed. Anne took the
child and held it in the air, at the same time praying in a singing
tone. While she was holding the child in the air, a ray of light
fell upon it; it opened its eyes, smiled, and then closed its eyes
again, whereupon the ray of light disappeared. The three women
who had assembled now each took the child in her arms and

prayed aloud in a singing tone. The child had blue eyes, and light yellow hair.

Third vision: Therese saw herself in the same room as in the second vision. Anne lay on the bed as before, completely covered with gray blankets. The child lay beside her, bedded down in a reed basket. The woman (nurse) was in the room. The other women were no longer present. An old man (Joachim) with rather long gray hair and a beard of the same color, entered the room. He was dressed in traveling clothes, having been absent at his daughter's birth. He took off his dusty cloak and a leather purse which was hanging at his side. Anne placed the child, which the woman took out of the reed basket for her, into his arms. He raised the child up, looking up to the window, and sang a long prayer in a loud voice. Then he gave the child back to the woman who laid her back into the basket.

When the Blessed Virgin grew up, her hair had darkened to a brownish-blond. The child did not have a pretty face, but she radiated a strong, healthy beauty. Her face was rather brownish, burned by the sun. Her expression was maternal. She stood rather tall, and she was strong and healthy.

Blessed Name of Mary: September 12
(Sources: N 1, 4; G 1, 265ff.)

Father Naber: September 12, 1928—Therese sees a priest with two attendants enter the house of Joachim and Anne; she hears them praying from a scroll, she hears first Joachim call her Mariam, then the priest call her Miriam, sees the priest cut some hair with a sort of scissors from three places in the child Mary's head, holding them with a pincer and then burning them over a small three-legged vessel. He then dips his fingers into a jar with something that smells good and touches the child's eyes, ears, nostrils, mouth, and breast. Finally, Therese sees them sharing a meal.

Gerlich enlarges on this account with the following notes describing the normal ritual observed by the Jewish people in naming a girl child.

On September 12, 1928, at 3:15 P.M., Therese had two visions of the naming of the Blessed Virgin. She was in the pastor's house and, since she did not feel well, had just lain down on the sofa. Suddenly she was carried away.

First vision: Therese saw herself transported into the house of Joachim and Anne at Nazareth—a large, simple room with three high windows and a door, by which she was standing. In front of the windows were green plants. On the walls there were tablets with two lines of Hebrew writing ("The same kind of scrawling as in the Temple"). On one wall there were two statues in high relief. One of them represented an old man, holding a tablet with Hebrew writing in his hands (Moses). The other represented an old man with a crown and a harp (David). In the middle of the room stood a table. The tablecloth was white, and seemed to be crocheted; it was trimmed with red. Above the table, suspended from the ceiling, was a double-beaked lamp. There were no chairs or seats in the room. In the background were men and women. Before the table stood an old man (Joachim); before him stood a priest and two servants. They were dressed the same way as at the feast of the circumcision. (Corresponding to the course of the Church liturgy, Therese had seen a vision of the circumcision of Christ before the vision for the Holy Name of Mary, and was thus familiar with customary priestly vesture).

The servants put a metal vessel with three feet onto the table; they then started a small fire in the vessel. The nurse brought the child to its father, and Joachim in turn gave the child to the priest, who gave it back to its father, whereupon he laid the child back into the reed basket. The child was clothed in a red dress, or in red material, with a white dress on top, and was bare footed. Before the nurse gave the child to its father, she had uncovered the child's breast. Then she put the red basket on the table. With a gleaming scissors-like "pincers" the priest cut three locks of hair from the child's head, forming a small tuft in the "pincers". Then he opened the "pincers" over the tripod and burnt the hair. Thereupon an attendant handed the priest a vessel with sweet-smelling ointment, with which he anointed the child's eyes, ears, the outside of the nostrils, the mouth, and the breast. During this operation the child made a small gurgling noise. During the ritual the priest sang some prayers, while all present were silent.

Then the father spoke a few words to the priest; Therese recognized one of them as Marian. The priest then held the child aloft and spoke a prayer, and this time Therese recognized the word Miriam. Then the priest gave the child back to its father who laid it back in the little basket. During the entire time Anne, the child's mother, was standing in the doorway and looking through the door-curtain. She did not enter the room.

Author's note: According to the Jewish law, since the days of Moses, a woman was considered "unclean" after childbirth and could not thus play any immediate role in any religious ceremony. Only forty days after childbirth was she allowed—and obligated—to enter the Temple for the ceremony of purification. Moreover, in the case of a first-born son, as later in the case of Mary and Jesus, there was the "presentation" of the child in the temple.

Second vision: The same room as before. The same men and women present, but this time without the priest, the two Levites as well as the nurse and the child and without Anne the mother. The two servants brought in a second table and several seats. A pastry was brought in that had been cut lengthwise along the grooves. There were also grapes and some fruit which Therese could not recognize. Some of it looked like lemons, others were gray with red sides. Glasses were also set on the table. There was no meat nor fish. Before the guests sat down a man spoke a few words, to which all present gave a brief response. Then, raising his eyes towards the window, he pronounced a long prayer in a singing voice; Therese was able to catch only the word *Elohim*. Then the others also prayed in a singing tone, but much more briefly, whereupon they all sat down and began to eat the bread and fruit and drink wine from the cups.

Surprise photograph by a journalist during Therese's fifteen days of medical observation, July 1927.

The Offering of the Blessed Virgin

November 21. Sources: N 1, 47, only a reference to the vision; account by Naber to the Author, based on statements made by Therese in the state of elevated calm, 1964.

On this day Therese had a vision of how Mary, a child of about thirteen, was brought by her parents into the Temple at Jerusalem and given over to the priest to be brought up in the Temple school as a Temple virgin. Hence the word "offering." This schooling and the corresponding service in the Temple lasted about ten years, after which time the Temple virgin would be released from the Temple and pronounced free to marry. The conditions for marriage were, however, very strict; the suitor must come from the same tribe of Israel as that to which the virgin belonged.

When Mary, at the age of thirteen, was officially registered, at first they could find no one who was of the tribe of David. Her registration was performed a second time later, and came to the attention of the carpenter Joseph of Nazareth, who was at that time thirty years old. He asked for the hand of Mary who, with or without her consent is not recorded, was betrothed to him. I mention this with respect to Mary's words to the angel Gabriel: "How shall this be, since I do not know man?" (Lk 1:34).*

The two of them made their way to Nazareth, where they lived in a small house which is described more fully in the visions that follow.

Annunciation: March 25 (Source A.)

Regarding this vision, the journals kept by Father Naber (1, 4 and 2, 58) contain only the notice that Therese had a vision of the Gospel for this day. Neither Gerlich nor Witt offer any further detail. But I myself was privileged to witness this vision on March 25th. In the midst of a conversation which ranged over a variety of mundane details, around 9:12 in the

---

* Mary had evidently dedicated her virginity to God, and Joseph seems to have agreed to this (Mayr).

evening, while she was sitting on her sofa, Therese suddenly experienced the vision which I immediately recorded as follows.

Therese sees a young woman, who appears to be almost still a girl, in a small house, praying. Suddenly a shining man is at her side; he did not enter, he is there. "With big wings?" I ask her, in an effort to lead her astray. She answered: "What are you thinking of? The shining men do not need any wings." The man bows down before the frightened maiden and says: "*Shelam elich, Miriam, gaseta. . .*" And a few more words follow. I say: "Wait a moment, what comes after *gaseta*?" She thinks for a while and answers: "You should have written it down faster; I don't know it any more." It is the greeting of the angel Gabriel: "Hail, Mary, full of grace."

Mary, still frightened, although, to judge from her expression, gaining confidence, is looking intently at the light vision which resembles a man but shines by itself. The angel continues to speak something powerful. The maiden interrupts him to ask a question and the angel answers her. When he is finished, the virgin bows her head and says a few words. At that same moment Therese sees a mighty light from above enter into the virgin, while the angel, after bowing once again, disappears into the air.

This is the way Therese described her vision in the state of prepossession which always followed visions (compare Luke 1: 26-38).

After this description of the events I asked Therese, when she returned to her normal state (wherein she was able to elaborate on her vision from impressions she received in other visions), how the house looked, and she gave the following description of the Holy Family at Nazareth:

The little house stands on a hill, and there is a well in front of it. A rocky cliff forms the rear wall of the house. The house has a flat roof upon which one could walk around. There is a vine on the front wall. Through a door which is closed off by a curtain, one enters into a small room. It is here that Mary, and later the Holy Family prayed. It had a single window, placed rather high, through which they prayed. It was not of glass, like our windows, but open and covered with a lattice-work of wood.

From this room another room enters to the right, through a door. It was here that Mary worked and where the angel came. There is an open fireplace there and a small opening above it for smoke to escape. It was here that Mary and the boy Jesus used to sleep, on a mattress which was turned up on one side as a pillow. During the day the mattress was kept rolled up. They slept covered by blankets. The room also contained some rather long chairs with a sloping arm on one side where a person could support his upper body while eating. From this room another door leads into the third room. This was the workshop and bedroom of St. Joseph. From the side of this room, there is still another door leading up to the roof. Directly across from it is a small stable for the donkey.

Visitation (Mary Visits Elizabeth): July 2
(Sources: N 1, 25; A.)

The angel of the Annunciation, apparently in an effort to convince Mary that he was really present and not just a product of her imagination, had told her the news that her cousin Elizabeth, who had long been considered barren, and whom even Zachary her husband (Lk 1:18) referred to as "far advanced in years," was six months pregnant, adding, prior to his departure, that "with God nothing is impossible." Mary immediately decided to visit this cousin. The visions of this visit are taken first from the journal of Father Naber (1, 25) and then expanded on the basis of personal experience of these visions. I feel that the circumstances surrounding these visions, as described in the account that follows, give an insight into the effect the visions had on all who witnessed them.

Father Naber makes the following comment under date of July 2, 1928: In the afternoon Therese sees Mary and Joseph together with the donkey which is carrying their luggage, and Mary sitting sideways on its back, as they pass through the mountainous region. In the evening Therese sees Joseph and Mary make their way through a rather large town (Hebron) to a smaller settlement with only about ten houses (Therese refers to this as Yutta), where Zachary and Elizabeth live in a rather large house which is located in a rather big garden set off by a natural fence. Wearing her veil, Elizabeth comes to the garden gate to meet Mary, who has hurried on ahead of Joseph. There they greet each other hastily, embracing each other and touching their right cheeks together. Then they make their way through the garden and the curtained doorway into the house, while Elizabeth removes her veil. Once again they greet each other, this time with greater emotion, embracing each other and kissing each other on the forehead, cheeks, and mouth. A ray of light passes from Mary to Elizabeth. Elizabeth then raises her right hand and speaks some inspired words, whereupon Mary, speaking in a powerful singing tone, speaks under inspiration much longer than Elizabeth. Then they make their way into a smaller room, where they sit down and eat some fruit which is brought to them by a servant girl. Joseph and Zachary make their appearance and eat some of the fruit. Joseph had been greeted by Zachary at another doorway. While the servant cared for the donkey, Joseph and Zachary went into a sort of vestibule with many columns, where they were conversing. Joseph speaking and Zachary writing on a tablet with a stone instrument.

Conclusion of Father Naber's account (cf. Lk 1:39-56).

First description by the author, July 2, 1947:

On Tuesday, July 1, on the Feast of the Precious Blood, Therese experienced great pain from the bleeding in her eyes, etc., even though she did not have her normal Friday sufferings during those two weeks, because of the octave of John the Baptist and the octave of the Feast of Peter and Paul. On the afternoon of July 1 she was quite exhausted and could not receive me. Instead she sent a message saying that I should come next afternoon and that I could witness the vision which would probably take place then because it was the Feast of the Visitation.

On Wednesday, July 2, at 2:00 P.M. I came to Konnersreuth. Therese was busy in her garden, planting. After paying my respects to Father Naber, I went into the parish house and had a rather lengthy conversation with him. About 5:00 both of us made our way to the Neumann house. Therese had finished her planting, had cleaned up, and gone into her room. After a while she called us and invited us to come up to her room, where we conversed with her for about half an hour on various subjects—but not about the visions.

In the middle of our conversation about publication plans, about 5:30, she was carried off into a vision. The priest showed me her complete insensitivity to all external influences, by striking her on the stigma in her hand and by waving his hand rapidly across her eyes, all of which did not produce the slightest reaction. Her radiant face was fixed on a point in the distance, and reacted with lively reflexes to what she saw: first astonishment, then a friendly smile, apparently at recognizing some person. Once she gave an unmistakable start, and then, apparently blinded by some brilliant light, sank back blinking her eyes. Then she immediately put on an expression of great astonishment.

This vision, which lasted for fifteen minutes, was immediately followed by the so-called state of prepossession, during which we queried her about her vision. She told us—in her own dialect and in very simple expression—that she had seen "the mother making a visit to an old lady" (Elizabeth). "The good man" (St. Joseph) had accompanied her with their donkey, and had handed this donkey over to another "old man" (Zachary). This man was not able to speak, but he opened his mouth as if to speak and formed the words with his lips like the deaf and dumb (she had made similar motions with her mouth during the vision as well). Later, while they were seated, this same man had also "scrawled on a little tablet."

Meantime, the mother had made her way, together with the "old lady," through a beautiful path, planted on both sides with shrubbery, towards the principal entrance to the house, and "then the old woman suddenly said something powerful. In that same moment a beam of living light sprang from the mother to the old woman; it almost blinded me. And then the two of them prayed together. But that was really magnificent (the Magnificat). Then they went inside the house, where a simple meal was waiting for them. When I asked her what they had eaten, she said, "Only what came down from the trees (fruit), and a hard loaf of bread and a sort of yellow spread (probably honey, which was customarily served with bread; cf. the vision of the multiplication of the loaves). Then, after a short pause, "There were also some water-skippers (fish)." But she kept coming back to the main point, the mother and the magnificent bright light that came from her.

At this point I set a book before her, the alleged words of Christ to a certain nun, but she would have nothing to do with it; she pushed it aside and said: "This I do not understand." And when Father Naber placed her fingers at another passage in this same book—she had closed her eyes and turned aside her head—she said: "Take it away." Then I put Aretin's manuscript on Gerlich into her fingers, and she was immediately interested. She felt the paper and said: "He has been with our Lord for a long time already. But now we must speak about the Mother once again." Around 6:00, this state passed into an obviously very refreshing sleep, which lasted for some ten minutes, whereupon Therese once again awoke and found herself in her normal state.

In her previous state, she had explained that today she had been "away" (that is, transported, in her ecstatic visionary state, to the locale of the vision) for the third time; early in the morning she had seen Mary and Joseph setting out with the donkey from "the same city in which the Savior had been for such a long time," (Nazareth), "but not from the house where they lived afterwards, rather from a bigger one, and the mother's (St. Anne) was there too, and the two of them had a long conversation." (To the question: "And the Father?" she answered: "Him I did not see." Joachim was, apparently, no longer alive.

That afternoon, about 2:00, she had seen her second vision, alone in the greenhouse. The subject of this vision was Joseph and Mary during their trip into the mountain country.

I should like to add here that, after the vision, when Therese was in her state of prepossession, Father Naber touched the stigmata on her hand in order to show me the difference, and Therese, with an expression of pain on her face, immediately withdrew her hand.

Therese Neumann, 1952. Photo for an identification card.

CHAPTER FIVE

THE CHRISTMAS VISIONS

(Sources: Lost description N; G 1, 179ff.,
partially abridged; TB; V)

December 22: Departure from Nazareth for Bethlehem

Joseph had just returned home and informed Mary that an edict had come out from Caesar Augustus ordering the registration of the entire population of the Roman Empire, and, since each citizen had to register in his own native city, that they must immediately set out for Bethlehem. Since Mary was at that moment expecting her child, this was a very difficult order. Nonetheless, she declared herself ready; there was no alternative, they had to obey. Joseph was concerned that the trip would prove to be too much for Mary, and wanted to go by himself. But Mary answered that God would help them, and that she would obey her superior. So they prepared for the trip.

As their mount and pack animal they took along a she-ass, because they would be able to use her milk. The gray tent-cloth was laid on the animal and over it the gray wool blanket. The rest of their baggage was hanging from both sides; on the left a pack which consisted of a blanket for Joseph, wrapped around a warm outer garment for him, and some bread and fruit. On the right were the packs; the front pack, smaller than the back one, consisted of a simple woolen blanket which could be cut up for swaddling clothes, wrapped around similar pieces of cloth and shirts for the expected child. The pack on the rear at the right side was of hemp, and it contained a warm outer garment for Mary and some other foodstuffs. Fastened to it, horizontally, were the three tent poles.

At about 6:00 in the morning they set out. Mary was sitting on the donkey with her feet hanging down on the left side. Joseph was walking beside the animal, on the left side and towards the front. He was leading the donkey with his right hand by a dark brown leather harness. In his left hand he carried a walking stick taller than himself and curving in a half circle on top. He was dressed in a dark yellow tunic and brown cloak. Mary was wearing a warm, grayish-brown tunic, a reddish-brown cloak, and a yellow wool veil under the cloak. The weather was rather cold and rainy, and the paths were rough and rutted. The trip proceeded well on this first day, but they could not reach a place to spend the night. They set up their tents in the open air, in a desolate region near a few trees, and spent the night on the blankets they had brought with them. The donkey was tied fast to a tree.

December 23; On The Way to Bethlehem

On the next day Mary and Joseph set out around 5:30. They traveled without interruption until around noon although they were constantly concerned with preparations for the birth of Mary's expected child. In order to spare the donkey, Mary went on foot from time to time. Especially around noon she was unwilling to burden the animal because she noticed it was very tired.

But since she was tired herself, they began looking for help. Then they saw a house in the distance; they thanked God and went towards it. Here lived a very old couple who had a boy and a girl. Joseph went into the little house and asked them for their help. The old man came out to Mary and forced her to come into the house. The people did not actually know Joseph and Mary; but since they were so friendly and since Mary, in her pregnant condition, looked very pale and sick the old couple gave up their warm dinner.

Our Lord rewarded them for it later. The old people died

as pagans, but good pagans. Their two children became Christians. They first listened to the preaching of John the Baptist, and the brother had himself baptized. He then followed our Lord, one of the 72 disciples, while his sister took over the management of their house. While she was busy removing every trace of paganism and idolatry from her house, and was in the act of removing an idol from the roof, her relatives came upon her and pushed her violently from the roof to her death.

The second night Mary and Joseph stayed in a small town in an inn where they had to pay for their lodging. They rested well and set out refreshed on the next day's journey.

Author's note: In later years this vision gave me much to ponder. This is what Resl actually said: "You can see how our Savior thanked them for having received his mother so well; they all came to him. And especially their daughter, how our Savior rewarded her; she went straight to him."

In Konnersreuth, the phrase "to go straight to him" always meant that the soul of the person referred to was privileged to enter together with our Savior into his glory immediately upon death. Therese would have a vision of the Savior appearing to each dying person a few minutes after his death, judging the soul in a single glance, whereupon the judged person immediately recognized both his fate and absolute justice of his Judge. Sometimes the soul was immediately bright and radiant and able to go with Our Savior; other souls remained more or less dark and had to wait behind, alone and abandoned—the poor souls. (Therese never saw the damnation of a soul, although she did have a very frightening vision of the fall of the angels).

To return to the death of the daughter of this hospitable family, we would more or less expect some reward in terms of earthly happiness, in some form or other. But we must grow accustomed to the fact that statements in a state of ecstasy, that is, statements made in the state of elevated calm, to the effect that "it will be made good" have a scope that looks beyond the limitations of death. When Gerlich was engaged in his battle against Hitler's regime, he was frequently told in ecstasy: "Even if it looks bad down here, the Savior is still winning, it will all be all right." And what was his fate! Five and a quarter years of "protective custody" and then murder at Dachau. Therese saw him immediately enter the presence of our Savior, right after his death. His protective custody had certainly been more than enough Purgatory for his passionate aggressiveness. When I heard of his death, I found myself at once thinking of this daughter from the vision whose "reward" consisted in her being pushed off the roof to her death.

December 24: Looking for Shelter

About 6:00 in the morning Joseph and Mary resumed their journey. After noon the donkey was too tired to go farther. At a small village they managed to get some food for the animal, without pay. The weather was rainy and cold. About a quarter to six in the evening, Therese saw Mary getting off the donkey at the north gate of Bethlehem, and then Joseph making his way through the gate behind the animal.

Bethlehem, at that time, had about 1100 inhabitants. The houses were like those of Jerusalem, flat-roofed. They were built with rectangular, narrow, and also round windows, without glass, covered instead with wooden lattices and curtains. Inside the gate and along the streets the panniers were already burning. These were pans which hung in a fork from six-foot long poles and which were used for maintaining a fire. The street was finished with large stones and was thus, very rough. The houses stood in a straight row, although there were gaps in the line.

Joseph went into the house on the right side of the street, while Mary held the donkey by the fence. Soon he would come back out. With a troubled expression he would tell Mary the bad news, that they could not spend the night there. Then they went on a few houses farther and Joseph asked at an inn. He was informed that there was no longer any room. Very disturbed, he went back to Mary who said something consoling to him.

Then they tried farther down the street, a house on the left, but again without success. This was the house from which Joseph had descended and in which he was supposed to register.

Since there was such a crowd, he decided to put off his registration until the following day. But Mary insisted on today, since her time was drawing near. Accordingly, they waited between two houses until the house was less crowded. Then they registered.

Meantime, however, it had become very dark. Finally, Joseph asked lodging of a man who was standing on a staircase without a railing which went down the right outside of the house located on the right side of the street. This man was friendly, but answered that he had no room left. He directed them to the south city gate, where a pannier was burning. They were supposed to pass through this gate and travel a short distance along the road where they would find, on the right hand side, a stable in which he told them they could spend the night. The man had an interest in the stable. His shepherds were among the group of shepherds who later came to worship. Mary and Joseph followed his directions.

Standing under the city gate, Joseph lighted a beaked lantern he had brought along. This lantern was enclosed in a small case constructed like a roof, open in front, and equipped with a handle on top. The two of them went ahead on foot, Mary behind Joseph, on the left, walking beside the donkey. They went about 600 feet along the street, heading south, before a footpath branched off to the right, leading to a stable about 150 feet away from the road. The stable had a sliding-door built into the middle of the wall. Joseph pushed the door to the right and then, about 8:00, entered the stable together with Mary and the donkey.

Therese added these remarks (tapes): "How miserable it all was. It was only a place for cattle. There was straw lying all around and hay and dirt from the cattle, and it was bitterly cold—just awful when you consider the mother's condition. Just imagine it. I really felt sorry for the mother, but the good man (Joseph) started cleaning up immediately, and putting things in order. If the people who had refused to let them in had only known who they were—but they did not know. Do you think we would have taken them in? I think so, but what if they didn't know us? And they were such simple people. Then she began speaking about the stable again: "Why, we just take it for granted that we have such beautiful houses, all bright and warm and dry, and they had such a miserable time of it."

Continuation of the account by Father Naber: The stable was about twenty-two feet wide and twelve feet deep. It was built on the eastern slope of the hill and connected with a rocky cave which was about three feet high and three feet deep on the northern side, and formed the rear wall. To the south, the hill sloped away and the cave disappeared. On the roof of the stable was a thatch-roof; it began about six feet high in the front and was almost two feet higher in the back; it was made of thick old boards which were attached on a somewhat slanting line. The front and the side wall were also built of boards. On the right hand side wall there was a small window, higher than it was wide. All around the stable were pens for the flocks.

Joseph tied the donkey to a pole in the rear left-hand corner of the stable, moving it later to another pole at the head of the child so that the donkey could help warm the crib. He hung his lantern in the middle of the stable, from the ceiling. Then he prepared a bed for Mary and for himself. For Mary he spread the tent on the straw along the right wall, covering it with the gray woolen blanket, while he made his own bed along the left wall. The sky was cloudy.

Thus far Father Naber's description.

December 24-25: Christmas Night

Gerlich (1, 184), who had come to Konnersreuth Christmas Eve with Professor Wutz, describes what follows:

After sharing in the pastor's hospitality, we found ourselves together with him that evening, before 11:00, in Therese's room.

At 11:13 that night, in the middle of a conversation about her goldfinch, she was once again carried off into a vision, which lasted until 11:19. Her face was radiant with joy. Her motions were extremely vivacious, even her feet were moving, and her fingers were trying to grasp something. Then she sank back and closed her eyes, only to open them after a moment and launch upon a lively account of what she had seen—she was now in her state of prepossession: "I have just been in the stable, and there was a little child there. He was wrapped in blankets. I saw his little hands. They were very tiny and the little child had his eyes closed most of the time. It was very cold." In her great joy she wanted to speak of nothing but the "tiny baby" and it was with difficulty that she could be brought to describe the entire scene.

Finally she told the following story which I took down in brief notes: "I was in a stable made out of wood which was built against a mountain; it was dark gray stone. The ground was not even; fragments (pieces of rock) were lying all around. The stable was set against the cliff and had a sloping roof. In the stable, along the wall in the back, and on both sides, there were posts more than three feet high." She herself had stood to the left, beside the door, as she explained in answer to a question. She was, accordingly, looking into the stable. What was the left side for her, was on the Christ child's right. "In the rear to the left, a donkey was tied to a post."

When she was asked if there were not also an ox there, she answered: "There was no other kind of animal there. The little child was lying in a crib. No, this was not the kind of crib, you know, that we use to feed our cattle; it was different. It was made of wood and stood on crossed feet. The back wall was two hands breadth higher, and straight. There were several cribs there. There were five of them. The one in which they laid the little baby stood more in the middle, almost directly across from the entrance. A little bit to the right side, you know. The little baby was lying with his head towards the back wall; the crib was situated diagonally in the stable, about five feet from the wall, and it was two feet high." Therese kept asking who the little baby could have been. When she was told that it was the Savior, her joy knew no bounds.

"The mother was standing beside the Savior, to the left, and was caressing the child's hands. Joseph stood to the right of the child; he had his hands folded and said something out loud that I could not understand. Mary crossed her arms. The child had dark blue eyes and fair, curly hair. The straw on which he was

lying was stronger than the straw we have and nice and dark."
(As she later explained in her state of elevated calm, there was
straw only on the bottom part of the crib, with reeds on top; this
was apparently the stronger, dark-colored straw.) "Along the
wall there were piles of wheat straw and this dark strong straw.
A gray covering was set on top. They also had a light. A lantern
was hanging down from the ceiling of the stable, with the flame
coming out of a small beak."

By constantly directing the object of her narrative, it was
possible to take down a simple sketch of the stable immediately;
the sketch corresponds with the already partially recorded details
that were given earlier, and it was later tested and enlarged upon
both by Therese's own recollections in her normal state and what
Father Naber recorded of her remarks in her elevated state of calm.

The Birth of Christ

Therese herself did not see the birth of Christ. The details
recorded by Father Naber on this subject come from her state of
elevated calm. Literally, they are as follows: "At about 11:00
that night Mary experiences an ecstacy. She rises to a kneeling
posture and crosses her hands over her breast. Around midnight
the divine child leaves his mother's womb, which remains intact
and immediately closes again without any complications, without
any labor pangs before or after. Joseph, who got up shortly
after Mary, prepared a crib with straw. He put wheat straw into
it first, with reeds on top, to make it softer. The crib was about
three feet long; not all the cribs in the stable were of the same
size. This was the crib in which Mary laid the divine child, after
she had dried him off, wrapped him in swaddling clothes, then
dressed him in a little shirt with long sleeves that went down over
his feet, and wrapped him in a woolen blanket. Then they began
to worship the child, Joseph on his right and Mary on his left.
Joseph prayed holding his hands across his breast with his fingers
intertwined. Mary had her arms crossed over her breast. At the
birth of Christ, the sky turned bright and filled with stars."

Adoration by Mary and Joseph had been witnessed by Therese in the vision that began at 11:13 and has already been described.

Personal note by the author: The first time I read this account, from Therese's state of elevated calm, I was very moved. At that moment I was not yet 30 years old, an age in which we tend to develop a critical attitude towards the religious instruction we get from our parents and our school. In the very pregnant formulation of the words describing the birth of Christ, I noted that several dogmas of the Church were precisely confirmed: the dogma of Mary's virginity after the birth of Christ ("intact and immediately closed") as well as the Immaculate Conception ("without any labor pains before or after") as an exception from the curse of the proto-evangelium ("in pain shall you give birth"), both of them most important dogmas of Mariology.

That is why, later, I could not understand how the events that followed could have taken place: Gerlich had asked the bishop's office at Regensburg for an Imprimatur for his book. The Imprimatur, as is well known, does not guarantee that the authority which grants this seal of approval shares the author's opinion in every detail; it merely confirms the fact that there is nothing in the book against faith or morals. Now, Gerlich was advised by letter, December 2, 1929, that his book would receive the Imprimatur as soon as he had removed four "passages that directly contradict the faith."

The first and second of the passages were as follows: "The state of elevated calm gives Therese Neumann the sensation of being united with Christ and participating in his blessedness and omniscience insofar as Christ grants this" (G 1, 174) and "in her state of elevated calm, in which, as we have said, she participates in the omniscience to the degree that Christ permits." It was the word "omniscience" that was objected to in both cases.

Gerlich was willing to change these passages, since they comprised impressions and formulations of his own. But he was unable to do so in time for the first edition, since the bishop's office at Regensburg had, on November 6, already telephoned permission for the printing and the book had meantime been printed excepting for the page which was to carry the Imprimatur. Among the passages, however, which were objected to as directly contradicting articles of faith, the following two sentences were also cited: 3. "which remains intact and immediately closes again, without any labor pangs before or after"; 4. "after she had dried him off."

(Both passages come from the account given by Therese Neumann herself in her state of elevated calm as recorded by Father Naber: Gl, 187.)

In a 14-page letter to Regensburg, Gerlich made a most emphatic appeal against any alterations or omissions in these passages. He was, he said, an historian and it would be a violation of his conscience to conceal statements that had actually been made by a person in any effort at extenuation. If these passages did in fact offend against articles of faith, then Therese must be a heretic and the Church would have to take corresponding steps against her; but under no circumstances would he play the role of hypocrite.

In the sharply worded logic of the letter he writes: "You have explicitly asked this author, who in his introduction to his book explains that he will never allow himself to deviate from the commandment, 'Thou shall not bear false witness,' to transgress this very commandment." Thus, his book appeared without any Imprimatur, but also without the omission of the passages in question.

In the course of time I have consulted several theologians who are both highly placed and still quite actively engaged in teaching, but none of them was able to find a single point of contradiction with the Catholic faith in the passages in question. Quite the contrary, they found them to be a real support for Catholic dogma. The objection to the phrase "after she had dried him off" is difficult to understand. A newly born child, who is still wet from the womb, cannot be swaddled while he is still wet. How could the drying, which happened at every birth, offend against the faith?

In this short and very precise account of the birth of Jesus we find confirmation not only for the dogma of the Virgin Birth and the Immaculate Conception, but also a third element: twice we find the expression "the divine child," which underlines the dogma of the Council of Ephesus, the Theotokos (Mother of God).

The. Glorified Christchild

In 1927, Therese had stayed home during the Christmas Mass. When the bell rang at consecration time she was carried off into a vision which she reported to Father Naber as follows: From the Consecration to the Communion of the Mass she saw the Christchild in a glorified state. He was approximately sixteen inches high, with a radiant white shirt that reached from his neck to his ankles and had long wide sleeves. He was standing on a luminous cloud, stretching out his hands with a friendly smile. His hair was bright blond and curly, his eyes dark blue. The whole vision was like a view of heaven. During the entire time, in the distance, she heard a wonderfully beautiful song.

Christ's Birth Announced to the Shepherds

The vision began at about 1:20 that night. Therese saw herself transported to the front of a hut that lay about half an hour south of the stable and some 160 feet to the left of the road, on a hill. The whole landscape was hilly. The hut was not quite six feet high, covered diagonally with reeds, and built into a corner of rock in such a manner that the front side was open to the rock with three thick round poles for support, while the south side had another such pole. The hut was about half as big as the stable at Bethlehem. There was room for eight shepherds to pass the night, lying on reeds with bundles of reeds under their heads. There were all sorts of blankets and hides lying around. There were also thirteen white and brown sheep, some larger, some smaller, which were the shepherds' favorites, as well as a medium-sized black dog and a small brown one, both of them long-haired and with drooping ears and tails. The hut was surrounded by seven tents, with approximately 500 sheep.

Suddenly there was a blinding light. Everyone in the hut was frightened; the shepherds all began looking out of their hut to see what caused this apparition. What could they see? About ten feet away from the west side of the hut, and about ten feet in the air on a luminous cloud was an angel of higher rank, in the luminous form of a young man with a radiant white garment with long full sleeves, flowing from his neck to his ankles, and girt in the middle. (According to the tape she said: "He was one of those, you know, like the one who said, *Shelam ich Miriam*," i.e., the Archangel Gabriel at the Annunciation.) His long hair fell from both sides of his head. His left hand lay on his breast, while his right was raised. He had no wings. The entire area was illuminated by the light that emanated from the angel.

As if to calm them, but at the same time clearly, friendly, and solemn, the angel spoke to the shepherds in their own language. Twice he pointed with his right hand off towards the left. When he finished speaking, many other angels appeared around him (about 600) in a similar luminous form and on a luminous cloud. After they had repeated a magnificent song about half a dozen times, apparently in the language of the shepherds, who paid the closest attention throughout this whole experience, the entire heavenly apparition disappeared. The shepherds spoke among themselves for about a quarter hour, determining what to do next. (Explanation from tape: They were good people, this you could see, but they were very poor, all they had to wear were a few rags; but then it wasn't so cold there.)

Then they all left in the direction of Bethlehem. The thirteen pet sheep and the two dogs ran after them. The stable in which the Redeemer had been born belonged to the master of these shepherds. They hoped to find the newborn boy there. Their hopes were raised when, from the road, they saw a light coming from the stable window.

The Shepherds Adore the Child

In a further vision, Therese saw the adoration of the Savior by the shepherds in the stable. First she saw the eight men with their sheep and dogs in front of the stable. The one who appeared to be the eldest shook the stable door, whereupon Joseph appeared and the door opened. (Tape: After considerable delay: "You know, he had to protect the Savior and that is why he didn't open up right away. And they had a little problem with the language.")

The shepherds were telling Joseph, as one might gather from their gestures, what they had just experienced. Joseph then spoke to them and pointed to the child and his mother. Then he led them to the crib in which the child was lying. The shepherds looked at the child with obvious love and joy. Then they spoke a few words to the mother who had been seated on a blanket which seemed to have straw under it, but now stood up. She spoke a few words to the shepherds and showed the child, who looked very alert, uncovering him a little so they could see. With amazement and enthusiasm they all looked at the child, especially the eldest. Then they all knelt around the crib (Tape: "They fell down on their foreheads") and prayed, while Mary crossed her hands reverently over her breast.

She was dressed in a reddish-brown tunic, girt in the middle, a yellow wool veil, and a large woolen shoulder-cloth, and had leather sandals on her feet. On the straw, in the left front corner, lay a cloak. Joseph's hands were crossed over his breast at about the height of his chin, his fingers intertwined; he was wearing a dark yellow tunic, girt at the middle. Mary and Joseph had girt their tunics with ties of the same color and apparently the same material as that of the tunics.

Joseph wore nothing on his head. His hair was rather black, somewhat dishevelled, and it fell about to his shoulders. His beard was of medium length, thick and not parted, and seemed somewhat brighter in color. The expression on his face was peaceful, gentle, and friendly. Of the shepherds, one was rather old, a second already well along in years, both of them gray-bearded; four were of middle age. The last were without beards, while the other four had full, uncultivated beards. Four of them had their heads wrapped, two wore round caps made of skins, and two were bare-headed. Almost all of them wore their hair shoulder-length. Some of them had tunics that reached to their ankles, while others reached only to the calf of the leg.

Author's note: At this point it is necessary to correct Gerlich's original records with the aid of the tape recording. Gerlich has taken the dialect form *"oi, oi,"* which expresses simply a plural number, which number can be made up of no more than two, as reading "some, others," thereby easily creating the impression of a much greater number, whereas, in the case of the proclamation to the shepherds, there were a total of only eight shepherds.

Some of them were dressed only in sleeveless skins, which reached to their knees and were bound around their waist with a sash of cloth. Others wore tunics and had skins over their shoulders. Some were barefoot, others wore sandles, some had wrapped their feet and lower legs with strips of cloth. About six of them had staves taller than themselves, bowed on the top. The eldest prayed with outstretched arms, while the others held their hands as Joseph did. The eldest had his head uncovered; he had long white hair and a white beard. He was dressed in a brown tunic which went to his ankles, a large, yellow wool fleece lay around his shoulders, and his feet were bound with swatches of cloth.

All eight shepherds were very reverent. The sheep and dogs had been herded to the inside of the group. Only one lamb remained standing inside when the stable door had been shut. (Tape: "But then they brought it outside again.") The shepherds gave one of their sheep to the Holy Family. (Tape: "It was not very old, but already fairly well grown, and needed to be properly fattened.") But Mary and Joseph soon gave it away again to a very poor shepherd. A mother sheep with her lamb, which was later given to them as a present, had to be sold in order to buy necessary provisions.

CHAPTER SIX

THE CHILDHOOD OF CHRIST
Circumcision: January 1

(Sources: N1928 lost, but recorded in Gl, 220.
N1, 53 (1929), N2, 22 (1930); Tape; A.)

According to the Law of Moses, every male child had to be circumcised, in keeping with God's covenant with Abraham. The corresponding passage in the Old Testament reads as follows (Gn 17:10-13): "This is my covenant, which you shall keep, between me and you and your descendants after you: Every male among you shall be circumcised. You shall be circumcised in the flesh of your foreskins, and it shall be the sign of the covenant between me and you. He that is eight days old among you shall be circumcised. Every male throughout your generation, whether born in your house, or bought with your money from any foreigner who is not of your offspring, both he that is born in your house and he that is bought for money, shall be circumcised. So shall my covenant be in your flesh an everlasting covenant." As a descendant of the house of David, the child Jesus also was subject to this law.

In the course of the spread of Christian doctrine, this practice was opposed by the non-Jews. Particularly St. Paul, the most zealous champion of the Mosaic precept before the time of his conversion, encountered the greatest opposition when, in his attempt to spread Christianity to the heathens outside Palestine, he did not demand that they be circumcised. A great part of the apostles were of the opinion that the candidates for Christian baptism must first be circumcised before they could be admitted to baptism (cf. Ac 15:1-5). It was this struggle that led to the Apostolic Council, at which Paul spoke out violently against this opinion. Therese sees him there, in one of her visions, stamping his feet in anger; that is why, in her state of prepossession, in which she does not know people's names, she refers to him simply by the term "the foot-stamper." It was, at length, unanimously decided not to demand circumcision in such cases (Ac 15:22ff.).

In her natural sympathetic sensitivity, Therese sees the circumcision of Jesus as an attack on the child which she strongly disapproves of, since she sees that the child is wounded and crying loudly in his pain. Some of her words will be recorded in conclusion to the following account of Father Naber's.

N January 1, 1928, as per deposition by G 1, 220:
1:00 p.m. in the parish house.

Therese was standing to the left of the door in the stable at Bethlehem. The stable had been cleaned. Joseph had just tied the donkey to the last pole on the left. A sheep and a lamb were running around the donkey. Mary, standing on the left of the child lying in his crib, was speaking with a woman standing to her right. Both women had their backs to Therese. This woman (according to N 1, 53, the account of 1929, she worked as a midwife) was wearing a long dark red tunic girt in the middle, and over it a yellowish cloak across her arms and breast, and over this a veil of the same color, of lighter material. Then three men came to the stable door. The eldest was a priest from Bethlehem. He was clothed in a yellowish-white tunic which hung in broad folds down to his leather sandals. Over this he wore another gown, white in color and woven with gold; it was folded over his neck and breast and held over his hips with a strong yellow sash, whose tasseled ends hung far down on the left side. This second gown reached as far as his knees. The golden border was sewn around the neck, the cuffs, and the bottom hem, from which there also hung brilliant tassel-balls. The sleeves were medium-broad and reached to the wrist. Over these tunics he wore a broad cloak, striped with many colors, closed at the left shoulder. On his head he wore a covering made of two hemispherical pieces, narrowing from bottom to top and separated by a split which ran along the middle, front to back: the two halves were held together, at their lower ends, by a three-inch wide stiff band of cloth wrapped tightly around the head. The head covering was white and sewn with gold. On both sides hung bands of the same material, about four inches wide. His shoulder-length hair, and his round, full beard were mixed with gray.

His attendants, two servants from the synagogue, were wearing long yellow-blue wool tunics, held together in the middle by a sash, and over them a cloak like that of the priest. Their heads were bound with a white, gold-striped cloth, which was tied together on the right side and hung down in two strips upon their shoulders. They had black full beards and black hair which was not quite shoulder-length. Joseph went to meet them as they entered and greeted them with bows and words. He helped the priest take off his cloak which he brought, together with those of the attendants, to a crib near the pile of straw. The three then approached the crib.

After exchanging greetings with the mother and the woman and after a few further words between the priest and the mother, the priest and his attendants went to the window, while Mary unclothed the child and wrapped it in a long white woolen cloth that reached up to the arms. Joseph then took the child from Mary who spoke a few words to him which he answered briefly. Then she went to the left front corner of the stable where she leaned against one of the cribs, alongside the crib that held the cloaks.

Joseph handed the child to the woman who brought it to the priest. He himself stayed near the crib at first, but later went to the side of the mother, and, towards the end of the circumcision, close to the priest. The woman brought the child to the priest near the window.

In front of the priest stood a rectangular table of yellow-brown wood, about two feet in length and not quite so high, with three gray-brown feet set at an angle. Previously this table had held two reed baskets with fruit (dates, figs, and fruits that looked like apricots, oranges, and melons). These baskets now stood on the floor, while the table was occupied, at the front, with an octagonal stone box, about sixteen inches across, made out of something that looked like grayish-white marble, covered on top with a recessed lid of the same material. This had been brought in by one of the attendants in a yellow wooden chest which he carried by means of a sash bound around it. Beside this chest lay the two scrolls that had been brought by the other attendant. In the box were three small copper-colored round vessels and a curved yellowish knife with a curved tip. There was water from the Temple well in one of the vessels and ointment in another, while the third was reserved for the piece of skin that would be cut off.

The attendant standing to the right of the priest (an assistant priest and would later become a priest) who had brought the vessels and the knife, took them out of the box, laid them beside the scrolls, put the cover back on the box, and then handed the priest the cloths which were apparently carried in the same box. The first of these was red with a red fringe. This covered the stone box down to the table top. A second cloth with a golden hem reached down only to the fringe of the red cloth. While praying from the scroll which was held for him by the two attendants standing slightly before him on either side, the priest spread the covers over the table.

In front of the little table, diagonal 'to the wall with the window, was a chair with crossed feet and a rectangular back made of sticks of wood that were covered with gray bark, and covered with brightly striped material. The priest sat down on this chair. First he took the child onto his lap, then looked through the window to his back, and up into the air in front of him; then he freed the child from the cloth, which the woman took, and laid the child with its upper body on the veiled box. The two attendants, kneeling on either side, each held a foot and an arm, while the attendant to the priest's right handed him the knife.

Then the somewhat excited priest (he had begun to suspect

that this child might be the promised Redeemer; later he actually became a follower of Christ) failed to make a straight cut so that he had to correct the cut and also had to cut away part of the outside skin. The particle of skin which, according to the precept of the law, had been cut away from the inner skin, he then deposited in the lowest of the three vessels, which the attendant on his right offered him. Putting this vessel aside, the same attendant offered him the largest of the three vessels, from which the priest took a water-soaked sponge, with which he daubed at the place he had circumcised, and which he then replaced in the vessel.

The attendant then handed him the middle vessel from which the priest took something which he rubbed over the circumcision. Finishing this, he took the sponge from the vessel which the servant proffered once again, this time in his left hand, while he cleansed the fingers of his right hand and wiped them with the little towel which the woman had laid on the table together with some wool. The attendant on the right hand side then used the little cloth and the wad of cotton to dry up the blood. The woman brought the little towel to the mother.

During the circumcision the child had cried rather loudly. The mother also had cried. Joseph was watching everything with a very sympathetic attitude. Therese too had cried and had reacted very angrily towards the men who performed the circumcision. The woman now wrapped the child again in the woolen cloth and carried it to the crib. The mother also went over to the crib and the two of them wrapped the child in a long white wool wrap from his feet, which they covered, individually, up to his armpits. They covered this with a dark red wrap which covered the child up to his neck, including his feet and arms (both feet together this time).

The woman put him in his mother's arms, the mother handed the child to St. Joseph, who presented the baby to the priest who was now standing. The priest laid the child on the covered box, raised his eyes to heaven, and, with outspread arms, spoke a few words aloud. Then he turned to Joseph, asking what name was to be given to this child, whereupon Joseph answered (according to the Tape, *Yeshúa*). Now the priest spent some time lost in thought. At a given sign, the two attendants held the scroll out for him, and he prayed from it aloud. After this all three of them sang in unison.

Then the priest took the child and gave it to the woman. The woman gave it back to the mother. She, in turn, laid it on the stone box, whereupon the mother and the priest, looking up to heaven, joined their right hands over the child for a short time. The mother now left, and the woman brought the child back to the crib. There it began to cry, and the woman brought the child into the front left corner of the stable to its mother. Meantime the priest was folding up the little cloths, saying prayers as he did so. The attendants put the vessels and the knife back into the box which they placed in the wooden chest. They laid the little cloths on top. Then all three of them went to the strawpile, the one attendant ·with the chest held by its sash and the other with the two scrolls. Joseph helped the priest put on his cloak. Then, bowing and extending their greetings, they said goodbye to Mary. Joseph escorted them outside, while the mother went to the crib with her child.

Further details to the above account, according to the Tape: Therese says (here the translation is from High German): The good man (her habitual way of referring to St. Joseph in her state of prepossession) simply should not have let them come in at all. The little Savior made me feel very sad. Father Naber attempted to appease her by explaining that this was only a custom, something prescribed. Therese: The child really made me feel sad. Just recently I was reading in a book, and it was all written very beautifully, but none of it is true. Whoever wrote that was not there.

The people who wrote that said that they put the child into a stone trough from which the cattle had licked out all the salt. That is not true, the child was laid in a wooden crib, from which the cattle used to eat their fodder. In a stone trough, that would have been really uncomfortable; you would have had to stoop over and it would probably be very cold. At that time it was always inclined to be very raw, even though they did not have any snow in those places. The child was lying in a woven basket, made out of something green, like the grass we get from ponds (reeds). I could see this very clearly because the Savior "carried me away" (this means that our Savior suddenly snatched her away as an eye-witness, just as he did in the case of many prophets in the Old Testament, seizing them "by the crown of their head" and transporting them suddenly into different regions). There is also the case of the deacon Philip in the New Testament; after he had baptized the eunuch of Queen Candace, "the spirit of the Lord caught him up; and the eunuch saw him no more, and went on his way rejoicing. But Philip was found in Azotus" (Ac 8, 39f.).

Therese continued in her child-like presentation of the scene: One of the three was more finely dressed (the priest). And the good man also gave them something for what they had done with the little Savior. I wouldn't have given them anything. Gerlich (G 1, 217) adds these impressions of his during the vision:

January 1, 1928, 1:00 P.M. Therese's expression was at first friendly, but then showed marked signs of disturbance and anger; she even made a fist. Then she began to shake her head and show signs of visible sorrow. But suddenly she was seized by another burst of anger. Both hands turned into fists, with which she threatened the object of her vision. Then she began to cry. But the tears gradually turned into a sympathetic joy, and then a joyous nodding and beckoning with the head and a corresponding movement of the hands. Then her face began to register real suspense, her head and eyes assumed a very attentive posture and expression, and then once again she showed great joy. Now she turned her eyes upward, as if seeking something; suddenly she showed great joy, her fingers moved as if she wanted to grasp something. Then she sank back on the pillows and began brooding about what she had seen. "If it had been the mother who opened the door, they never would have got in; the whole thing never would have happened." Suddenly she put her hand to her face and eyes: "Am I wet? What's this?" Asked where she had been, she said: "I have seen the little Savior in the stable. It was the same stable as before, but it was all cleaned up."

Presentation of Jesus in the Temple
Purification of the Virgin Mary, Candlemass: February 2
(Sources: N 1, 59; 2, 42, although only references to the vision; Tapes; Author's own description.)

In introducing the vision of the Blessed Virgin Mary's name-day, it has already been mentioned that every mother, forty days after the birth of her child, had to go to the Temple for the ceremony of "purification," and that, according to another law, the child, if it were male and firstborn, had to be brought along for the presentation. This explains why the word "presentation" is commonly used to describe both ceremonies; the law commanded a special consecration and dedication of the firstborn to God. The firstborn had to be bought back from God symbolically, by a sacrifice. The ceremony was also important by reason of the fact that the right of the firstborn, which was officially established by the separate ceremony, had a role to play in Jewish law, from the time of the patriarchs, quite similar to our modern practice in the case of the nobility. In order to avoid any division of the family holdings, the firstborn inherited all the land and flocks of the father, while later children, and all the daughters, remained simply fellow-laborers in the family, unless they married into some other family.

Mary, accordingly, had to present the child Jesus in the temple on the fortieth day after his birth. The old priest Simeon, coming to the Temple "upon the impulse of the Spirit," gave the child a name: "a light for the revelation of the gentiles". That is why, in reference to the word "light," the feast was always celebrated, from earliest Christian times, with processions of burning candles, a custom which has given the feast its modern name of Candlemass. In the East the feast is celebrated as a feast of our Lord, while in the Roman Church it had become a feast of the Blessed Virgin. (With the recent liturgical changes it is now called the Presentation of the Lord.)

Therese's account of her vision: The Savior carried me away. There I saw the mother and the good man and the little Savior who was wrapped in swaddling clothes. They went up under the trees towards the big house. There was someone there waiting to take the donkey from the good man. The mother, who was carrying the Savior under her cloak, and the good man then went into the big house with many columns inside. The people inside seemed to have known all about it; they had a little table all ready, and they laid the Savior upon it. The good man had to buy something down below, and when he came back up he had to hand it over. Then he went back to where the men were and the mother was escorted by two "old women" (Temple widows) across a huge roomy passageway. The good man was not allowed to go away. Then they came to a place from which a stairway led up into the big house. At the corners there were lights burning, and there was a table "with little vessels on it."

Then the men took the beautiful clothes out of a chest and put them on; then they took one of the little vessels and laid the Savior in it. The mother was not allowed to follow them any farther; "she had to give up the little Savior and then simply wait." Then they sang many prayers from the scrolls, that I could not understand. Then a very old man, standing somewhat to the side, held the Savior up in the air and prayed and then said something magnificent (Lk 2:29-32): "Lord, now let thy servant depart in peace, according to thy word; for mine eyes have seen thy salvation which thou hast prepared in the presence of all peoples, a light for revelations to the Gentiles, and for glory to thy people Israel.")

Then they came for the mother who was standing behind a lattice. Then the mother had to lift up the Savior. That was rather difficult for her. This I could notice (apparently the offering of the child). The old man then took the Savior from the vessel and handed him back to his mother, then held his hand over them and said some powerful words (the words are very probably "Behold, the child is set for the fall and rise of many in Israel and for a sign that is spoken against" and "A sword will pierce through your own soul also" (Lk 2:34f.). They had to wait a while longer and then a woman came up the stairs that led to the room. Try to picture a long, gloomy passageway. First the woman said something friendly, this I could notice. Then she went with Mary into the passageway, after she had been allowed to take the child in her arms for a moment. Then the mother took the child back and held him under her cloak.

Meanwhile the good man was waiting below. He was not allowed to come up with the rest. Why? *Father Naber*: That was the custom. *Therese*: Yes, and then I saw something else. There were many women there, all behind the lattice. They were not allowed to enter. And there were also many sheep. *Father Naber*: Did the good man buy any of them? *Therese*: No. He had a couple of little birds in a small basket, little doves, two of them, and then something that had grown in the trees (fruit). Oh, how cold it is! *Father Naber*: Why, was it just warmer? *Therese*: Yes, you can certainly feel it when you are there, how nice and warm it is. Now there is something else I forgot; they also had a fire there, the people out in front (in the Temple court) and it smoked and stank whatever it was (holocaust? burning of the entrails?). But I didn't go to see it; I stayed with the Savior. You could see over a stone wall. When the mother was little she was there too (Temple school). The old woman already knew the mother. By old woman she means the prophetess Anna, who, at the age of 84, had already lived 60 years as a widow, after her husband's death, always in the Temple—Lk 2:36-38.

From the Presentation to the Visit of the Magi

Concerning this period, there is, in the available sources, no written record of the vision, but Father Naber has accumulated a few details which he gleaned from another vision or from answers to interrogations regarding other visions, or from interrogation in the state of elevated calm: The Holy Family stayed about three days after Christ was born, in the stable in Bethlehem. It was there that the circumcision of the child Jesus took place, and it was from there that they traveled to Jerusalem for the presentation of the child. Then, through an arrangement with some relatives of St. Joseph, they were able to live in Bethlehem itself. Here they stayed for about nine months, while St. Joseph went about his work.

Then, apparently as the result of an edict, many stragglers came to Bethlehem for the census, and the Holy Family had to move back into the stable. They were there for about two weeks when they received the angel's warning which told them to seek refuge in Egypt. Joseph got up that same night and set out with Mary and Jesus. But since they had to plan for a long absence, they wanted to conceal their escape. Accordingly they headed for the Dead Sea and crossed the Jordan, in order to return secretly to Nazareth by a route that lay outside the boundaries of Herod's power.

They did not live in the little cottage that belonged to Joseph, but spent the time they required in preparation for their long journey with Mary's mother, St. Anne, the grandmother of Jesus. St. Joachim was no longer alive. But Mary's sister was there, Mary Cleophas together with her child Cleophas who later became a disciple of the Lord, one of the two to whom he appeared after the Resurrection on the road to Emmaus. The Holy Family, after making only the most essential provisions for their journey, took an early leave. St. Anne blessed her daughter Mary by laying both hands on her. They both wept.

The Holy Family then headed south, along the coast—Resl could see the water—to the boundaries of Judea, where the desert land begins (the wilderness of Beersheba, today frequently called the Gaza Strip). There they were delayed for some reason or other, probably because of the poor roads—it was winter and thus the rainy season, about one year after the birth of Jesus— and found an unoccupied stone house, already somewhat dilapidated, which some shepherds were using to store their hay. The shepherds offered it to the Holy Family and they stayed there for more than half a year.

This finally was the place where the three Wise Men and their retinue found the Holy Family. It was from them that they heard the angel's warning that they should not return to King Herod, who meantime had ordered the slaughter of the Holy

Innocents. These Wise Men wanted to take the Holy Family back into their own country with them, but Joseph absolutely refused, since the angel had bidden him to go into Egypt and wait there. Immediately after the departure of the caravan of the "Three Kings," frightened by the news they had given them, he took the mother and child and made his way towards Egypt. Among their baggage Resl was particularly taken with a sort of water-skin, made of an animal hide, which they used to transport liquids (cf. the words of Jesus: "Does one put new wine into old wineskins?").

Cardinal Kaspar (p. 100), in his book, describes the journey through the desert as narrated by Father Naber: Resl mentions a terebinth tree, from which she sees "little brooks" falling, two towns, which she calls Heliopolis and Materia, and an oasis in which a robber family is living. There she says the Holy Family met a very friendly reception. The mother of the robber family was so strongly impressed by the child Jesus that she bathed the third of her four children, who had been attacked by leprosy, in the bath water in which Mary had washed the child Jesus, and the sick child was immediately healed. He adds here that the child was the robber Dismas who was crucified as one of the thieves, at Jesus' right. Father Naber did not tell me that—but one can hardly expect, considering his advanced age and the lengthy conversations, all lasting several hours, which we had together after Therese's death, that he would remember every detail. With respect to this last part of the account, accordingly, I rely fully on the above named source. I was, however, unable to find, in the authentic reports, any mention of where the Holy Family lived during their approximately four years in Egypt, and how they managed to make their living.

Slaughter of the Children at Bethlehem
December 28, Feast of the Holy Innocents
(Sources: Lost report by N, contained in G1, 211; Tapes; A.)

Gerlich witnessed this three-part vision on December 28, 1927, and made a precise record of the times. The content is reproduced in the form of question and answer in dialect. This is difficult to work through and would easily tire the reader. What is reprinted here, in conjunction with Gerlich's indications of the times involved, are the notes taken by Father Naber, December 28, 1926, the day on which this vision first appeared. This account is enlarged upon by excerpts from my own records of the year 1950 and phonographic reproductions, which, judging from the text (war), must have been made around 1943. These are particularly valuable for the insight they give into Resl's drastic manner of sharing both joy and suffering; they also display her often almost unrestrainable temperament.

Gerlich notes (1, 208): In the middle of a conversation about windows, occasioned by a discussion of chill and drafts, Therese was carried off into a vision, about 1:15 in the afternoon. The first vision lasted until 1:18. Interrogation established the content as Herod's order for the slaughter of the Innocents. The second vision began at 1:21 and ended at 1:27. Contents: the slaughter of the little boys. The third vision lasted from 1:37 to 1:41 and, as distinguished from the first two grisly subjects, was joyous in content: the children in glory.

The beginning and end of the visions—and this holds for all Therese's visions—depending upon the physical condition of the visionary, and sometimes on other circumstances, do not occur every year at the same time. That is why Father Naber, for the year 1926, records the beginning of the visions as 2:00.

First Vision: Herod Orders Slaughter of the Innocents

A large hall in the castle of Herod, the same hall in which the Savior was later mocked. The hall is about thirty feet wide, forty feet long, rectangular, without any back walls, with pillars on all four sides; at some distance from the wall, on the columns, a cornice and a flat vault. Everything is made, apparently, of marble, the columns of a somewhat darker variety, but all of it unpolished. In the front third of the room about twelve steps of darker polished marble lead to the throne of Herod, which is made of white polished marble and has a large back wall. To the right and the left there are small columns, with various decorations in between them; on the seat and side arms as well as on the back of the throne there are red cushions. On either side of the throne, right and left, there are six arm-chairs with red cushions and carved backrests of brown wood on the polished white marble pavement.

Herod is wearing an undergarment with red and white stripes, sewn with gold: it is folded across the breast and gathered in across the hips, reaching to the ankles, and it has wide, loose sleeves. He is also wearing a purple cloak which reaches to the floor and shoes of shining gold and silver. His head is adorned with a golden ring with triangular points and precious stones. His reddish hair falls to his shoulders, his face is round and ruddy with a bristly full beard; he is of average height and rather stout. The armchairs are occupied by well-dressed elderly men. In the back, and on both sides, there are many servants. Fifteen Jewish soldiers are standing in front of the steps. After Herod has spoken with the twelve elders sitting around his throne, he gives some instructions to the soldiers who immediately depart.

Second Vision: The Slaughter of the Innocents

In Bethlehem there are some young people running around with stiff, gray head coverings which look like pointed cones with turned-up rims. They are wearing gowns which fit tightly across the breast, closely gathered at the hips, and falling in wide folds to the knees; in most cases these are striped. They are also wearing sandals laced to the knees. These men were the policemen. It was their job to force the mothers who had little boys under two years old to bring their children to the marketplace of Bethlehem, if they should refuse to come when they had been ordered. The births had all been entered on the official records, and this served as the source for determining who was to be summoned. The soldiers were also going in the houses in order to search for children. They encountered much opposition from the parents. The soldiers attempted to maintain order for the execution of the demands, and the policemen (the words

from "attempted" to "policemen" were inserted into Father Naber's original 1926 description on the basis of later information
from the tapes) seized the children which had been brought out
of the houses and carried into the public place, some of them
naked, others clothed in long gowns, held them by the right arm,
and then plunged their foot-and-a-half-long swords into the children's breasts and threw them to the ground. The number of
children murdered in this fashion from Bethlehem was fifty-five,
from the surrounding countryside nineteen. From some families
two children were killed.

Third Vision: The Children in Glory

The murdered children hover over the stable at Bethlehem
in luminous form with brilliant white gowns that reach their
ankles and have wide sleeves. They are singing soft and tenderly.
After some time they glide upwards toward the northwest, in the
direction of the child Jesus on his flight into Egypt.

Subsequent details: Resl refused for a long time to add any
further details (state of childlike prepossession), "because it was
all so sad." Even after Father Naber both asked and begged her,
she wanted to concentrate on the third vision only. With great
patience and difficulty the pastor persuaded her to elaborate on
the entire sequence (cf. tapes and A).

1. "The Savior took me off into a large village (Jerusalem)
into the very hall where he was to be mocked, spit upon, laughed
to scorn, and where they clothed him in a white gown. It was
not the same man; this one was much older, but he was dressed
almost the same way."

She then refers to him as "the poor wretch, the redhead who
doesn't need to have any golden crown, the butcher. To slaughter
the little boys like that, nobody would do that. There were some
upright men present (soldiers); he said something to them and
gave them something scribbled down" (this is Therese's way of
referring to the letter).

2. "Now they are coming into the village, set on a steep
mountain, the same place where the mother and the good man

came. (When Therese said this, I suddenly began to wonder if perhaps the slaughter of the Innocents might not have been intended as a punishment for the inhospitality shown to the Blessed Virgin. A.) "I am glad that the mother was not there anymore. The women were glad at first to see the upright men (soldiers) and they made themselves pretty and were happy to come with their little boys. Some of them brought two boys. Some of the boys were still very tiny, and others could already walk. All of a sudden other men appeared, not the ones who had gathered them together. They took the young boys by the arm and ran their knife through them and then tossed them aside. Then the women began to scream and cry terribly. They picked up some of the children by their feet, and threw them together on a pile. It was terrible, terrible. It was just like in wartime, when the people shoot everything up and throw everything in a heap, only it was a little worse. And the women kept crying and screaming, but they didn't hear a word of it, they kept stabbing them just like butchers."

3. Resl is excited and happy: "But it all came to a good end. The murdered children were there up in the air. They hovered back and forth, all luminous, over the stable where the Savior came into the world, that's where they stayed. And then they glided onward right straight up into the air, in the direction where the little Savior went off. And the old fox thought that he had got rid of the Savior. Somebody should have told that to the women so that they would have at least some joy. I would have been glad to tell them." There followed a conversation between her and Father Naber, as to where the children went. Resl said: "They could not yet come into heaven; heaven was closed until the Savior died. But then he took them with him immediately. That was beautiful, to see how they all went gliding out after the Savior. Yes, it all had a good end. If only somebody could tell the mothers."

Father Naber did not ask her whether the information described in these last sentences was something she had just seen or whether it came from other visions, perhaps a vision of the time after the death of Jesus. Apparently these partial bits were intermingled with each other, just as Christ passes from the description of the destruction of Jerusalem to the end of the world. First the children alone in glory, blessedly awaiting the time of judgment, gliding off in the direction where the child Jesus was making his flight into Egypt, and then the picture passes over to a vision of these same children as they glide onward into eternal happiness with the Risen Savior. In the case of such visions of glory, both the visionary and the recorder of the vision are at a loss for words.

The Three Kings: Feast of the Epiphany of Our Lord, January 6 (Sources: G1, 24-29, according to the lost record of N; N1, 53 [—G1, 293]; Tapes; A; Kaspar 99/100; Mayr, manuscript.)

Every year, Father Naber and the members of the family would be joined by some of their friends in the neighborhood of Konnersreuth to experience these magnificent and stirring visions. The time and place were a favorite meeting point. I myself witnessed this vision when I had an opportunity a few years after the war to spend the time from Christmas to the middle of January in Waldsassen. Resl had sent me a Christmas package in 1939 and surprised me by a visit to the hospital in 1940. From Waldsassen I made the ten mile journey to Konnersreuth almost every day.

The reader must forgive me for dwelling on personal events if I mention that these were unforgettable days for me. I was invited to spend a few evenings with Resl—I must now use this familiar name for her—and Father Naber in her room. She had lighted the candles in various sconces, and set up an illuminated little crib. We were sitting together talking about everything that had impressed us or caught our attention, about plans for future work, about visitors, about departed friends, nothing particularly religious, and yet one could feel the scriptural promise, "There I am in the midst of them." I count these hours among the happiest of my entire life. They gave me, sober-minded man of the world that I was, a stronger sense of union with God than any religious exercises could have given.

The attacks which have been raised even today against Therese
Neumann by many people, even theologians, whose accusations
furnish magnificent headlines for obliging newspapers, justify,
in fact demand, that those who are privileged to count themselves
among the witnesses should confess and describe their innermost
experience and make known what a wealth of inspiration they
have experienced by the privilege of being connected with Konnersreuth. In these same happy days I was able to share the vision
of the "Baptism of Jesus," when I was taking Father Naber and
Resl home from a visit we had made on January 13, around
11:00 in the evening. I have always regarded it as a particularly
special privilege that I was allowed to witness this vision in my
own car, especially since St. John is my patron saint. The content
of this vision will be described in its appropriate place in the
sequence.

Drawing on my own records of the vision for January 6, of
this year of my visit to Konnersreuth, I shall give a brief account
of the impressions received during the evening vision. It began at
5:40. That year, 1952, the morning vision had occurred while
Therese was all alone. She gave the following brief description
of it that evening in her state of prepossession: "The three of them
with their men and their animals are making their way through
the water (crossing the Jordan River); then they came to the
big town of that dishonorable man, Herod. He is the man who
had them come out with the scrolls (the scribes who informed
King Herod that Bethlehem would be the birthplace of the
"king of the Jews").

The impression of the evening vision was as follows (on the
basis of my short-hand notes taken on that occasion; the explanations included in parentheses are from Father Naber, based
on his previous experiences and his interrogation of those present):
Resl's face shows great fright (because the star comes rushing
straight down, with brilliant light, glowing hot, frightening everyone, and disturbing the horses, camels, and elephants, all of whom
make their own appropriate cries of alarm). Then radiant joy
(the Magi have reached their goal). Once or twice she reaches
out her hand (she wants to take the child into her arms, as the

three Wise Men are doing). She sniffs with her nose (the incense and sweet-smelling ointments). A perfectly astonished expression (the child Jesus, who can now walk, comes out and gives his hand to the retinue). Resl jumps up from the sofa and runs through the room, tripping against the bed as she does so. Her expression has changed to one of ineffably radiant joy; then she sinks back unconscious on the bed (she ran toward the child Jesus and he offered her his hand too; she was able to take his hand and feel that it was warm and living. She fainted from sheer joy). Father Naber and her sister Ottilie led her back to the couch, where she awoke some moments later in the state of prepossession: "Why do I have to go now? The most beautiful thing has just occurred."

Then come the questions about what she has seen and experienced. I shall omit them now, and enlarge upon Father Naber's presentation only in conclusion. Father Naber wrote the following precise record of the first appearance of this vision of January 6, 1927:

Therese had this to say in her state of elevated calm (that is, in the ecstasy which followed the reception of Holy Communion, a state in which she speaks High German, by way of contrast with the child-like state of prepossession which follows her visions): the names Kaspar, Melchior, and Balthasar for the three Wise Men are approximately correct. They were actually ruling princes, very, very rich, not jealous of their ruling power, but on very good terms with their people. Balthasar came from Nubia, a land rich in gold. He was in his early forties and was traveling with about seventy servants, twenty soldiers, eight scholars, each of which had two servants—Balthasar had about twenty such scholars—and a wife. Melchior came from Arabia, a land rich in grain and spices. He was in his middle fifties and had with him about forty servants, fifty soldiers, five scholars with two servants each, and two wives. Kaspar came from Media, a land rich in resin and incense and fruit. He was in his mid-forties, and accompanied by about twenty servants, forty soldiers, and four scholars with two servants each.

In all three of these countries study of the stars was particularly cultivated, especially in Media. They used to build tall, solitary wooden towers to observe the stars. The princes each had his own astrologers, called magi. Jews who lived in the dispersion there, many of whom—and this was a special privilege they seemed to enjoy—grew to extreme old age, some as much as 200 years, had brought with them the knowledge of the one true God and the promised Redeemer, particularly the prophecy of Balaam: "A star will rise up from Jacob" (Nb 24:17).

In Nubia the star had been seen by two of the magi already three weeks before the birth of the Savior. They came to the king and told him that they had seen a remarkable star in the sky; it was of extraordinary size and particularly powerful light and had a very peculiar tail, which was long and curved at the end. The king now assembled all his scholars. They could not, however, give him a satisfactory answer, whereupon he sent ambassadors to his friend King Melchior in Arabia, in the hope of gaining some further knowledge.

In Arabia and Media, just as in Nubia, the star had been in their towers. Only in Arabia had there been a scholar engaged in observation; he had seen this peculiar star and advised that it be further examined into. But the magi were not all together and so the suggestion was never followed up on. The king himself did not bother about it any more. But now the king himself visited the tower and then sent ambassadors to Media, to inquire if they too had seen such an extraordinary star.

In Media the king himself had visited the tower in the days of the Savior's birth and had discovered the star. He had assembled his scholars for counsel, but they were unable to find a satisfactory explanation. But when the ambassadors came from Arabia with their message, he suddenly saw the light and ordered his servants to make ready for a journey to Arabia for a consultation. While the Arabian ambassadors were enroute to Media, the King of Nubia journeyed to Arabia, and then both kings went to Media where they encountered the king of that country just as he was preparing for a journey to Arabia.

From Media all three went together, following their star, which often could not be seen for days and months at a time, so that they were hesitant about continuing their journey. (Further detail from the Tapes: When the sky was overcast, and they could not see the other stars, then, naturally, they could not see this star either.) The men were monotheists, were familiar with the prophecies of Balaam, and believed that it was this star that they saw before them now. (Thus far the account from the state of elevated calm. What follows is from Father Naber's record based on information given by Therese a year later in the state of prepossession and upon interrogation in her normal state.)

On January 6, 1928, at about 6:00 in the morning Therese saw a spacious but low building, with many gold-decorated columns, just as the sun was rising. She saw a man with a large retinue (King Balthasar) make his way down a long, broad staircase. The building was surrounded by many widely scattered round and square huts, which appeared to be sheathed in bark and roofed with reeds, in either a lean-to or pointed form. The house of the man (the king) was made of dark gray stone, with columns of somewhat lighter stone, and adorned with gold from top to bottom. The stairway was dark like the walls.

The man (King Balthasar) was quite large and strong, his skin was dark brown, he had curly black hair of medium length and a full black beard. What struck Therese particularly were his red lips, his white teeth, and the white of his eyes. His head-covering consisted of a brilliant white ring surrounded by a hanging gold band; on the top of his crown there were little gold rods with little gold globes, each of which was decorated with precious stones. Inside the circle of rods and globes, and rising somewhat above them, there was a sphere-shaped white cap, sewn with gold. He also wore a striped, brightly colored tunic, gathered at the waist with a colored sash. The tunic reached his knees and had a broad gold hem and somewhat narrower borders on the long, full sleeves and around the neck. He wore a sort of slipper, with golden bands wrapped crosswise around his feet and lower legs. His tunic was richly adorned with gold embroidery over the breast.

Around his neck he wore about five golden chains of various forms, each adorned with pearls and fastened to the tunic. Hanging from these chains were various kinds of gold coins with various ornamentations stamped on them. His cloak, which covered only his shoulders, was clasped in front with silver bands and buckles. The interior of the cloak was white, with flowers of various colors worked into the background and a gold border. It had a train of many folds which was carried by two servants.

The king's wife followed him, accompanied by four maid-servants. She was wearing a gown embroidered with a fine flowery pattern, held together in the middle with an embroidered girdle; the gown had many folds, reaching to her ankles, and ending in a train. From her neck hung several golden chains, adorned with pearls, crossing and fastened over her breast. Around her neck she wore a gold circlet; on her ears she wore gold and pearl orna-ments which reached down to her shoulders. In her black, curly hair, which reached down to her shoulders, she had fine gold chains adorned with pearls, and over each ear two curved brooches with precious stones. The slippers on her feet were fastened by embroidered bands crossed over her ankles. Over her gown she wore a white cloak, embroidered with large flowers; it hung forward over her right shoulder, and from there, over her back and her left shoulder. It was thrown back over her right hip so that it touched the floor and formed a train. There were two maid-servants on either side, supporting the queen's train. They were wearing gowns of yellow, embroidered with flowers; de-signed with many folds fastened in the middle with yellow sashes, whose ends hung down on the side. The gowns were long enough to form a small train. Around their necks they wore some gold chains with a few stones, with similar ornaments in their medium-length hair. They also wore rings in their ears. These three were followed by some finer maid-servants, carrying small objects.

There were also servants carrying baggage. The maid-servants were wearing simple colored or striped robes, reaching down to their ankles, and rather long in the back. They had jewelry only in their ears; their hair was curly and medium-long.

The king had two servants on either side, carrying his train. They were wearing a yellow-colored tunic with brightly em-broidered ornaments. Their clothes hung to their knees and were held together in the middle with a sash whose ends hung down on the side, ending in golden tassels. Around their necks they wore some gold chains; they had golden bands around their heads. Their foot-wear was similar to the king's. They, in turn, were followed by many other servants. Before the king, too, was a troop of servants. Some of these were completely clothed in brightly colored garments, but without any jewelry; only some of them wore earrings. The servants immediately around the king carried a curved dagger with a white or copper colored handle. Some of these servants had only a colored loincloth, or a loincloth and another cloth slung over their shoulders and breast, held in place underneath the loincloth; they went barefoot.

This is the end of Father Naber's account for 1928. He continues it on January 6, 1929, and on October 10, 1949, he dictated two additional notes which enlarge upon the account of January 6, 1929, and are included below. He writes (N1, 53):

January 6, 1929: About noon Therese sees the three Wise Men together with the princes, with a retinue of about 300 persons (scholars, servants, soldiers, and wives) on their way to Jerusalem. There is a black man from Nubia, a brown man from Arabia, a yellow man from Media, all led onward by a comet. Upon their first questioning of King Herod as to where the newly born king might be, they head towards a Bethlehem far in the north. Only after a second inquiry do they set out upon the road for the correct Bethlehem. But the star leads them far beyond Bethlehem into a stable, in which the Holy Family, who are already on their flight to Egypt, have already been staying for a long time.

At first they are disillusioned at seeing the simplicity and poverty which greets them, and they feel they must have made a mistake. Nonetheless, St. Joseph cautiously comes outside. Only the brown man can speak a language that St. Joseph understands. He brings them inside, where they bow to the mother and speak with her. Then the child Jesus, who is already almost two years old, looks them in the eye with a "divine look." Immediately they recognize that this child is the goal of their journey and they throw themselves to the floor. Touching the ground three times with their foreheads, at long intervals, they adore the child. "Therese hears the chains around their neck striking the floor with a clanking noise" (this last detail from Mayr).

Then they offer their presents. The mother honors their request by putting the child into their arms. Finally she takes the child, who could already walk, outside in front of the stable, to meet the retinue of the Magi, who give it a friendly greeting and many presents. Therese was very envious of the kings because they were allowed to take the child in their arms, but finally her own glowing love is rewarded when the divine child, while he is greeting the retinue in front of the house, also looks at her, whereupon she runs to greet him and he offers her his hand. She feels that the hand is warm and living, and is ecstatically happy. She had this experience for the first time in 1931 (N2, 25) and every year since then.

Excerpts from Therese's words spoken to me after the vision of 1952: They made their way traveling by night, and by day they rested because during the day they could not see the star, and then at night they would set out on their journey again. All of a sudden "it became very gray (twilight), and then the star swooped powerfully down; you couldn't see anything but fire. The animals cried and bellowed. There was no longer any doubt that they were at their destination, and they didn't need to ask any more. The black man was the richest, and he also had the biggest animals, with huge blankets on their backs, and then cushions and more blankets on top of them, and a good many people sitting on top of the elephants; and the others were all humpy, with round humps on their backs (camels), and beautiful horses."

Dr. Schorer, Eichstätt, interjected this question: "Were they more beautiful than your own Lotte?" (This was Resl's name for her shaggy pony which she rode on her visits to the sick in the neighborhood). Resl: "Now you don't have to make fun of my Lotte; she doesn't have to go so far. And the mother's (Mary) was even worse. It had such long ears, it was a donkey."

It is not my intention, as has already been stated in the introduction, to attempt any theological explanations, or to offer any hypotheses, only to present a faithful witness of everything I have observed and recorded in Konnersreuth. But, when all is said and done, descriptions such as the above story of the star do force us to ponder over their probability, unless these visions or parts of these visions are to be regarded simply as the product of imagination, rather than historically possible, that is, to ask whether it is possible for a star which was visible in the sky for two whole years to suddenly fall to earth as a fiery ball and then extinguish. With respect to meteors, and based on our modern experience in space travel, where our space capsules need to be protected by heat shields, one likely explanation suggests itself. Perhaps the comet that led the Magi was very small and very close to the earth and finally touched upon the earth's atmosphere, which brought it to a fiery glow. Or perhaps part of its tail, which would be very long in comparison to our conceptions of magnitude, came into contact with our atmosphere and thus caused this sudden outburst of fire. In the Gospel of St. Matthew we read (2:9): "Behold, the star which they had seen at its rising went on before them until it came and stood over the place where the child was." For the star to have flared up and then extinguished over a particular place is, in terms of astronomy, much more probable than for the star simply to have remained stationary in its course. At least, that is what the term "stood" would seem to mean in the Gospel narrative.

God sent his angels to announce the birth of his son to the shepherds because these simple people would never have understood the message of the star, and because they were already too close to the locale of Christ's birth. For the learned Magi, wise in the ways of the stars, representatives of the pagans who were searching for the true God, he arranged for a star to take the very course it needed in order to serve as their guide.

The Boy Jesus in Nazareth (Source: Mayr)

Professor F.X. Mayr narrates the following: Father Naber recounted to me the following vision of Resl's. Jesus is a small boy. Joseph is going out to work. Jesus wants to go along. But his mother will not allow it. When Joseph comes home that evening, the boy Jesus runs out to meet him. After the return from Egypt, the Holy Family had received a gift of several sheep. The boy Jesus is supposed to look after them. His mother gives him his lunch. Once a very sick leprous man comes along. The boy Jesus, in sympathy, gives him some lunch. Then he "wipes" the man's face. The man goes away. On his way he examines himself and finds that he has been cleansed of the leprosy.

This man later came to a very respectable position. He was in the assembly when Jesus was sentenced to death. Together with a few other men, he did not agree to the sentence.

The boy Jesus was on friendly terms with the other children in Nazareth.

Mayr did not indicate on what day this vision occurred, but presumably it was on the Feast of the Holy Family.

Jesus in the Temple; Luke 2:40-52
(Sources: N1, 55; N2, 27; Tapes.)

Every year a great multitude of people went from Nazareth to Jerusalem on a sort of pilgrimage to celebrate the Feast of the Passover. Joseph and Mary made the trip every year. When the boy Jesus was twelve years old, they took him along on this pilgrimage. Whether they had ever brought him before is not recorded. (Therese, at all events, had never seen him, and it is not mentioned in any of the Gospels.) The boy went the greater part of the way, not with his parents, but with a crowd of boys. He went barefoot; Joseph was carrying his "slippers with thongs" in a small sack slung over his shoulders together with other things they needed for the journey. The boy Jesus also carried a small pack, with "something to eat during the day."

The various groups were often separated by some distance. "They had walking sticks taller than themselves. The boy Jesus, too. These staffs were bowed somewhat at the top. When they got too hot from walking, they would hang their cloaks from these bowed tops." Someone interjected this question: Did they pray along their route or did they carry on a conversation? *Resl*: You can imagine how they spent most of their time talking, especially the boys; after all, it is a long journey, a couple of days. They didn't have any cars, the way we have today, where they could sit around and go faster. They had to cover the whole distance on foot. *Pastor*: Someone should have gone along to see everything. *Resl*: No, not me; when the Savior carries me somewhere, everything is a lot quicker, and I see just about everything. But I can't decide when this is going to be. The Savior takes me when he wants to.

Next, Therese sees the child Jesus in the Temple. Among the scribes she sees a very old man whom she recognizes. He is the one she saw when Mary and Joseph were making a visit before the birth of the Savior (Zachary). There is a second man there whom she also recognizes, a man in his middle years, who, later, when he was much older, came to visit the Savior during the night (Nicodemus). Father Naber, in his journal (2, 27), under date of January 11, 1931, offers the following note which sheds considerable light on the entire vision (here abridged). About 7:30 in the evening Therese sees the pilgrimage of the twelve-year-old boy Jesus to Jerusalem. Zachary, who apparently had Temple service during these days—for Therese sees him at the altar of incense too—has introduced his young relative to the scribes as an extraordinarily talented and intelligent boy. Among these scribes he also sees Nicodemus. Thus far the note of Father Naber.

In her state of prepossession, Therese Neumann gives the following description of the Temple: The whole area is surrounded by a strong wall; it looks like a little village. When you go inside, you have to climb up six broad semi-circular steps. Then comes a big gate with shining slabs on it; that is the main door. Father Naber offers this explanation: Probably bronze plates, the so-called "Beautiful Temple gates". Then the people go in to pray, into the big house (the Temple proper). This is a very big house, with beautifully carved pillars (perhaps she means artistically hewn). The room is just about as high as one of our big churches. With many smaller rooms and passages all around it.

Outside you can look down, there are open halls, they have a roof, but no side walls. The people out there cannot come into the big house. These are the people whom the Savior chased out of the Temple when he was bigger. And farther down you can see open fires burning: these are the courts for the animals. A question was asked here: When the mother was a little girl, did she also go through the great gate? *Therese*: No, never. They went up the rear way, not through the big gate, but through a winding stair-case from the other side.

A second vision follows: On another day, it is already night time, it had already grown gray, the mother is looking for the boy Jesus. She cannot find him. She goes through all the boys and asks. They shake their heads. Frightened, she turned to Joseph. They go to all the groups of relatives and acquaintances, but no one has seen the boy. The next day all alone and very upset, Mary and Joseph spent the whole day going back to Jerusalem. They had acquaintances there, an elderly couple. The mother spoke with the wife. Since it was late in the evening, they could no longer go into the Temple.

On the next morning they immediately went into the "big house." There the mother spoke with a man who kept order. He went in with them and led them to a special room. There were men sitting there on chairs, and the boy Jesus was in the middle. He was speaking to them and they were astonished. Now I mean really astonished; you could tell by looking at them. You know, like when we say, "Oh, come on now". But they did not say any such thing. When someone asked her if the chairs were arranged in a circle, she at first gave the rather reluctant answer that she was being drawn away from the "main story," but afterwards said that they were arranged in a sort of half circle and permanently fastened: "Nobody could move them." Now the parents see the boy and the Temple guide leads them into the room. The mother spoke a few rather harsh words to the boy and the little Jesus answered in astonishment ("Did you not know that I must be about my Father's business?"—Lk 2:48). (Therese heard the words, but did not understand them. She could only see the as-tonishment on the little face). Joseph did not speak a word. But the boy Jesus immediately followed them and went back to Nazareth with them.

Therese honored by her townspeople. The marketplace of Konners-reuth is renamed "Therese Neumann Square" and a statue was erected to the Little Flower, St. Therese of Lisieux.

CHAPTER SEVEN

THE PUBLIC LIFE OF JESUS

Preliminary notes: The following excerpts from the public ministry of Jesus, up to the time of his triumphal entry into Jerusalem, are recorded among the visions which Therese regularly had on Sundays during the year—and Lenten Tuesdays as well—on which there is no special feast, as a vision of the Gospel for that day. She enjoyed such visions, however, only when the Gospel selections described some active appearance of some activity on the part of Jesus. When the Gospel consisted only of a parable, there would be no vision. This is perfectly understandable and very enlightening: It speaks well for the lack of fantasy and the reality of what takes place in Konnersreuth.

It is to be regretted that Therese did not live to see the new liturgical order with the three-year cycle of Scripture readings. For, given the strict liturgical connection between her visions and the Gospel of the day, she would, in the course of the three-year cycle, certainly have had a visionary experience of the newly added Gospel sections. Thus the picture afforded by the visions accorded to her would have been essentially more complete and differentiated.

The sequence in which the rest of her visions is arranged in this book is not coupled with the sequence of the Gospel readings assigned throughout the liturgical year; otherwise the accounts would not follow the chronology of the life of Jesus. We have attempted to organize the various visions in the framework of a Gospel synopsis (including pertinent sections from the Gospel of St. John), in a temporal sequence, and have utilized the synopsis by Joseph Scmid (Regensburg, fourth edition, 1964). In the case of each vision, however, there is always an indication of what date in the liturgical year the vision took place.

Baptism of Jesus
(Source: Author's own experience, January 13, 1952, or, 1953.)

My experience of this vision, as I have observed earlier, occurred under the most extraordinary circumstances. On the afternoon of January 13, Father Naber had asked me if I were interested in seeing the Bernadette film (based on the story by Franz Werfel). When I said that I would like to see it, he thought that Resl and he would also like to go along; he asked if I would take them with me. I was delighted to acquiesce. We also took a fifteen-year-old nephew with us. On the way home we were talking about the film and Resl was expressing her delight at the fine presentation, the beautiful settings, and especially the obviously good effects such a film must produce. "But," she said, "if one believes that the Mother of God actually appeared to Bernadette, then one must notice how ineffective all our technical means are to present such a supernatural illumination from a heavenly apparition. A body radiating light from itself, bright as the sun and still able to be looked at without your eyes hurting you, that is something quite different than a movie actress, no matter how brilliantly she is lighted on the screen."

Suddenly Resl stopped speaking and her nephew sitting beside her in the back seat of the car exclaimed: "My godmother (she had been his sponsor at baptism) is having a vision." I stopped the car at the next turnout—it was between Pechbrunn and Mitterteich—and turned on the inside lights. Father Naber and I carefully observed Therese's gestures and expression during her ecstasy. Her face registered great attention, joy, a happy, surprised look, and fright. The vision lasted for a long time, at least so it seemed to us. It was a night of heavy frost and very cold, the sort of damp chill that can easily creep through the car when it has stopped. Resl, on the other hand, lifted her shawl and seemed close to perspiring.

Meantime, Father Naber had told me that on this day, the

octave of the Epiphany, the theme of the Gospel reading was the baptism of Jesus (Jn 1:29-34), and that this was apparently the object of Therese's present vision.

When Resl, after her vision, entered her state of childlike pre-possession, she quickly covered herself in her thick woolen shawl, and her first words were: "My heavens, but it's gotten cold, and the sun was just burning so warm on my back."

Question: "Where were you then?" "By the water, but not a large standing water (the way she sees Lake Genessareth), but a flowing water, the same water where just recently the three men with all their people and all their animals had to cross over (she refers to the passage of the Three Kings over the River Jordan, on their way to Jerusalem, and describes it as recently because she had had that vision only a week before). The man with the animal skin (John the Baptist) was there, and then the Savior came. They spoke with each other."

John had bowed down to greet the Savior and at first would not let him come into the water. Then, after further conversation, he gave in, and poured water on the Savior "and now, as the Savior was coming back out of the water, all of a sudden there was a white bird over his head, with radiant light, and you could hear somebody speaking loud from the sky, but with a voice like a thunderclap. I was quite frightened—but the luminous bird, that was beautiful." Resl then dropped into a brief, refreshing sleep, as she usually does after a vision and its following state of prepossession. Meantime, we continued our journey home (cf. Mt 8:13-17).

Temptation of Jesus; Mt 4:1-11; First Sunday of Lent
(Source: N 2, 43.)

Entry for February 22, 1931: Therese sees the Savior in the desert, a place where there is a lot of shrubbery, as well as wild animals, lions (she sees him petting one of the lions, although she herself is quite frightened), gazelles (Father Naber puts a question mark after this), and birds. There was also a spring in this place, but the Savior did not drink from it; he only washed there. For forty days he had neither eaten nor drunk. Therese sees the devil (Lucifer) as a gloomy human shadow figure. The first temptation takes place in the evening, the second at the southeast door of the Temple at high noon (the next day), and the third takes place in the evening of the second day.

At the first temptation, the devil offers the Savior two stones, on the second and third temptations he puts his right arm around his neck and carries him on his shoulders through the air (by fits and starts on their way up the mountain). On the occasion of the second temptation the devil shouts from the foot of the tower, where there are people, up to the Savior. After this temptation the Savior wanted to return to the desert. On the way back, the devil led him aside up the mountain from which he showed him Jericho and all the territory to the east. Like a lightning bolt (this is the comparison Therese uses) he finally went down the mountain and disappeared. After that many angels appeared around the Savior, two of them carrying him down from the mountain, holding him upon their arms. The angels also supply the Savior with food (Therese speaks of fruit).

It would be difficult to accept the content of this vision as an historical event. Yet, comparing it to the Gospel narrative, there is perfect harmony. In the three synoptic accounts, we find the statement that, when the Spirit of God came down upon him at his baptism in the Jordan, Jesus was "led by the Spirit into the wilderness". In St. Mark, whose account is the briefest (1:12f), we read that Jesus lived there among the wild animals, that he was tempted by Satan, and that "the angels ministered 'to him". What he faced was a temptation to use the divine power he enjoyed for his own individual advantage, namely, to transform stones into bread because of his hunger, or to demonstrate his power over the elements in an unnecessary display to a great crowd of people by the imposing spectacle of his gliding down to earth unharmed from the pinnacle of the Temple, or, finally, to prove untrue to his Messianic mission by accepting an earthly rule instead of saving the world from the hands of Satan. It is an open question whether these temptations actually took place as described, or whether they describe a spiritual, and perhaps visionary temptation.

The temptation stands at the beginning of Christ's public ministry, immediately connected with the theophany at his baptism. It calls attention to his divine nature and his supernatural power to dispose of the material world, elements which show up frequently again (e.g., when they attempted to throw him off the cliff at Nazareth, when he miraculously disappeared, when he walked on the water after the multiplication of the loaves, when he was transfigured on Mount Tabor, and all the miraculous details of his time on earth after the Resurrection).

The Marriage at Cana; Jn 2:1-11; Second Sunday after Epiphany (Sources: N 2, 26; Tapes; A.)

I should like to preface some remarks from the Old Testament scholar, Professor Franz Xavier Wutz of Eichstätt, which explain some of the background for this vision. It was the custom at that time, he reports, to celebrate more important weddings for at least eight days. In order for the celebration to last that long, it was customary for those invited to bring their share of the food and drink. As Jesus and those invited together with him had not done anything to observe this custom, his mother was quite embarrassed when the wine began to give out.

Father Naber records the following in his journal for 1931: At about 8:00 in the evening, Therese is in the living room, surrounded by about twenty relatives and friends. While she is sitting at the table at which some of the guests amuse themselves in a harmless game of dice, she is suddenly carried away to the marriage feast at Cana. In her state of prepossession, which follows the vision, she chatters very comfortably about what she had seen in this vision, particularly how the Savior behaved, how he cut up and shared the roast lamb that was brought to him, how he made his way among the guests and carried on friendly conversation with them, how Mary helped to serve the guests. If she (Therese) had been able to share in the activity, she would have gone to Mary and helped her.

Transcript of tape recording, twenty years later (the manner of expression is, wherever possible, retained, but the dialect has been translated into written German): Resl has severe pains in her heart, and can hardly tell her story. Father Naber consoles her. She says: "Well then, why don't we try it. After all, I'm not dead. So let's go ahead." *Her description*:

She is in a large room, there are many people, obviously a festival. The men and women are eating in separate places, with an embroidered cloth stretched between them. That is the custom. But you can see over it. Among the guests she sees the Savior, and the mother is there too, and some of the men who go around with the Savior, not all of them, but the young John is there. They are apparently relatives of the host or at least well acquainted, because Jesus' mother is helping to serve the guests. They ate and drank and the Lord spoke. Another day the mother goes to the Savior and says something to him. The Savior gives an astonished answer, but is then very friendly. Therese did not understand what was said.

Note: Mary tells Jesus that the wine has run out. Jesus answers, according to the original text of St. John's Gospel: "*Ti emoíkai soi?*" literally translated, "What to me and to you?" These words have frequently been translated in what appears to be an important sense: "What do I have to do with you." But in the Greek language as in Latin, the word *ti* or *quid* includes the subject "that" or "this." It would be contrary to usage to say "*Quid id mihi et tibi?*" But if we translate: "What is this to you and to me?" (namely, the fact that they have no more wine), we come very close to the correct interpretation. Otherwise, the rest of the story, Mary going out with calm assurance and ordering the servants to do whatever Jesus commanded, would be quite incomprehensible.

After this exchange, the mother goes out into a broad corridor, where there are some "big tubs" (wine jars). They are beautifully shaped, like big vases, with thick sides, as if made from stone; they are placed in frames, which can tilt in the middle, so that it is easy to pour from them. "Otherwise they could hardly lift them, they were so big." When asked how many of them there were, Therese said that she had not noticed particularly, but that there was a whole row of them. (According to Scripture, there were six such wine jars.) There were some servants standing there. The mother tells them something (according to the Gospel, "Whatever he tells you, do it").

A little bit later the Savior went out and ordered the men to do something. Thereupon, they filled the wine jars. When they were full, the Savior went out and held his hands over them, looked up to heaven, and said something. Then he ordered them to do something else. They drew out of the vessels and brought it into the guests. One of them, who was a "higher-up," tested it first. Then he was very upset; he did not know what had happened, and went straight to the master. The servants then explained what had happened. Then the master was very happy that they had something to serve, and the mother was particularly happy because she had been able to do them a favor. Word of what had happened quickly spread. I knew it too, because I saw it.

Now that was no work at all for the Savior. When you know him, that is nothing very special. Before he came down to earth, after all, he created all the water to begin with. Now that was something, but to make water taste better, that is nothing for him. Next comes a long conversation, of some depth, from which I record the following: *Resl*: Why it is a much smaller thing to give the water "a different taste" than to make the water to begin with. When I neither eat nor drink anything and still live from the Savior, that is really nothing for him, and still people make such a fuss about it. (The reference here is to her daily reception of communion.)

Father Naber: But Resl, turning water into wine is something that not just everyone can do. *Resl*: But making the water out of nothing, that too is something that not everyone can do. When the Savior did that, he was still with the Father in heaven, and now he was in the world and wanted particularly to help these people, and he made the water taste "better". I mean, the mother was in a quandary, and she asked the Savior for something, and that is why he went out a little later. The tester then went out to the man in charge and asked him something. Then they found out from the servants what it was all about. But for the

Savior, that was nothing. When he was still with his Father, he was able to do much more. Wherever the Savior is, there the Father is, and where the Father is, there is the Enlightener (Holy Spirit) and they are all one together. And if he could make water to begin with, then it is easy for him to make the water have a different taste.

Father Naber: But no one of us can do that. And that is why they were so astonished. The Savior did this so that people would recognize the fact he was more than simply human. *Resl*: Yes, that's true, but people should recognize that simply by the fact that there is water. Everything is a gift of God, and water especially, and our Savior created that when he was with his Father. What would you do in the garden, if you had beautiful little flowers, and all of a sudden no more water? We must never stop thanking God for water. But people want to ask only when they need something; they never thank. And yet when there was no water in the whole world, no seas and no ponds and no running water, the Savior made it all.

Ferdinand Neumann interjected at this point: 'Well then, it came about all by itself. *Resl*: See, that is the way they talk, all these clever people. The Father created water and what the Father created the Savior also created; he says it himself: I and the Father are one. That was a long time before he had to come down to us in this world. I am thinking now of how it was when there wasn't any water and no mountains and not even any life, and the Father simply said: "So let it be," and then everything happened. And the Savior was with him then, and the Enlightener too.

The Miraculous Catch of Fish; Lk 5:1-11
Fourth Sunday after Pentecost
(Sources: N1, 21; Mayr; A.)

The Savior was so crowded by people at the lake (Capernaum) that he couldn't find any decent place to stand and speak to them. So he sat down in a small boat that lay along the shore and told Peter to set out a little from the land. Then he began speaking to the crowd along the shore. Since the lake was shallow here, though somewhat turbulent, Peter got out of the boat and held it steady. The Savior then stood up and delivered a powerful sermon to the people.

After his sermon, he said something to Peter (telling him where to fish), but Peter did not want to follow his orders at once. But when the Savior pointed in that same direction once again, Peter set out onto the lake. They caught a great multitude of fish in the nets. The second little boat had to come out after them to help them carry the fish. Some of the fish were quite large. They cut them open with bone knives.

Peter, astonished and alarmed, threw himself onto his knees before the Savior and said something to him ("Lord, depart from me, for I am a sinful man"), whereupon the Savior answered in a friendly tone ("Do not be afraid; from now on you will be fishers of men").

Mayr, who writes of the same vision on July 3, 1949, the Fourth Sunday after Pentecost that year, adds the following details in his account: Since Resl cannot recall the normal expressions for various objects that she sees in her state of child-like prepossession, she coins very fitting substitute words; instead of ship she says "box of boards" and instead of fish "water skippers."

The Centurion from Capernaum; Mt 8:5-17
Third Sunday after Epiphany
(Source: N2, 36.)

The content of this vision does not entirely harmonize with the Gospel for that day. In the Gospel we read that the centurion from Capernaum sees Jesus himself: "As he entered Capernaum, a centurion came forward to him, beseeching him and praying, Lord, thy servant is lying paralyzed at home, in terrible distress. And he said to him, I will come and heal him. But the centurion answered him, Lord, I am not worthy to have you come under my roof; only say the word, and my servant will be healed. (5-8) ... and to the centurion Jesus said, Go; be it done for you as you have believed. And the servant was healed at that very moment."

Therese's vision then extends beyond the Gospel selection for that day and adds Mt 14-17 (healing of Peter's mother-in-law and various other cures). The principal section of the vision, while it departs from the text of Matthew's Gospel, does correspond, in content, with the parallel section from the Gospel of St. Luke (7: 1-10), which I reproduce at the end of the vision, for the sake of comparison.

Father Naber records, under date of January 25, 1951: "Today Therese had a vision of the conversion of Saul, that is, the Gospel of the Third Sunday after Epiphany. Then she saw the following: She sees the Savior accompanied by the people coming towards Capernaum. At one of the gates of the outer city walls, the centurion's representatives come forward to ask Jesus to come to the centurion's house and cure his sick servant (the centurion was in the service of Herod Antipas. The reason he was so fond of the servant was that the servant had saved his life during a hunt. He was a monotheist). [The notes included in parentheses in this account are present in Father Naber's journal, apparently information gleaned from interrogation in Therese's state of elevated calm].

The Savior walks a short distance together with these representatives, and then stays behind. When they announce to the centurion that Jesus of Nazareth is coming, he begins to have second thoughts as to whether he is worthy of such a visit. Finally he decides that he is not at all worthy even to meet with Jesus, but sends more of his friends who are to ask Jesus in his name: "Oh Lord, I am not worthy for you to enter under my roof; but only say the word, and my servant will be healed." At some distance from the centurion's quarters (house) these friends meet with the approaching Lord, throw themselves on the ground before him, and deliver the assigned message.

The Savior takes these trusting and confident words of the centurion as an opportunity to address some serious words' to his followers about the house of Israel, then he turns toward the centurion's house, raises his eyes to heaven, raises his hands as if to lay them on the servant, and prays. Then he departs through a gate in the inner wall, in the direction of the synagogue, in front of which he continues to speak to the people, and then, upon the request of Peter and Andrew, goes with them to Peter's house near Lake Genessareth.

As soon as the Savior entered Capernaum, Peter had hurried to his house to look in on his mother-in-law, whom he knew was sick. He found her in very serious condition and quickly went back to get the Savior in order to ask him to come to the patient. The Savior came at once, laid his hands upon the sick woman while looking up to heaven and praying, she was immediately cured, got out of bed, and waited upon the Savior and his company. Though already dark, there was a great crowd with sick people outside the house, waiting for the miracle-worker to emerge. The Savior did go out, drove out devils with stern words of command, and healed the sick. Therese noticed that the Savior did not heal all the sick of their diseases, that he simply consoled a part of them; but that these people went their way just as contented as those who were actually healed. (The house of St. Peter, says Therese, was not really small; down along the lake shore there was also a fish hut)." Thus far Father Naber's description.

The Gospel of St. Luke is as follows: "After he had ended all the sayings in the hearing of the people he entered Capernaum. Now a centurion had a slave who was dear to him, who was sick and at the point of death. When he heard of Jesus, he sent to him elders of the Jews, asking him to come and heal his slave. And when they came to Jesus, they besought him earnestly, saying: he is worthy to have you do this for him, for he loves our nation, and he built us our synagogue.

"And Jesus went with them. When he was not far from the house, the centurion sent friends to him, saying to him, Lord, do not trouble yourself, for I am not worthy to have you come under my roof; therefore I do not presume to come to you. But say the word, and let my servant be healed. . . ."

In St. Luke's Gospel, however, this event is not followed by an account of Peter's mother-in-law. This obvious departure of

Therese's vision from the Gospel for the day, taken from St. Matthew, makes it perfectly obvious that her visions are not the result of any suggestion—for she always used to pray the daily text for the Mass when she was in church or, if she did not get to Mass in church that day, at home. The accuracy of the presentation, the obvious lack of influence by any external impression, from people who could not know all the details, and the synopsis of the Gospels all argue for a genuine illumination in the visions.

The Young Man from Naim; Lk 7:11-16
Fifteenth Sunday after Pentecost
(Sources: N1, 39; G1, 265; Mayr.)

Father Naber, and following him, Gerlich, record the following under date of September 9, 1928 (Fifteenth Sunday after Pentecost):

Therese had a vision of the resurrection of the young man from Naim, the subject of today's Sunday Gospel. On the way to Naim, she sees the Savior heal a blind girl. Before the Savior raises the dead man, he sprinkles people with Jordan water, which has been brought along. Therese hears, from the Savior's very mouth, the word "Etpheta," whereupon the dead man opens his eyes and his mouth. After the Savior said the word "Kum," the young man rises up from his bier.

Therese says (apparently upon interrogation in her state of elevated calm - A.) that this young man's name was Martialis; his father had given him that name after a Roman friend of his; his mother owned several vineyards; he himself became one of the Savior's disciples and a lay apostle.

Msgr. Mayr gives an essentially more explicit account based on his own experience:

Sunday, September 14, 1952. Today is also the Feast of Exaltation of the Holy Cross. The Sunday Gospel, on the other hand, described the raising of the young man from Naim. Around 5:00 in the afternoon Father Riedl and I went to Resl's new garden where we found her together with Father Naber, her sisters Mary and Agnes, and several children. We sat in the garden house and Resl showed us the technical books on gardening which she kept there. Suddenly the book fell from Resl's hand, and she passed into a state of vision. Her face was calm. We were asking each other what she was seeing in her vision. At first we could not determine whether it was a vision of the discovery of the true cross or something else. Suddenly her face took on an exceptionally joyous expression. Then we knew that she was seeing the Savior. It was, accordingly, a vision of the Naim story. It lasted for a relatively long time. Then Resl returned into her childlike state, which also lasted a rather long time. This is what she told us:

The Savior was on the road. Accompanying him were the apostles and several other people, women as well, and "the mother" (Mary). The harvest had already been finished, so it was in the fall. Our Savior encountered a blind woman and healed her. Then he went on toward a city. A funeral procession was coming out. The people were all "draped in gray" and many were crying. Some men were carrying a bier. The Savior went up to the mother of the dead man and greeted her. It was easy to tell that he already knew the woman, and she knew him. Then he ordered the men to set down the bier. Some of them began murmuring and wanted to continue the procession. But the Savior insisted on his order.

Then a basket-shaped piece of wickerwork was removed from the bier and the dead man could be seen. He was wrapped in cloths, in the way that the Jews prepare for burial. They took away the cloths, so that the corpse itself was visible. Jesus spoke a few words, one of which sounded like "Kum." He grasped the young man's hands, and the young man stood up. The men were all dumb with amazement. Some of them started crying: "Marsiali" or "Masiari" (1 and r could not be accurately distinguished). That was the young man's name. He stood up and they put a cloak around him. Then he thanked the Savior and wanted to go with him. But the Savior would not allow this; he gave him back to his mother. She was a very wealthy and well-known woman.

During this account Resl once again passed into a state of vision. Once again her face was very calm. The pastor himself did not know what Resl would be seeing in the vision. He thought that it might be a vision of the finding of the true cross. But then her face took on a friendly expression, indicating that once again she had seen the Savior. So we could not possibly imagine what she would be seeing. The vision did not last as long as the first one. After it was over, Resl told us the following:

She saw the house of this well-known woman, whose son had just been raised from the dead. In one large room preparations had been made for a banquet. In front of the house there was a large hall, with many poor people and sick people gathered around. The woman gave directions and orders. She was obviously the lady of the house, and a widow. The young man, Marsiali, was running all around. Then Jesus came. He passed through the rows of the poor and the sick. He healed many of the sick, but not all. He spoke so lovingly to those whom he did not heal that they went on their way satisfied and consoled. Then, together with the men who accompanied him, the apostles, he went into the banquet room and reclined on the pillows at the lowest table. It was already evening. Many of the acquaintances of the family were there as well, and they kept calling to Marsiali.

This young man, as Father Naber records, later joined the Savior and became one of his disciples.

Storm on the Lake; Mt 8:23-27 (cf. Mk 4:35-41; Lk 8:22-25)
Fourth Sunday after Epiphany; (Source: Mayr.)

From Mayr's record: January 31, 1954, Fourth Sunday after Epiphany. After dinner I was at the pastor's house, in the kitchen. Resl was sitting with us, engaged in lively conversation. Suddenly she had a vision:

First her face was very calm. Suddenly it grew very bright and she smiled; obviously she was seeing the Savior. Later she showed surprise, anxiety. Then keen observation of her surroundings; listening closely, then registering astonishment, and finally a look of great joy.

Later, upon interrogation in her state of childlike prepossession, she gave this explanation: She had seen the disciples and the Savior go into the boat; she called it "a box of boards." Not all the disciples were in the boat, and there were no outsiders. There were, however, many other ships headed in the same direction. It was windy and already late. You could see stars. The Savior stretched out in the back of the ship and began to sleep. Then the storm got very bad, so that "mountains of water" rose up and the waves were breaking over the boat.

The disciples were frightened, but for a long time they hesitated to wake the Savior. First they tried to influence the "young man" (John) to awaken the Savior. It seems that this disciple had the least fear and also the greatest confidence in him. But he refused to awaken the Savior. Finally Peter did so. He had to shake the Savior for a while until he was awake. The Savior then spoke to the disciples, apparently rebuking them for their lack of courage. Then he stood up in the ship which was violently listing, spread his arms over the water, and immediately the wind and the waves died down. The water and the storm had both been immediately calmed. The disciples looked at the Savior with an expression of fear and astonishment ("What sort of man is this, that even winds and sea obey him?" Mt 8:27).

This exercise of power left a profound impression on everyone, Resl too. She was breathing heavily in her excitement. She was very proud and happy at this mighty show of power: "That's what the Savior can do!"

Healing of the Lame; Mt 9:1-8 (cf. Mk 2:1-12; Lk 5:17-26)
Eighteenth Sunday after Pentecost
(Sources: N1, 42; A.)

Father Naber, September 30, 1928, records only a reference to the Gospel. Therese sees the Savior in the house in which he lived at Capernaum. A huge crowd of people is thronging around the house and into the open side of the house. The Savior is preaching. Some people are carrying a lame man on a stretcher, but they cannot get through the crowd. They climb onto the roof, make a small opening, and lower the lame man, together with his stretcher, to the Savior's feet. He said something to him, full of sympathy ("Take comfort, your sins are forgiven"). Then the scribes and Pharisees scattered among the crowd look at the Savior with some misgivings (cf. 5:21—"Who is this that speaks blasphemies? Who can forgive sins but God only?"). The Savior, reading their thoughts, continues speaking to the crowd, and then he says some words of power over the lame person, stretching his right hand over him. The man jumps up, picks up his stretcher, and goes his way, expressing his joy and gratitude. Every one who saw it was astonished.

According to Naber's journal, entry of May 29, 1931, Therese had the same vision on the Friday after Pentecost, for which the Gospel of St. Luke (5, 17-26) was the prescribed text.

In His Own Town; Lk 4:23-30 (The vision covers 14-30)
Monday after the Third Sunday of Lent
(Sources: N2, 51; Tapes; A.)

Therese finds herself carried away into the town in which the Savior grew up. She follows him into a rather large house, but nowhere nearly so big as the house in the big city (Jerusalem). It is simple, but bigger than the houses all around it. In this house (the synagogue at Nazareth) many people are gathered. Some of them are sitting, some of them standing up. A couple of them are speaking something out loud. You have to go up a little bit to them. "There are linen scrolls, the kind that can be rotated." The Savior wants to go up to read too, but they will not let him. This was his first time. But now he did go up, did read something, then preached to them. Everybody listened to him attentively.

But then the "people who wanted to be so clever" (Pharisees) spoke against him. The argument went back and forth and so I noticed some words that were repeated several times: "*Liam, gamál* (?), *salém.*" Then they suddenly became violent. They simply would not listen to what the Savior said. Then he got up and came down a few steps. Then they threatened him and tried to lay hold of him. But he was not afraid, and went on out. There they surrounded him: "A handful here and a handful there and another handful and still another handful. There were about that many, although there could have been one or two more or less. They wanted to take hold of the Savior right outside the door, but he would not allow them. Then they took off after him. There were many people, even some friends.

"All of a sudden they began shoving the Savior, and kept shoving him ahead of them. Then they forced him up onto a high place, and he spoke to them again and they spoke against him again and the Savior spoke one more time. Then they carried him off again and, in their fury, charged into him. Then they forced him up to the edge of a high cliff, from which you could look far down, and began to push him over. But the Savior paid no attention to it. He simply turned around in the air in front of the cliff, in a show of power, and moved calmly towards them. They all stood there looking at him, and then they suddenly separated and let him pass through. Those further in the rear, who had not seen what happened, wanted to take up the fight with the Savior again, but he simply disappeared. The Savior can do that. Once before, when all the people were shouting *"malka, malka"* (king), he also suddenly disappeared because otherwise they would never have let him go." (Therese is referring to the events which followed the multiplication of the loaves, recalled from the previous vision—A.)

"That was something to see; all these people had contradicted the Savior and were so high and mighty and didn't want to let him get in a word, and he showed them all how powerful he was, what he can do when he wants to. The old man in the big house, when the Savior was there as a little boy (Simeon, cf. the Presentation in the Temple), had already told the mother that he would be contradicted, and now it has happened once again. They should have known the Savior, because he grew up there. But usually that's the way it is, that nobody is worth anything at home and that nobody will believe anything. You frequently do a lot better with people you don't know. They were mistrustful and did not want to believe him. But with people like that, who always know better, you only waste your effort. But why were they so furious?"

Father Naber explains the reason to Resl: "Because, since they would not believe but kept demanding the Savior to work miracles as he had in Capernaum to show his power, and our Savior answered them that in the days of Elijah and Elisha it was not the unbelieving in Israel, but rather simple foreigners who were specially chosen out by God. In the final analysis however, it was true that by hovering in the air and by disappearing he did show his power, although in a quite different manner from what they had been demanding."

This explanation of the events makes it easier to understand what is presented so simply in the Gospel text: "By passing through the midst of them he went away." We might also refer to the text of Mark (6:5ff.): "And he could do no mighty work there, except that he laid his hands upon a few sick people and healed them. And he marveled because of their unbelief." And Matthew writes (13:58): "He did not do many mighty works there, because of their unbelief." We might recall the same passages in view of the fact that many people demand today that there should be some miracle in Konnersreuth in order for everyone to believe. What has happened and what has been sworn to by witnesses, that they will not allow. But what Scripture says is not "demand and you will receive," but rather "ask and you shall receive." These are two quite fundamentally different attitudes towards God.

Daughter of Jairus Raised to Life; Mt 9:18-26 (cf. Mk 5:21-43; Lk 8:40-56); Twenty-third Sunday after Pentecost. (Sources: N1, 46; G1, 272; Spiegl, pp. 55-56.)

With respect to the content of this vision, both Naber and Gerlich record only a brief reference to the Gospel. Father Naber's entry for November 4, 1928, is as follows: Towards evening, Therese had a vision of the content of the Sunday Gospel: The cure of the woman suffering from the hemorrhage (her name was

Veronica) and the resurrection of the daughter of the president of the synagogue, Jairus of Capernaum.

Anni Spiegl reports concerning the vision: Resl had a vision of the resurrection of the daughter of Jairus. She was amazed by the noise of the flute-players. She was even more annoyed by how they mocked the Savior when he said: "The child is only sleeping." Resl describes the house in some detail, the surroundings and the little girl. She was particularly pleased to note how dismayed the flute-players were when the child arose.

The Samaritan Woman; Jn 4:5-42
Friday after the Third Sunday of Lent
(Source: N2, 52.)

Father Naber, under date of March 13, 1931, has this single note: "Therese has a vision of the Savior with the Samaritan woman at the well of Jacob." Since, during Lent, there was a vision almost every day, it would seem that he had not found sufficient time for a more thorough interrogation and recording of this vision, but had to content himself with a simple reference. If, in this case and some other cases, there is no other eye-witness account to be found, and if the author too has not shared the experience of this vision and recorded it, careful attention to the principles of faithful recording prohibit any attempt to present the material as if it were the content of a vision. On the other hand, the reader of this book must not be expected to rest content with simple references. For this reason the author, after consultation with several witnesses, has decided to reproduce the content of the Gospel section in question insofar as this is not already evident from the text of Father Naber's journal. In these relatively few cases, in order to make the distinction clearer, the word *Jesus* is used, whereas in the description of episodes seen by Therese in her visions, the word is always *Savior*.

The vision of the encounter between Jesus and the Samaritan woman at the well of Jacob in Sichar: what takes place is primarily a conversation between the two, a very profound and lengthy conversation on the subject of "the living water." Since this conversation was carried on in a language which was not intelligible to Therese, she could only have reported this as a long conversation between the two, although the descriptions of the locale and other particulars would have been most interesting.

The Pharisees Demand a Sign; Mt 12:38-50
Wednesday after the First Sunday of Lent
(Source: N2, 45.)

In this case too, under date of February 25, 1931, Father Naber notes simply: "Therese has a vision of the day's Gospel reading."

Content: Jesus has just healed a deaf and blind possessed person, and has been accused by the Pharisees of driving out devils through Beelzebub, the prince of devils. He then called the Pharisees "a brood of vipers" and told them that "on the day of judgment men will render account for every careless word they utter; for by your word you will be justified, and by your word you will be condemned." Now the scribes and Pharisees demand that he work some miracle in order to justify his speaking such words. He refuses but proclaims his own death and resurrection in words his hearers cannot understand: "An evil and adulterous generation seeks for a sign; but no sign shall be given to it except the sign of the prophet Jonah. For as Jonah was three nights in the belly of the whale, so will the Son of Man be three days and three nights in the heart of the earth."

When someone told him that his relatives were standing outside, waiting to speak with him, he stretched out his hands over his disciples and said, "Whoever does the will of my Father in heaven is my brother, and sister, and mother."

Driving Out Devils; Lk 11:14-28; Third Sunday of Lent
(Sources: N1, 60, —G1, 296; N2, 51.)

Father Naber (and Gerlich also), under date of March 3, 1929, and March 8, 1932, refer only to the Gospel of that Sunday, Jesus driving out demons and a woman from the crowd praising the Blessed Virgin Mary.

The event here is the same as that described by Matthew in the preceding vision; but this time it is from the Gospel of Luke and is read on the Third Sunday of Lent. There is one addition, the words blessing Mary: "Blessed is she that bore you, and the breasts that you sucked," whereupon Jesus answered: "Blessed rather are those who hear the word of God and keep it."

Feeding the Five Thousand
Jn 6:1-15 (cf. Mt 14:13-21; Mk 6:32-44; Lk 9:10-17)
Fourth Sunday of Lent
(Sources: N1, 3; 2, 54; G1, 229; Tapes.)

Father Naber's entry of March 18, 1928 (Fourth Sunday in Lent): "Towards evening Therese had a vision of the miracle of the multiplication of the loaves as described in today's Gospel." Gerlich records essentially the same thing. Father Naber's account for March 15, 1931, Fourth Sunday of Lent, offers nothing to enlarge upon the content of the Gospel, but it is instructive with respect to all Therese's visions, since it makes it very clear that it is not any wish fulfilled or imagination or suggestion from anyone present that introduces the vision. Gerlich's entry:

"The vision of the multiplication of the loaves. We all arrived too late to witness this; Therese often has a vision without anyone being present, certainly a sign that her visions are not induced by anyone else. Sometimes we have found the room locked from the inside when Therese was having a vision. In those cases, as we stood before the closed doors, she would tell us, in her state of prepossession, what she had seen in her vision."

There is, however, a very lively description of this beautiful vision, this time from the years around 1950, preserved on tape. Content: Therese finds herself on a grass-covered mountainside, with big rocks sticking up. The mountainside slopes down like a terrace towards a great body of water (Lake Genessareth). There are very many people there, some of them "big humpy animals" (camels), which are tied to posts. It is evening, everybody is tired, the Savior too. He sits down on a stone and asks all the people to sit down too. Therese's peasant instincts and the poverty of her youth are apparent when she says that she "pitied the beautiful grass, when they were trampling all over it; if we had had grass like that!"

Upon interrogation she says that there were also women and children in the crowds, but that they were not together with the men; they were somewhat farther down the mountain while the men were above. There were, however, fewer women than men. "The mother was there too. The Savior had been speaking with those who were always with him, and he did something for them." Then they brought in some large broiled fish. *Naber*: How many? "One and one more, as long as your arm, each one on a little board, and there were green leaves on the boards and on top of them the brown water skippers (the broiled fish). Other people brought bread, oblong, flat, and not very high and grooved on the top, all on a great big platter." How many? "One and one and one, crosswise, and one more and one more" (a total of five). They had honey too, "naturally that always goes with bread, and they passed this out afterward."

The Savior then made order, then had the people sit down in rank. "Then he looked up to heaven holding his hand out over the loaves and the water-skippers, and said some prayers." He had them bring the baskets, divided the fish and broke the bread into pieces, and put it all in the baskets. Then the people around him (Apostles) had to hand them out "and they just kept on cutting it into pieces and breaking it and it never ran out. All the people were hungry and ate quite a bit. And when they had all had enough, the Savior had them gather up what was left over into the baskets which were all full again. At first the people were sleepy, but when they had eaten they were refreshed.

"The Savior's men then went back down to the water and went away again with their box of boards (boat). The people shouted "*Malka, malka*" (king). Then the Savior quietly departed on the left side. But the people saw him and when they started running after him and would not stop shouting "*Malka*," the Savior simply disappeared. Nobody saw him this time, not even I. But the men with the baskets had already gone onto the water. They were going to share them with the poor people, I think.

But the water, I think, is the big body of water where the wind sprang up and the Savior came to them walking on the water."

Author: This story of the walking on water, here recalled by Therese's memory, is, in the Gospel texts of Matthew and Mark, joined immediately to the story of the multiplication of the loaves, and thus is a later occurrence. Still, Therese can recall this as something already experienced, because the Gospel narrative is liturgically set for the Saturday after Ash Wednesday, and she had a vision of this event three weeks before the vision of the multiplication of the loaves. Moreover, it is difficult to say to what extent her recollections in the state of prepossession draw upon the visions of later years.

In conclusion to the above account let me report a conversation which, in a certain sense, develops from the concluding words of Therese's vision of the miracle at Cana, and should not be kept from the reader. The text follows.

Therese: The Savior can do everything. It is he that makes everything grow and whether he makes it grow slowly on earth or whether he makes it grow fast on earth, that's all the same for him. Or if you eat and don't die or if you don't eat and still don't die, or if you do eat and do die, that's all the same to the Savior. You are in the Savior's hands, no matter which way it goes. It all depends on him, the way he wants it.

Naber: But certainly we must eat and drink so that we don't die; and you?

Resl: Why, I don't need to eat anything. Look, the way the Savior does that is nothing different from the way he makes bread grow out of the earth. But this happens every day, until people think it has to be that way. But the Savior makes this other business a little more exceptional.

Jesus Walks on the Water; Mt 6:47-56 (cf. Mt 14:22-23;
Jn 6:16-21); Saturday after Ash Wednesday
(Sources: N2, 43; A.)

In the Gospel account this story follows immediately after the multiplication of the loaves. The Apostles had set off that night in their boat upon Jesus' express wish, and had left him behind on the mountain where he had performed the miracle of the multiplication, and where, as we have seen in the last vision, he disappeared from people's sight. At the time when Jesus met them on the lake, "about the fourth watch," that is, about 3:00 in the morning, they were about three miles from shore, in the middle of the lake. They were having a hard time with the waves, because there was a strong wind against them (Matthew), and it was churning up the water. Therese sees the Apostles struggling to row their boat.

Suddenly the Savior comes to them, walking on the water. The frightened men in the boat cry out in their fear, but the Savior speaks to them gently. Then Peter speaks a few words, to which the Savior gives a brief answer. Peter gets up out of the boat and goes to meet the Savior. Suddenly he sinks and cries for help. The Savior stretches out his hand and lifts him up, as if he weighed nothing. They both go into the boat and immediately the wind dies down before the Savior. Upon interrogation, Therese says that the Savior did not walk directly on the surface of the water, but was hovering a little bit above the water, although his motions suggested he was walking on a flat surface.

Therese had the same vision on July 5 (octave day, in the earlier liturgy of Sts. Peter and Paul) on which the same event is read in the liturgy, this time the Gospel according to St. Matthew (N1, 26).

The Syro-Phoenician Woman; Mt 15:21-28 (cf. Mk 7:24-30)
Thursday after the First Sunday of Lent
(Source: N2, 45.)

Entry from Father Naber, February 26, 1931. Therese sees a vision of the Canaanite woman begging the Savior to heal her possessed daughter. When I came to Therese's room, I found it locked and we (in addition to Msgr. Härtl and me, there were also Msgr. Geiger from Bamberg, Father Baierlipp from Berneck, and a pastor from that same district) could not come into the room because Therese was already having her vision and, in the state of prepossession which followed it, spoke to us from the sofa on which she was seated, but did not open the door. We could observe her, however, through the ventilator.

Healing the Deaf-mute; Mk 7:31-37
Second Sunday after Pentecost
(Sources: N1, 35; G1, 261; A; 1950)

The Savior had returned from the territory of Tyre and Sidon (modern Lebanon) to the Lake of Genessareth. Therese sees them bring a man up to him, a man who is deaf and can only stammer, and beg the Savior to cure him. The Savior takes the sick man aside and puts his finger into his ears. Then he spits upon the tips of his fingers, puts them on the tongue of the dumb and says: *Effetah* (or: *Etfetah;* the final *h* is a hard *h*, to be distinctly heard at all events, and was confirmed by both Naber and Gerlich as early as August 12, 1928. This is at marked variance with the written form, in which, in the Greek text, we find *ephata* and, in the Latin text, generally *ephpheta*). The man immediately begins to hear and speak correctly. Therese sees that everyone present is amazed at the Savior's work, but he raises his hand to show that it is God who must be thanked.

Second Multiplication of Loaves; Mk 8:1-9 (cf. Mt 15, 29-39)
Sixth Sunday after Pentecost
(Sources: N1, 26; A.)

Therese sees the Savior once again speaking to a huge throng of people on an inhospitable height overlooking the Lake of Genessareth. The people appear to be quite fatigued, and have apparently been with him for a long time. Once again, as in the case of the first multiplication, he does not want to send them away without some sustenance. He asks his disciples something, whereupon they bring him seven loaves and a few little fish. He looks up to heaven, holds his hands over the food, and has it divided among the people. The people all sit down, and when, after some time, they are all satisfied, the Savior has the left-over food gathered together, and there are seven baskets full. Then the Savior departs from the crowd and, together with his disciples, embarks upon a boat which sets out from the land.

The Pool of Bethesda; Jn 5:1-15
Friday after the First Sunday of Lent
(Sources: N2, 46; cf. February 17, 1931; A.)

Therese sees a pool in Jerusalem, surrounded by several porticoes. It is situated along the city walls, near a gate. Many sick people of all kinds are lying around observing the water; they are waiting for something. The Savior comes and has pity on a particularly serious case. He speaks with the sick man, who answers him. Then the Savior holds his hand over him and gives an order ("Get up, take up your bed, and go"). The sick man, who does not know the Savior, gets up, and goes off with his bed. (This cure took place on a Sabbath, whereupon the Jews reproach Jesus, and he defends himself in the Temple.)

Feast of Tabernacles; Jn 7:1-13; Tuesday after Passion Sunday
(Source: N2, 55.)

Father Naber, under date of March 24, 1932, notes simply: Vision of the Gospel of the day.

The Gospel account records Jesus leaving Galilee for Jerusalem, to celebrate the feast of Tabernacles, although somewhat later than his companions, since he wanted to go up privately, and avoid any notice. Still, from the middle of the festival week, he appears openly teaching in the Temple.

The Feast of Tabernacles was one of the three great Jewish feasts on which every man, according to the Law, was obliged to undertake a pilgrimage to Jerusalem. It is true that the old precepts were no longer strictly observed at the time of Jesus. It was enough to make one pilgrimage every year. Each of the three festivals was celebrated for an entire week; the Passover, beginning on the Sabbath after the first full moon of spring, in commemoration of the Exodus from Egypt; Pentecost, seven weeks after the Feast of Passover (the name comes from the Greek number *pentecoste,* "fiftieth," i.e., day) was a festival of thanksgiving for the grain harvest and the Mosaic Law. Finally, the Feast of Tabernacles, which fell in the middle of our month of October, was the great, general feast of thanksgiving, for both the grain and oil harvest, as well as for the gift of the Promised Land. It was the greatest of the three feasts. During the time of its celebration the Israelites were obliged to live in huts made from green branches, generally palm or olive branches, or branches from the vineyard. The weather was generally very dry and warm at this time.

Christianity introduced the feast of Easter to replace the Passover, because Jesus arose from the dead on the morning after the Passover Sabbath; and the feast of Pentecost (descent of the Holy Spirit during the Jewish Pentecost feast) in place of the Pentecost Sabbath. For the feast of Tabernacles, however, there is no corresponding Christian commemoration. Thus, this commemoration has passed out of the Christian sphere, even though harvest thanksgiving festivals and church dedication festivals can prompt similar commemorations. The third and greatest of the Christian festivals is the Feast of the Birth of Our Lord, Christmas.

The following three visions recall events which took place during the time Jesus spent in Jerusalem for the Feast of Tabernacles, in the Temple.

> Jesus, Source of Living Water; Jn 7:32-39
> Monday after Passion Sunday
> (Sources: N2, 55.)

Father Naber, under date of March 23, 1931, makes this reference to the Gospel for the day: Therese sees the Savior teaching in the Temple.

The Gospel speaks of how the highpriest and Pharisees sent out some people to seize Jesus while he was teaching in the Temple during the Feast of Tabernacles. Jesus says: "You will look for me, but you will not find me, and where I am, there you cannot come." The Jews do not know how to interpret these words. But Jesus goes on: "If anyone thirst, let him come to me and drink. He who believes in me, as the Scripture has said, out of his heart shall flow rivers of living water" (the grace given by the Holy Spirit; cf. the conversation with the Samaritan woman at Jacob's well). The Gospel goes on to inform us that, impressed by Jesus' words, the men returned without having carried out their orders: ("No man ever spoke like this man"), and were severely criticized for their failure. Only Nicodemus stood up for Jesus.

The Light of the World; Jn 8:12-20
Saturday after the Fourth Sunday of Lent
(Sources: N2, 55.)

Once again, under date of March 21, 1931, Father Naber simply refers to the Gospel of the day, a vision in which Therese sees the Savior teaching and disputing in the Temple.

In the Gospel section quoted, we find those most significant and majestic words of Jesus which figure so prominently in ancient Christian art, especially the Byzantine representation of Christ as Pantokrator (Jesus as ruler over the universe), or in pictorial representations of Jesus, written in Greek or Cyrilic script: "I am the light of the world. Whoever follows after me does not walk in darkness, but has the light of life."

Jesus and Abraham; Jn 8:46-59; Passion Sunday
(Sources: N1, 4; 2,, 55.)

The introductory remarks to the visions just described also apply to this vision, dated by Father Naber on March 25, 1928, and March 22, 1931: Therese once again sees the Savior in the Temple in serious conversation with the scribes and Pharisees, who eventually pick up stones, but then can no longer see him. The conversation itself Therese cannot understand.

I quote from the Gospel: "Which of you convicts me of sin? If I tell the truth, why do you not believe me?" "Truly, truly, I say to you, if anyone keeps my word, he will never see death. Your Father Abraham rejoiced that he was to see my day;

he saw it and was glad." Then the Jews said to him, "You are not yet fifty years old, and have you seen Abraham?" Jesus said to them: "Truly, truly, I say to you, before Abraham was, I am."

Cure of the Blind Man; Jn 9:1-38
Wednesday of the Fourth Week of Lent
(Sources: N2, 55.)

Under date of March 18, 1931, Father Naber records: Vision of the Gospel of the day, the cure of the man born blind.

St. John records that (after he had concealed himself from his opponents when they wanted to stone him and made his way out of the Temple; cf. the above described vision) Jesus saw a man born blind as "he was passing by." His disciples asked him whether it was this man or his parents who had sinned, with the result that he was born blind. Jesus corrects this Old Testament conception of things. He makes a sort of clay with dirt and spittle, spreads it over the blind man's eyes, and orders him to go wash in the pool of Siloam. The man does as he is ordered. The Pharisees, however, are upset because the cure took place on a Sabbath. The blind man speaks vigorously for Jesus, and is thrown out of the Synagogue. Jesus hears about this. Then comes the most moving part of the whole account. Jesus meets the man once again and identifies himself by asking: "Do you believe in the Son of man?" The answer, "Lord, who is it?" "You have seen him, and it is he who speaks to you." The formerly blind man says, "Lord, I believe," and falls to his knees before Jesus.

The Adulteress; Jn 8:1-11
Saturday after the Third Sunday of Lent
(Sources: N2, 53.)

Under date of March 14, 1931, Father Naber records as follows: "Therese sees Jesus and the adulteress." The Savior is in the Temple. They bring a woman up to him and publicly accuse her. (According to the Gospel narrative, she was caught in open adultery, and the Jewish Law prescribes death by stoning as punishment.) The Savior stoops down and begins to write something with his finger on the floor. The people keep speaking to him, and he stands up and looks at them, each one individually, saying something very pointed, while his eye searches and penetrates each man ("He who is without sin among you, let him cast the first stone"), and one after another they all begin to withdraw. Then he stoops down again and keeps writing with his finger. Once again he straightens up and speaks earnestly to the woman ("Go your way and sin no more.") She thereupon departs.

In the Gospel of St. John this episode occurs during Jesus' teaching activity during the Feast of Tabernacles. Many New Testament exegetes are of the opinion that this passage about the adulteress may have been introduced into the original text by a later copyist, since it is not to be found in many of the most ancient manuscripts and does not fit in harmoniously with the accounts of Jesus' teaching in the Temple. The narrative begins (8:1f.) with these words: "Jesus went to the Mount of Olives. Early in the morning he came again to the Temple. . . ." We shall see, in the description of later visions, namely, those regarding the Apostle John, that Jesus had lodging regularly available to him on Zion, in the vicinity of the Mount of Olives, in an inn that belonged to Nicodemus, and that he used to take advantage of this generosity whenever he was staying in Jerusalem. He probably used to spend the late evening hours lost in prayer and meditation on the Mount of Olives. It is certainly logical to suppose that, in these turbulent days of the Feast of Tabernacles, he would have sought some repose and relaxation in the garden, a presupposition with which the passage cited above, the Gospel of St. John, and the whole narrative of the adulteress taking place at the Feast of Tabernacles is in perfect harmony. Still, I have treated this passage separately from the sequence of St. John's Gospel, in order not to interrupt the teaching offered by Jesus during this feast.

Transfiguration; Mt 17:1-9 (cf. Mk 9:7-13; Lk 9:29-36);
August 6. The same Gospel account is read on the
Second Sunday of Lent.
(Sources: N1, 33; 1, 60; 2, 46f.; G1, 261; 1, 296; Witt 1, 245; A.)

The most explicit account of this vision (describes the first occasion of this vision, August 6, 1926) is offered by Father Leopold Witt. I reproduce his account in an abridged form, together with some notes taken from conversations with Father Naber. Therese says:

"The Savior is standing on a mountain. The mountain is rather flat, not like Mount Calvary, but still somewhat rocky. The Savior is wearing a red-brown tunic and over one shoulder he has a cloth like a sort of shawl (apparently the customary cloth for wiping off perspiration). He is praying in a standing position. Three of those who are always with him are sitting on the ground, and leaning against the rock, sleeping. The one to the right of the Savior has short hair; he seems to be the oldest of the three. On the left is the one I saw under the cross. He does not have a beard. The other, who is somewhat older, is sitting toward the front.

"The sun is just setting. Suddenly the Savior begins to hover about two feet in the air. His face becomes radiant, brighter than the sun, and still you can look at it without being blinded. I see his eyes and his features. His clothes are white, more radiant than fresh snow in the sun. Under his feet is a thick white cloud. He is looking upward, but still he looks straight at me. To his right, standing on his own little cloud, is a man with a rather long beard. His clothing hangs in folds, like a cloak. On the left side, again upon a cloud of his own, stands another man, with a short beard and a garment that seems to be gathered in the middle. Both are luminous figures of light, but the one on the left seems to be of flesh and blood (Elisha, whom Therese also saw on the Feast of All Saints, together with Jesus and Mary as brilliant and luminous figures; but this time she sees him as a luminous figure of flesh and blood, as opposed to the other blessed, who appear to consist entirely of light, even though their faces can be recognized—A), whereas the other is pure light. They are speaking with the Savior.

"Suddenly the three men are frightened out of their sleep; one gets the impression that they don't quite know what to do, but they recognize the Savior, and the one who is sitting on the right says something. Then suddenly the little clouds become one big cloud and I no longer see the luminous figures. But from the cloud comes a clear, strong, and powerful voice. What it says I could not understand ("This is my beloved son in whom I am well pleased; listen to him"). The three men are frightened and, in their fear, they prostrate themselves. Suddenly the Savior is standing there again, just like before. He goes to the three men, raises them up, and takes the one on the right by his arm. Then they go down the mountain. The light in which I saw the Savior on the mountain was much more beautiful and brighter than the light that I otherwise saw (she refers to the light visions when she was healed)."

Father Naber (and Gerlich after him), in his journal entries, adds the following details:

August 6, 1928. Around 8:00 in the evening Therese sees the vision of the Savior on Tabor, as it is recorded in the Gospels, followed by the cure of the epileptic (which took place on the same day—Mt 17: 15-18).

February 24, 1929 (Second Sunday of Lent). At sunset Therese sees a vision of the Transfiguration of the Savior. And then the cure of the deaf and dumb possessed boy at the foot of the mountain of transfiguration.

March 1, 1931 (Second Sunday of Lent). Vision of the Transfiguration of Christ. Therese explains that, on the occasion of her first vision of the Transfiguration of Christ (August 6, 1926), she left behind all hunger and thirst on the mountain. At that time, I had the impression that from that time on she had no need of food and drink, but needed only drink. Solid food had formed no part of her diet since the beginning of the year 1923. From August 6, 1926, Christmas of that same year, Therese took, upon her mother's insistence, only some fluids— in the course of a week this would amount to about one cup—

but she would always bring it back up. She used to fool her mother, as she says, by using the liquids to water flowers, but then the flowers all died.

From Christmas, 1926, until September, 1927, Therese took only a little water occasionally, when she received Communion, because I felt that she could not otherwise swallow the host which, on account of the pain in her neck and her impaired ability to swallow, I simply handed to her. From September, 1926, she no longer took even the least bit of food or liquid, not even a drop of water. The discharge from bladder and bowel, which, towards the end, had grown increasingly rare (every two weeks or so a little bit of water and every two or three months, with great pain and difficulty, a small viscous discharge from the bowels), completely ceased at the beginning of the year 1930.

When anyone would ask Therese what she lived on, she would say simply: "The Savior." She means: Holy Communion. She represents a *literal* fulfillment of the word of Our Lord: "My flesh is food indeed and my blood is drink indeed." Therese's leaving her hunger and thirst behind her on the mountain of Transfiguration, upon her vision of the glory of the Savior, reminds me of the words from Scripture: "I shall be satisfied when your glory shall have appeared."

Cure of the Man with Dropsy; Lk 14:1-7
Sixteenth Sunday after Pentecost
(Sources: N1, 41.)

Father Naber's entry for September 16, 1928: Therese has a vision of the Gospel for the day, the cure of the man suffering from dropsy and the banquet during which the cure took place.

Brief content: Jesus was invited to dinner, one Sabbath, by one of the leading Pharisees. He sees a man suffering from dropsy and asks if it is allowed to heal on the Sabbath. There is no answer. He heals the sick man and asks once again whether, if their child or one of their animals were to fall into a well on the Sabbath, they would take it out. They cannot answer. Then, noticing how the guests all try to get the best places at dinner, he rebukes them for it and suggests that they go instead to the last place at the table and give their host opportunity to tell them, "friend, move up higher. For everyone who exalts himself will be humbled, and he who humbles himself will be exalted."

Cure of the Ten Lepers; Lk 17:11-19
Thirteenth Sunday after Pentecost
(Sources: N1, 38; G1, 263; Mayr.)

Father Naber's entry (taken over by Gerlich) from August 26, 1928; Therese sees the activity of the Gospel for the day, the cure of the ten lepers.

Professor Mayr experienced this vision in 1952, and recorded it. He writes: On the Thirteenth Sunday after Pentecost in Konnersreuth. Resl sees the ten lepers. Her looks and gestures show great revulsion.

The lepers see the Savior, but stand at a distance and call to him. The Savior goes over to them. Peter jumps up and tries to hold back the Savior. Calmly Jesus puts him aside. Then he speaks with the lepers and gives a sign with his hand that they are to go away. Resl follows the lepers with her eyes and sees how their leprosy suddenly falls away and they become clean. Her look expresses considerable astonishment and joy.

One of those who were cured comes back and bows deeply before Jesus. He is dressed differently from the others; he has something red in his clothing. The Savior speaks very friendly to him. Resl cannot understand this. She says that the Savior had sent them all away; the others are all following his directions, but not this one. And yet the Savior is still friendly to him. Father Naber explains the situation to her, as it is recorded in the Gospel text; then she was happy once again at the fact that the Samaritan showed gratitude.

Cure of the Blind Bartimaeus; Lk 18:31-43 (cf. Mt 10:46-52).
Quinquagesima Sunday
(Sources: N1, 59; 2, 43.)

Father Naber records on both occasions, February 10, 1929, and February 15, 1931, that Therese had a vision of the content of the Gospel for that day.

In the midst of a great crowd of people, Jesus is going towards Jerusalem for the feast of the Passover. In the neighborhood of Jericho a blind man is sitting along the road, called Bartimaeus (Mk 10:46), "son of Timaeus." He asks what the noise is all about. They tell him that Jesus is passing by. He cries aloud: "Jesus, son of David, have mercy on me." They try to stop him from calling. But he only cries louder and louder. Jesus hears him, has the man brought before him, and asks him what he wants. He begs to be cured of his blindness. Jesus says: "Receive your sight; your faith has made you well." Immediately the blind man sees and all praise God.

Zacchaeus; Lk 19:1-10; Feast for the Dedication of a Church (Sources: N1, 43; G1, 271; A, following N.)

For October 21, both Naber and Gerlich state: "Therese had a vision of the content of the Gospel for the dedication of a church: Jesus visits Zacchaeus, the chief tax collector." Since there is no other written record to establish this vision, I can only reproduce a few details from Father Naber's presentation.

Therese says that she saw many people standing beside the road along which a few low trees were growing. In the midst of the crowd the Savior is making his way. The location is one she already knows. Not too far off was a big city (Jericho), but not the great big city (Jerusalem). Suddenly the Savior looks up, into a tree, and shouts to someone. There is a man sitting up there, but it is not this man who calls the Savior, as the other men in that same place were doing (cf. the immediately preceding vision of the cure of the blind man, which she had seen a half year earlier), but rather it was the Savior who calls to him. Then the man is filled with joy, climbs down from the tree, goes with the Savior, and takes him along into his house. There the Savior spoke some marvelous words to him ("Today salvation has come to this house"—Lk 19:9); then he sits down with him and his guests at dinner, and later spent the night there.

On the Way to Jerusalem; Mt 20:17-28
Wednesday after the Second Sunday of Lent
(Sources: N2, 49.)

Together with his Apostles, and his Mother and the women who were close to them, and some other companions, Jesus is on his way to the Feast of the Passover, the last Passover of his life, which would lead to his suffering and glory.

The Gospel recounts that Jesus foretold his capture, mocking, scourging, crucifixion, and Resurrection to the twelve. The Apostles took little notice of it, but were arguing who deserved to sit next to Christ, on his right hand. Jesus said: "Whoever would be great among you must be your servant, and whoever would be first among you must be your slave; even as the Son of man came not to be served but to serve, and to give his life as a ransom for many."

Father Naber describes this vision under date of March 4, 1931: Therese has a very impressive vision of the Gospel for this day. She sees the Savior and his Apostles. Before and after the meal they raise their eyes and their outspread hands to heaven. During this vision, and afterwards, recounting it in her state of childlike prepossession, Therese displays a considerable degree of understanding for the content of the words spoken in the vision, although she was unable to understand them as they were spoken.

Three days before this vision, in a state of elevated calm, Therese had predicted that she would have a vision of today's Gospel, and had spoken of its content, although neither she, in her normal state, nor I had any idea whatsoever of what the Gospel selection for today was.

The Raising of Lazarus; Jn 11:1-45;
Friday after the Fourth Sunday of Lent
(Sources: N2, 55; Tapes, and accounts by witnesses.)

Father Naber, under date of March 20, 1931, relates that Therese saw a vision of the raising of Lazarus. The further, acoustical record of this very important sequence of visions of one of the most impressive miracles worked by Jesus, made some thirty years ago, has, unfortunately, suffered so badly that it is possible to understand only fragments. Since I myself did not witness or record this vision for any year, the entire account that follows is dependent upon these fragments and upon what I have been able to put together from incidental conversations with Therese herself and with Father Naber and other eye-witnesses. There i' a sequence of three visions, two of which describe what immediately precedes the miracle, while the third is a vision of the resurrection itself. Therese's brother Ferdinand took some very impressive photographs during these visions.

Background for the vision: On the occasion of the feast of the dedication of the Temple (a feast which lasted eight days, called Hanukkah and celebrated in December, somewhat like our feast of Christmas), Jesus went up to Jerusalem, where, upon being asked by the Jews if he were the Messiah, he makes, in answer, the majestic claim to equality of essence with the Father: "I have told you, but you do not believe me. I and the Father are one." The Jews wanted to stone him as a blasphemer, "but he escaped their hands." He avoided Jerusalem and went to the eastern side of the Jordan, to the territory of Perea, towards the north (Jn 10:22-42). He probably stopped in the house of his friends in Bethany, where he was to spend the time that followed. Otherwise, how could the messengers who are described in what follows possibly have found him?

First vision: Therese sees the Savior and the Apostles in the vicinity of the region where "the man with the animal clothing (John the Baptist) poured the water over him and the luminous white bird suddenly appeared." Men are coming up to them, to announce something to the Savior (messengers from Mary and Martha in Bethany, informing him of Lazarus' sickness). The Savior sends them away again. After a brief pause, not long enough to admit of questioning, she passes into the *second vision*:

Therese sees the Savior still in the same district, but he is obviously giving his Apostles an order. They argue against him and refuse to obey; Peter even goes so far as to stamp his foot.

Finally, after conversation on either side, they stop talking and go with the Savior.

Explanation: Jesus had already spent two days in this territory near the Jordan in Peraea, some two days' journey from Bethany. The Apostles are opposed to the prospect of Jesus' returning once again to the place where they wanted to stone him. But he informs them of the death of Lazarus, which has meantime occurred, and they all go with him (Jn 11:6-16).

Third vision: The Savior and his followers come to Bethany, Martha comes out to meet him and speaks with him for a long time. He consoles her. She hurries away and then comes out of the house together with her sister Mary and many people. "The maiden" (Mary) throws herself at the Savior's feet and speaks to him in tears ("Lord, if you were here my brother would not have died"). And the Savior weeps too—Resl also wept during the vision—and has them bring him to the tomb. He points to a stone slab lying over the tomb. (The tomb was cut into a cave in the gently sloping terrain. The slab lay almost horizontal and, as Thérèse herself explained to the author in her normal state, it led to a series of steps down into the tomb.)

The Savior obviously wanted them to take the slab away, but Martha tried to stop him. (She said: "Lord, he already smells; he has been here four days.") But the Savior speaks again very insistently, and they take away the stone. A horrible, rotting smell seems to emanate from the tomb; Therese, standing in her vision at the edge of the tomb, holds her nose. The Savior looks into the tomb. The dead man comes out of the tomb. This was a chilling spectacle, a man who had been dead, his hands and feet bound and his face covered with wrappings, coming up from the tomb. Everyone is speechless. Then, upon a word from the Savior, he is freed of his bindings, covered with a cloak, and led back into his house. No one can quite grasp what has happened, and no one even begins to rejoice until the reality of what they have witnessed finally bursts out into tears of joy. Resl, too, was crying toward the end of the vision, but this time obviously for joy.

CHAPTER EIGHT

BEFORE THE PASSION

Entry Into Jerusalem; Mt 21:1-9; Mk 11:1-10; Lk 19:28-44; Jn 12:12-19; Feast of Palm Sunday.
(Sources: Tapes, second part.)

First vision: Therese is standing near the foot of the Mount of Olives facing Jerusalem. She looks in the direction of Jerusalem, but she cannot yet see it, since it is covered by the mountain. Behind her lies the town of the "man who came back to life" (Lazarus, Bethany). She notes that he too was in the procession. Nearby, alongside, is a small village (Bethphage). It is a time of festivals and there are many pilgrims who have pitched their tents there. Therese sees the Savior speaking to them (preaching) and then giving an order to two who are not always with him (disciples, as opposed to Apostles whom she describes as those who are always with him). These two go down into the little village, which is "nice and fresh" lying down below in the valley.

There are also many pilgrims there with animals, primarily donkeys. The two men "simply took away" one of these animals that had a young one. At first the people argued against it, and would not give in. But when the men told them that the Savior needed the animals for a short time, they had no further objection. The Savior, meantime, had spoken some powerful words and looked up to heaven. He was not wearing his beautiful white wool cloak, but a brown one. More and more people kept arriving. The Savior continued speaking to them until they came to the little city in front of the big one (Jerusalem); it lies on a slope, "where the growth was already coming up nice and green" (spring). There were also many people here on the street, for they had heard that the Savior was coming. There are sick people there too. The Savior helps some of them, and speaks kindly to others.

Meantime, while he is helping the sick people, they come up with the "animals". One they led, the other came running along. Now it is got ready for the procession (Jerusalem). Jesus' mother is there too, with many other women (Therese describes some of them whom she knows from other visions) and among the men, there were not only those who always go around with the Savior, but many others. A couple of them manage to arrange and keep a very good order. "Two by two, side by side; for it is a deep and stony path, not a real road, lined on either side by high vineyards, growing into a solid hedge. They get the animal ready, laying blankets on it so that only the head shows; that was beautiful."

The Savior put on his fine yellow robe; it was long, hemmed, and bound with a simple broad girdle. Two men placed the Savior on the animal, one of them lifting while the other helped from the other side. He did not take the old animal, but rather the young one. They had no leather bridle, simply a band that was tied under the head. They had to hold the animal steady and lead him very carefully (according to the Gospel this was the foal of a she-ass, which no one had yet ridden—A). The old animal went alongside, without being led. Many other people went along with the procession. In the little town there were trees with branches hanging down, trees without nice bark (palms); the people cut off whole armfuls and threw them down along the path that the Savior would take. They also threw down pieces of cloth from their clothing. "One woman threw down her own cloak and the cloak of one of her children."

There were many children going with them; it was a very long procession and it went very slowly. They sang and kept crying, "*Bargafidam, bargafidam*" (or *bardafidam* ("Son of David")— the words cannot be precisely distinguished). At first the procession went in perfect order: the men went first, then came the

Savior, immediately behind his Mother and some other women, then some more men who were often with the Savior. But where the road starts to go up and these trees are growing, then the men and women ran on ahead to throw the branches in the road. The Savior wanted to have them back in the rear; he didn't want to have any people out in front, but they could no longer be contained. "So finally the Savior was the last of all. He didn't say anything against it, however, for there was sheer jubilation." Very many curious people also came along, just to see what was going on, and when they heard, they joined the jubilation. Then the procession climbed higher, up over the mountain.

Second vision: The procession followed the high road overlooking the valley toward Jerusalem. It was already near evening. Then the Savior dismounted and the other people sat down and had something to eat; they were tired. The Savior sat all alone on the stone. What Therese says literally is "next comes something not very nice." The great city lies there, shining and beautiful in the setting sun, and the Savior looks down upon it, and suddenly begins to weep. "I saw him weep that way once before, the time that he woke up Lazarus, but then he did not weep as much as he did now." When John saw the Master weeping, he came up to him and began to weep too, and "the tall, stiff man of those who were with the Savior"—Father Naber says it was Bartholomew—comes and weeps too. Father Naber asks, "Did you weep?" Resl: "When the Savior weeps, you have to weep with him."—she actually had wept considerably during the vision, hence Father Naber's question.—The Savior said something sad to them (the lament over Jerusalem, Lk 19:41-44).

After they had sat together there for a while, and the people had recovered their energy, they set out once again. They set the Savior upon the foal once again, this time covered by a particularly beautiful blanket. "Do you know where they make such beautiful blankets as that?" Therese asked. In the big house (Temple district), down below, where the mother used to be when she was little, after her parents led her up the winding staircase (Temple school; cf. vision of the Offering of Mary). There are many rooms there, each with its own curtain. And inside there are looms and all the equipment that they need for this work, and there is where they make such beautiful things. I didn't go there today, but I have already seen that they make them there. They also made the beautiful broad girdle that the Savior is wearing, with something written on it (Hebrew letters embroidered onto it). Today is the first time I ever saw it on him, and I never saw it before or after.

By then they had already gone into the outer city, where, just recently, we also went in during the night, where there are many children, and they all cried out: *"Slam, slam, slam"* (dialect for *shelam*—"peace, hail"). They were wearing hardly anything at all; the people there are so poor, but it isn't very cold. Oh, they came rushing up to the Savior again, and the men didn't want to let them, but the Savior went out among the children and put his hands on them. (Therese' is here speaking of her memory of the vision of Christ blessing the children: Mt 19: 13-15; Mk 10: 13-16; Lk 18:15-17.) The people began shouting again, but I could not understand anything: there was a lot of noise. This was in a suburb of Jerusalem (probably Ophel).

Then, today, the procession started upwards again and went under the great gate through the walls and up the mountainside. Then the sun suddenly seemed so beautiful, shining down on a very white place below the big house. Here there were only "lattices" all around (probably animal cages with folding lattice work), and that was what I liked best. There were a lot of sheep around there, all beautifully decorated, with colored bands; and there was a lot of grass which they were eating. But that was not by the big house, that was further down. Then we came to the inner walls, in front of the courts of the big house. There the Savior said something very serious. Here he got off the animal and made his way through the big gate.

There were a lot of people there, oh so many people. And they used to do their business there. They had money set out in rolls on little tables. Then the Savior became very energetic; he overturned the tables and drove the animals to the gate. The businessmen didn't dare to say anything. This was not yet in the big house itself, it was further outside where the people come up when they come from a great distance. But even here the merchants should not have been allowed (this court already belonged to the consecrated Temple district). The people inside had been waiting for the Savior a long time. A good many people had gathered, strangers, but not those who later cried out "*Shelappo, shelappo*" (crucify him). Where do you suppose they were? It certainly wasn't the people in the Temple; they shouted out in jubilation when he came. The Savior then healed some sick people and, finally, went back outside the city with his own men.

Cleansing the Temple, and Cures; Mt 2:10-17
Tuesday after the First Sunday of Lent
(Sources: N2, 45; Tapes.)

The content of this vision, recorded by Father Naber under date of February 24, 1931, has already been recorded in the description of the entry into Jerusalem, because the event follows immediately upon Christ's entry, and more probably belongs to this event. It takes place at the precise moment in which the procession from Bethany arrives at the Temple in Jerusalem.

Monday after the Fourth Sunday of Lent; Jn 2:16-25
(Sources: N2, 55; Tapes.)

The Evangelist John describes the "cleansing of the Temple" at the beginning of the Gospel, after his account of the marriage feast at Cana. But Therese sees the very same scene as on Christ's solemn entry into Jerusalem. Perhaps St. John has arranged these events not on the basis of temporal sequence, but rather in keeping with a spiritual principle of order, and perhaps parts of his Gospel have been transposed by copyists; this speculation lies outside the boundary of this book; our only concern is to record what Therese saw.

The Tax Question; Mt 22:15-21 (cf. Mk 12:13-17; Lk 20:20-26
Second Sunday after Pentecost
(Sources: N1, 44; G1, 271; A.)

In the few days that passed between the entry into Jerusalem and the beginning of the Passion, Jesus was teaching daily in the Temple and many of his discussions with his adversaries, his harsh words against them and the parables, are recorded in the four Gospels as coming from these days. The nights were spent either in the house of Lazarus at Bethany or in the quarters available to him at Nicodemus' inn on the Mount of Olives. The content of the following vision also falls within this period of time.

October 28, 1928: Therese has a vision, in the evening, of what the Gospel for the 22nd Sunday after Pentecost describes: the Pharisees ask Jesus whether it is lawful to pay taxes to the Emperor. The hypocrites are directed to examine a coin with the bust of the Emperor stamped upon it and then directed to "render to Caesar what is Caesar's, and to God what is God's". (Therese did not understand the content of the words, but only saw what happened.) At the end of the vision she sees the Savior leave the Temple and go to Bethany where he has dinner at the house of Lazarus.

Anointing at Bethany; Jn 12:1-9; cf. Mt 26:3-13; Mk 14:3-9
Monday after Palm Sunday
(Sources: N2, 57; Tapes.)

. Therese is transported in her vision to the region of Bethany. She says she is standing by the house behind the mountain. The phrase "behind the mountain" must be understood from the point of view of Jerusalem, from which point of vantage it is Bethany that lies behind the Mount of Olives. "The house is situated perfectly on the slope of the hill, in the sun, and oh how beautiful it is." It is the house of Lazarus and his sisters. She sees Lazarus and says that you can still tell he has been sick, and dead. In terms of time, we are now in the days that follow Jesus' entry into Jerusalem, the time he spent teaching every day in the Temple, while he spent the nights at the house of Lazarus. Since the Passover Festival was near, the many pilgrims are still there in their tents and every day there are more of them; they have already been mentioned in the vision of Christ's entry into

Jerusalem. News of the resurrection of Lazarus spread like wild-
fire, and the house was "overrun with strangers, all of them eager
to see the man who came back to life and to talk with him".

Therese sees the Savior coming and carrying on friendly
conversation with the strangers. Around him are his Apostles and
disciples, and the mother of Jesus is there and the maiden (Magdalene); "in fact she seems to be at home there," and other
women whom Therese knows. Then a well-dressed and dignified
man comes up; he is wearing a cloak which is embroidered with
"little flowers," and a beautifully embroidered girdle; something
shining was hanging from his arm. He certainly must have been
very sick once; you can still see that: his face is full of little
pock marks, which have all healed (Simon the leper; Mt 26:6).
He has another man with him, who is dressed less elegantly; he is
wearing his good everyday clothes, with bare arms. The well-
dressed man makes a very deep bow before the Savior and in-
vites him, politely and earnestly, to come to a banquet with
all his followers, an invitation which the Savior accepts. All
the men and women around him follow him. They go down around
the mountain path, apparently in order to avoid the strangers,
the Savior with the man in front and the others following behind,
and they come to the man's house.

"And there was a big open hall, without any walls at the
sides, only columns, and between them green bushes and little
trees, some of them in blossom." On the columns rests a large
roof with a skylight in the middle, which can be covered with
a latticework in case of rain. Long tables had been set up. The
Savior enters with the man, on the side, and the men sit down
with him. On the other side there were places set for the women.
But you could look over, it wasn't the way it was before, where
there was a curtain between the men and the women (cf. vision
of the marriage at Cana).

The other man (who came with Simon)—he is the "man in
charge of the household"—presents the Savior with a broiled lamb
which he cuts, first lengthwise, and then in smaller pieces which
he distributes first to his host and then to the men with him.
Then he gives it back and the serving man gives portions to the

other people. The women too are served a very good dinner. "During the dinner, the Savior stood up and spoke, spoke quite a bit, also to the people who belonged to the man" (probably expressing his gratitude for the hospitality and service; we continually note from these visions the great natural sensitivity and tact and graciousness with which the Savior conducts himself in his dealings with his fellow man, or with the sick and poor, whereas he could, when occasion demanded, speak very sharp and unequivocal words—A). Then he sits down and continues dinner.

He was wearing his white wool cloak and he sat half-reclining as was the custom, "on a sort of half sofa, which had an arm rest on only one side," with one of his feet hanging down a little, while the other was resting on the cushions. "Suddenly, and very quietly, as if she were afraid, a girl came up from behind, one who had come up before when the Savior was barefoot (banquet at the house of the Pharisee, Lk 7:36-50), and today he was wearing sandals, tied on." The girl, Magdalene, was wearing a bright cloak and concealing something underneath it. It was not easy for her, "she wept the whole time, and I don't know why".

She came up quietly behind the Savior's back. The men who saw her looked at her in such a way that you could tell that they didn't think it was right. Then they all looked at the Savior and felt that he would have to turn around, "but the Savior doesn't do any such thing, he keeps looking straight ahead. Then she untied the strap and his sandal came off; you could hear it fall." She knelt down on the floor, poured ointment over the foot, and cried. The Savior then put his other foot down so that she could pour some of the ointment over it as well. To rub in the ointment and to dry the feet she used her veil. "She did not directly touch the Savior at all, I noticed that very carefully."

The people around the Savior were muttering and complaining, especially the false one, but not the tall one. No one thought it was right. The Savior said something to Magdalene, who then rose and you could tell she wanted to leave. "But she did not leave, she obviously had planned to, but then the Savior said something else to her. Then she took something else out from beneath her cloak, something white and shimmery with different colors, like mother-of-pearl. She poured it over the Savior's head. Oh Father, I can't tell you how good that "tasted" (Therese's dialect for "smelled"), and not an artificial taste either, but a real living taste (fragrance)." Everybody was astonished; they could smell it all the way over on the women's side of the table.

When she wanted to leave, "the false one (Judas) held up his arm in such a way that the girl could not get by." He said something to Magdalene and she began crying again and was very disturbed. The others all looked at her in a most unfriendly manner. "Then the Savior stood up, he would not stand still for this, and said something that was very hard; I could feel that he was talking about death. The mother also wept. Then the Savior sat back down and there was a sort of tension in the air. They could not understand what the Savior had said ("She has prepared my body in advance for burial" Mk 14:8). Then, after a short time, one of them jumped up furiously, stared wildly at the girl and the Savior and ran out. It was already night and the beaked lights were already burning. I didn't begrudge the girl for how the Savior acted towards her. She had certainly meant it well. The Savior really liked to be out with all these good people, but you know, she'd stepped out of line a bit. She was afraid."

Author's note: In order to appreciate Magdalene's courage, we must keep in mind the customs of the Ancient Near East, where, even today, a great many women wear the veil in public and the men, as a rule, will not allow a woman to be photographed on the street without permission. Certainly these conventions were much stricter two thousand years ago; we need think only of the marriage at Cana where, according to Therese's vision, the men and women were separated by a curtain, or the Samaritan woman at Jacob's well, when the Apostles were amazed to find Jesus in conversation with a foreign woman.

Even though here in Bethany, because of the intimate and friendly connections between people, the situation was somewhat more relaxed, we must, in view of the many people who were invited to the banquet, concur in Therese's expression that "she'd stepped out of line a bit". Here comes a girl, perhaps encouraged by Jesus' words or compelled by some presentiment, makes her way through the whole company, "calls attention to herself," as we would say today, by her behavior, and is thus viewed with hostility and muttering remarks from every side. For no one else can interpret this anointing as a preparation for Jesus' burial; no one but Jesus himself knows that in a week's time he will no longer be alive. But Jesus, who knows this, glorifies her act by these words: "Wherever this Gospel is preached in the whole world, what she has done will be told in memory of her" (Mt 26:13). And after his resurrection the Apostles and disciples understood it, just as they also understood the words spoken by the prophet: "Fear not, daughter Zion. Behold, your king comes seated upon the foal of an ass" (Zc 9:9), and recognized the fact that they too had cooperated in this fulfillment.

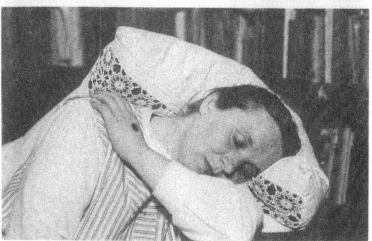

Above: Vision in Eichstätt, c. 1931.
Below: Refreshing sleep after the vision.

Vision of the raising of Lazarus. Above: Interested
participation. Below: the stench of corrupting flesh.

CHAPTER NINE

THE PASSION

Mt 26, 27; Mk 14:12ff., 15; Lk 22, 23; Jn 13, 19.

Visions of the Passion

The most impressive of Therese's visions were the visions of Christ's passion, the so-called "Friday passions", in contrast to the other visions which were repeated in the course of the Church year in strict liturgical sequence. Therese has these visions more than 700 times over the course of her life: the Passion and the evening preceding the Passion were presented in thirty-five to fifty partial series of individual visions, with different beginnings and endings. Every Thursday night and Friday they would be repeated, but they never occurred in the joyous liturgical seasons (from Christmas to Septuagesima and from Easter to the Friday after the Octave of Corpus Christi) and throughout the rest of the liturgical year on those Fridays on which a feast day fell (as well as on Fridays in the octave of feasts), for example, feasts of the Blessed Virgin and the Apostles, St. Joseph, and also the feast of the patron of the church at Konnersreuth, St. Lawrence (August 10), or on the feast of the diocesan patron, St. Wolfgang.

The liturgical connection was so strict that in these last two cases the Friday sufferings were interrupted only if Therese happened to be in Konnersreuth for the Feast of St. Lawrence, and somewhere in the diocese for the Feast of St. Wolfgang. Since she had no experience or awareness of this fact, twice in her life she was "surprised" by a Friday Passion, because she had counted on having the next Friday "free" and thus planned a trip or visit.

The Friday visions are distinct from all the other visions also in the fact that they left their mark on the body of the visionary. Starting with the vision of the Garden of Olives, the blood would begin to flow from within her eyes and flow down over her cheeks, and the stigmata would begin to bleed. The blood from the scourging, on Good Friday, would soak through her shirt and bed-jacket. The crown of thorns would bleed through her white headcloth in nine big areas and several smaller ones. At the Crucifixion, during Lent, her shoulder would swell and a large bloodstain would appear on her bed-jacket. The witness to these visions always saw a complete and very moving image of a martyr, but always noble and edifying, never unesthetic. Her hands would move towards her head in an effort to tear out the thorns. In her visions of the nailing to the cross, the fingers of her outstretched hands would jerk violently in pain, and her tongue would run over her parched lips.

The bleeding phenomena were not the same on every Friday; they always increased in intensity during the Fridays of Lent, reaching a climax on Good Friday. On Holy Thursday and Good Friday the visions were also prolonged beyond their usual duration. They generally began with the vision of the passage to Mt. Olivet, shortly before midnight, and ended with Jesus' death on Friday about one in the afternoon. But on Holy Thursday they would begin with the preparations for the Last Supper and end on Good Friday with the vision of the burial. The hour of death, one o'clock in the afternoon, coincided with the death hour as marked in Jerusalem. There the clock is two hours ahead of the time in Germany at that season of the year; it is three o'clock in Jerusalem. Thus according to the system of reckoning used in the Roman Empire, in which the hours were counted from six in the morning, it was the ninth hour. These last visions, of Jesus' death, she sometimes used to have on the Friday before Palm Sunday, "Sorrowful Friday" or Friday in Passion Week (in the former liturgy, this was the commemoration of the Seven Sorrows of the Blessed Virgin, while the washing of the feet and the institution of the Blessed Sacrament occurred not only on Holy Thursday, but sometimes also on the morning of Corpus Christi).

As Therese grew older, her Friday sufferings also began to decrease in Advent and other times outside the feast days and festal seasons mentioned above, or at least they were shortened whenever Therese was sick or too exhausted from her sufferings of reparation. In the last years of her life she had visions of the Passion outside Lent only on the Feast of the Sacred Heart, commemorated on the First Fridays of every month.

Below we present a catalogue of the visions as they used to occur on Holy Thursday and Good Friday. Essentially I am following the notes of Father Naber and Cardinal Kaspar, as expanded and completed by Therese's own notes and descriptions of her visions. Another source of real significance were the recordings that Ferdinand Neumann made of her conversations (in a state of prepossession) with Father Naber during and after her visions. They made it possible to achieve a very special control and expansion of the material already on hand.

Course and Content of Passion Visions

Holy Thursday, about 11:30 P.M.: *1st vision*: The Savior on the street with ten Apostles: Peter and John are missing (they had been sent on ahead).

2nd vision: A hall (she called it "a beautiful, big room") into which the Savior is being led by a "good man"; it is furnished. The number of men was more than had been on the street by "one and one more"—that is how she counted in her state of prepossession between visions. Peter and John were present this time.

3rd vision: Further description of the room: there were no chairs, only seats with slanting backs to lean on, dark brown plates, not completely round, knives but no forks, only hook-shaped "little scrapers". A big knife in front of the Savior. There is a fire burning. There are three lights set up in a triangle, with "little beaks" from which the flame burns. A man with a "pointed cap" brings a lot of greenery and the Paschal Lamb on a spit. The Savior paints some of the blood on the doors and sprinkles some into the fire.

4th short vision: Beginning of the supper.

5th vision: The Savior walks around with the men. They are singing; the Savior begins the song (Therese made a sign of the cross during this vision) and the others all join in. "The Savior led the song beautifully." Then they all go out of the door. Asked whether she heard any of the words, she answered yes, "*Halleluia, Elohim, Adonai.*"

6th vision: The Savior washes the men's feet. One of them doesn't want his feet washed, but he gives in after being asked to (Peter).

7th vision: Therese looks reverently upwards, then against her will and very sadly, to her side, then with a happy expression, upwards once again. (Before the words of consecration in the Mass the priest says the words "Jesus looked up to heaven," before transforming bread and wine into his body and blood. Therese was following his gaze.) Content of the vision: the Savior says "something big" (the words of consecration) and gives everyone a piece. He says something else and one of them, "the one with the red hair," hurries out. Then the Savior speaks again and gives the men something to drink.

8th vision: The men are talking together. The Savior gets up and prays (the "high-priestly prayer"). "It's hard for him," says Therese: i.e., he is sad. When he sits down again, the "young man (John) rests his face on the Savior's left side. Some of the other men are standing and some are sitting." After this the Savior goes out the door with all the men.

The group of visions recounted above were experienced only on Holy Thursday and partially on Corpus Christi. The next vision begins the regular weekly occurrences, about a quarter to twelve on Thursday and on Friday.

9th vision: (normally no. 1): Therese searches all around her. It is dark, and she is following the others on their way to Mt. Olivet.

10th vision: The Savior goes over a little bridge (across the

Brook of Cedron) with the men, up the mountain to his left, and into a garden. First he comes to a little house, then a big one. Here part of the men remain. Asked how many were left behind, Therese counted them in her usual manner, looking over the group, "one and one more and one more, etc." to the number of eight. The Savior goes on ahead with three of them.

11th vision: The Savior is praying in the garden, on his knees; then he goes back to the three (first prayer). Therese begins to shed watery tears.

12th vision: The Savior's second prayer. Once again he comes back and then leaves again, after he finds the Apostles sleeping. Therese's eyes begin to bleed, the first drops of blood coming from behind her eyes.

13th vision: The Savior prays for the third time. He is sweating blood. An angel ("luminous man") comes and comforts him. He goes back to the three and wakes them. They were the "younger man and an older one and a still older one."—Therese already has streams of blood on her cheeks, drops of blood on her bed-jacket, and the wound over her heart begins to bleed.

14th vision: The crowds come with "burning boughs" (torches) from the street. One of them is leading the way, the one that "ran out after the Savior gave him the bread".

15th vision: Clash between the Apostles and Judas. The Apostles keep crying *"Machada, machada"* (What's wrong?). They recognize Judas and start shouting: *"Ganapa, magera"* (You villain, a sword). Peter does draw his sword and starts to fight (later, in her state of prepossession, Therese calls him the "ear-lobe-cutter.")* They ask the policemen whom they are looking for and they answer: *"Jeshúa Nazaréa"* (Jesus of Nazareth). Jesus answers: *"Aná"* (I am he). All the policemen now fall down, but not the "upright men" (Roman soldiers). When Jesus says *"Kúme,"* (Get up), they all get back up.

*Some critics have found fault with Therese for not having been able to find a more dignified expression for Peter. The first historical vision that Therese witnessed was the vision of the Passion; she had seen Peter at the Last Supper, but not in any position of authority; otherwise she had not seen him before at all. And now she suddenly sees this courageously

16th vision: Therese smiles. She takes Judas' kiss for a sign of friendship. But her expression takes on a note of horror. She complains of pain in her hands: they tied up our Savior's hands, after he had just "put the wounded man's (Malchus') ear back on." The stigma on the back of her left hand is inflamed and begins to bleed. (The earlobe had been still hanging from Malchus' head, but after the Savior touched it, it was fully healed. After being cured, the man did no more harm to the Savior; he stood back— Tapes.)

17th vision: They lead the Savior away. He is tired and thirsty. They took the cloak from a "young man" (cf. Mk 14: 50ff.). When they tried to seize him, too, he undid the clasp on the right side and ran away.

18th vision: "They pushed the Savior into the water; he drank from the dirty water" (in crossing over the brook of Cedron). The stigma on her right hand and the stigma on her feet begin to bleed.

19th vision: The procession passes through a suburb in which many poor people express sympathy with the Savior, kneeling down on the street and shouting *"Jeshúa bardafidám, Jeshúa Nasaría, Jeshúa málka."* They start to follow him, but are forced to stay behind. They take the Savior, who is barefoot, further along a stony road into the inner city and into a large house with a court in which fires are burning.

20th vision: John, who has followed the Savior into the outer court, speaks to a woman at the gate, telling her that she should let Peter in too. Standing at a certain distance, they observe the further course of events. An old man with a long beard comes out, and the Savior is brought before him (Annas).

---

fighting man on the Mount of Olives, cutting off the earlobe of one of the Savior's opponents, and she is quite struck with him. Her conversations take place in the state of childlike prepossession. She does not know the name of anyone whom she sees for the first time, and has no idea of his earlier or later history. She simply refers to him by any expression which corresponds to his behavior. Then, as a rule, she retains this form of reference even for later visions, in which she recognizes the people involved. In her normal state she always spoke with great reverence of St. Peter, whenever she was discussing a vision in which he appeared.

21st vision: He stands before this old man, but at first will not speak to him. Finally, with a proud bearing, he gives him an answer. "Then somebody strikes the Savior for no reason at all. The Savior said something sharp to him." Blood flows from the stigma on the left hand over the back of her hand. Therese groans at the pain from the wound over her heart.

22nd vision: The Savior is mocked. The stigmata in her hands bleed once again. One might note here that the surface of the wound sinks somewhat when blood flows out (Gerlich 1, 284). The old man scribbles something on a scroll, puts this into the Savior's girdle, and has him led away.

23rd vision: The Savior is standing before another man, with a brilliant robe, with "something like little horns on his head and something special on his breast"; Therese traces a pattern with her hand, marking stripes horizontally and vertically across her breast. She is referring to the breastplate (ephod) of the high-priest, on which there are twelve little plates engraved with the names of the twelve tribes of Israel.

24th vision: Fire in the outer court. "The earlobe-cutter is being spoken to," and denying that he knows the Savior. Therese hears the rooster crowing, and describes it later in her state of pre-possession, with these words: "The animal made its noise" (using a dialect expression "be-igen" which can be applied to all animal noises; the term occurs again in her description of the vision of the Three Kings, when the camels and horses make noises of alarm after the star shot down from heaven over the place where the Holy Family were staying).

25th vision: "The man with the little horns tore his cloak. He cuts it with a little knife, and then rips it the rest of the way." The highpriest Caiphas tears his clothing as a gesture of condemnation. Some spoke against this, "but that didn't help anything".

The Savior is once again mocked; they put a dark brown cloak on him, put a crown of straw on his head, with a pointed cap on top, and spit at him from every side, while they shout out in contempt: "*Málka, málka, shelám málka*" (King, king, hail to the King!).

Peter is addressed by an old woman and once again denies that he is acquainted with Jesus. Again the cock crows. At that same moment, the Savior is being led by him, and looks at him, "sadly but kindly." He goes out weeping.

26th vision: The Savior is brought into a dark, cold hall, passing through a narrow, low corridor; they have to stoop to go through it. The prison is a narrow cell in which at the most two persons could stand side by side. There something is fastened around his neck so that he can neither sit nor lie down, and he stays locked up into morning. "The one who came to him that night (Nicodemus) had protested against this treatment."

Afterward, many people went away. John also goes out to the mother and the women who are waiting. "I went out with him; oh how the mother suffered." She was escorted into a house in the vicinity.

At this point, at about two o'clock in the morning, the visions are interrupted. The series, from the passage to Mt. Olivet up to this point, lasted for a good two hours, each vision lasting about five minutes, and all of them interrupted immediately by the state of prepossession in which Therese answered questions about the visions in the expressions of a child. During the visions she would sit upright in her bed, her hands raised and somewhat extended. In the state of prepossession she would sink back on her pillows exhausted, and her hands would fall to the bedclothes. After this last vision, she would usually enter the state of elevated calm, in which she would say, with normal energy in her voice, that the Savior was now strengthening her.

In the morning, the streams of blood that trickled out of her eyes over her cheeks were all dried up, the eyes were stuck shut, and the bed-jacket was drenched with blood over her heart, although, at the beginning of the Passion, Therese had put special compresses over the heart wound. There were dried streams of blood around her wrists, too, from the wounds on her hand.

27th vision: In the morning the priests and those with them bring Jesus before Pilate. "They remain standing in front of the steps. Pilate comes out and has them bring a sort of sofa, on which he sits." Therese, who is also standing there in her vision, can feel that Pilate has no hate for Jesus, but would like to be just. "But he let himself be manipulated by all these people." He can tell from his speech that Jesus is a Galilean, and so he sends him to Herod, the King of Galilee, who is in Jerusalem for the Passover Feast.* First he had him washed because "he was full of blood and had been spat upon all over". The whole crowd of his accusers and many Pharisees and idle and curious people go with him.

The Savior stands proudly before Herod. You can tell that he despises him. "He looked down on him while he was trying to be nice to him and he wouldn't give him a single answer. This made the man so angry, but he didn't try to do anything against the Savior; he had him clothed in a white gown, in order to make a mockery of him, and sent him back to 'I-can't-make-up my-mind' (Pilate)."

28th vision: While the Savior is being led from Herod to Pilate, Therese sees Pilate's wife begging him for something. He gives her "something beautiful, something sparkling. This apparently meant something to her and the woman went away happy".

°The king in question is Herod Antipas, one of the four sons of King Herod, who was about sixty at the time of Christ's birth and who ordered the slaughter of the children at Bethlehem. This man, acting as a vassal of the Romans, hostile to the Jews, had achieved a position of power by dint of several murders and absolute disregard of everyone else; Emperor Octavian Augustus had made him king of the Jews. His residence was in Jerusalem (cf the visions of the Three Kings and the Holy Innocents) and he survived the slaughter of the Innocents by only a few years, dying apparently from cancer of the genitals. He divided his kingdom among his three sons, in a will which was recognized by the Roman Emperor. Archelaus received Judea (cf. Mt 2:22), Samaria, and Idumaea. Herod Antipas became tetrarch of Galilee and Peraea. Herod Philip became tetrarch of Ituraea and Trachonitis.

It was this Herod Antipas who had repudiated his first wife and married Herodias, his brother's wife. John the Baptist had reproached him for this unlawful union and was beheaded by this obviously weak and vain man upon the instigation of his wife Herodias (cf. Mt 14:1-12; Mk 6:14-29)

29th vision: The procession with Jesus comes back to Pilate.
"You can see that he does not like the idea of their bringing the
Savior back to him." He continues his interrogation of Jesus,
and "he is the only one for whom the Savior will have any answers
to his questions". Then Pilate tries again to save him, but the
excited mob continues to shout the same refrain: *"Shelappo".*
(crucify him). Then Pilate has the robber Barabbas brought out
and shown to the crowd and asks them a question. They all shout
"Barabbas". Then Pilate gives an order and Jesus is led away.

30th vision: Therese looks on in horror and turns her head
from one side to the other. She is seeing the scourging. The Savior
is stripped completely naked, and he looks very much disturbed.
His hands are bound once again, and then, with his face towards a
pillar, he is raised up with his arms stretched upwards by the
same thong that binds his hands, until he is standing on the tips
of his toes. Then three angry groups (two men in each group)
of drunken policemen begin to whip him with various kinds of
scourges, as hard as they can and with undisguised pleasure.
When they see that the exposed parts of his body are already
swollen and would be torn to shreds by further scourging, they
turn the Savior around and scourge him on the front in the same
way. When they are finished, the Savior is so sore and exhausted
that he can hardly stoop over to pick up his clothes which are
lying on the floor. Then a half-grown boy kicks the Savior's
clothes so that they land a few feet away. During this vision of the
scourging, Therese's wounds on her breast and back open up
and bleed through onto the bed-jacket. She is particularly angry
at the young servant and speaks some rather sharp words to him:
"If I'd have caught him, I'd have taken him down a peg or two."

31st vision: Crowning with thorns. The crown of thorns is
not made up of one single crown of thorn branches, as it is so
frequently depicted; it looks more like the crowns worn in the
East, not open on the top, like the crowns worn in Western
countries, but closed and round (cf. the present-day head covering
of the Eastern Church Patriarchs), like a sort of basket, with
many long pointed thorns, which is forced down on Jesus' head,
and, in order to keep the soldier's hands from being wounded,

pounded into place with sticks. During this vision, Therese's wounds from the crown of thorns bleed through the cloth wrapped around her head: after every Friday Passion there are nine particularly large areas of dried blood, always at the same places.

32nd vision: Pilate has the Savior brought before him again. He is wearing the crown of thorns on his head and a badly torn red cloak. And he walks stooped and trembling. Pilate views him with obvious sympathy and calls something down to the crowd. But the answer is only *"Shelappo."* An "upright man" (soldier) comes in and gives Pilate a tablet together with the ring which he has just given to his wife and he is visibly disturbed. ("Have nothing to do with this just man. . ." Mt 27:19.) In the crowd Therese sees the mother and John. Pilate now tries all the harder to change the crowd's mind, "but the old man" (Annas) and the "cloak cutter" (Caiphas) were still working; "it didn't take them very long." They kept agitating and shouting out against Pilate, and finally everyone started shouting *"Shelappo"* once again.

33rd vision: Pilate has them bring out a basin and pour water over his hands. He called something down to the crowd, and then everybody below shouted something back. Then he called for his cloak and put "something sparkling" on his head. He stands up and shouts something down to the crowd, "which pleased them" (death sentence). There were a few who tried to speak against it, but they were shouted down by the maddened crowd.

During the general mocking of Jesus that followed, Therese heard the torturers shout out *"Shelám rabúsa,"* (Hail, Your Grace . . . translation by Teodorowicz). "Out of sheer thirst, the Savior had his mouth open, and they spat into it."

Pilate wrote something and gave it to them. Then he writes something else which he has sent somewhere. They bring him a brown piece of wood, "then, you know, he scribbled something on it (this means writing in a script which Therese could not read), one row and another row and one more row, each time in a different script" (The text "Jesus of Nazareth, King of the Jews," in Hebrew, Greek, and Latin). And then everybody was in a hurry to be off.

Pilate has several soldiers assembled, "with blowers among them" (trumpeters). They take off the Savior's red cloak; "it had stuck to his back and when they tore it off the Savior's blood came streaming down." Then they brought in two "really wild men"—they had bundles of wood bound on their back. One of them complained and kept shouting, while the other one was quiet.

Then they bring in some boards for the Savior, "a long board and two shorter ones". These were tied together and thrown onto his shoulder. Then they tied the "girdle with the little hooks and the ropes" around him again and led him out. It was not the soldiers who did this, but some small brown men, with scrubby hair and something tied around their middle; otherwise they were almost naked.

Since Therese did not realize that the crucifixion was about to take place, she thought they were loading some building beams on the Savior's shoulder. The wooden cross that she saw does not have the form familiar to us; it consists of three pieces of wood, not yet joined together, but bound into a single load, one long unfinished upright piece and two shorter, rough-hewn beams (these seem to have been hewn some time before; Therese notes that they are somewhat weathered). The Savior's shoulder, badly wounded by the scourging, begins to swell under the pressure of this load and starts to bleed again. A large bloodstain becomes visible on Therese's right shoulder and stains her bed-jacket.

34th vision: Jesus is on his way to Calvary. He stumbles under the cross and is roughly jerked back to his feet.

35th vision: On the way of the cross Jesus sees his mother accompanied by John and some of the women. Therese hears him say *"Immi"* (My Mother). One of the "good-for-nothings" who are carrying the executioners' tools, when he hears that it is Jesus' mother, opens a little box and mockingly shows her two of the nails for the crucifixion, whereupon Mary faints and is caught by John as she sinks to the ground.

36th vision: They are signalling to a stranger that he should help Jesus carry the cross. Therese, too, is continually signalling with her left hand. She obviously wants to persuade the stranger to help the Savior.

37th vision: The man, (a Greek, Simon of Cyrene), recognizable as a foreigner by his strange clothing and the way he wears his hair and beard, comes up with a walking stick under his arm and two boys, a big one and a much smaller one. They want to see what is going on. The man is ordered to help carry the cross. He protests violently. One of the jailers forces him to obey. He is very angry at being talked to and treated this way, continuously complains, and, by his efforts, causes Jesus' second fall. When the Savior gets up, he turns to him and gives him a "divine look". (This detail comes from Therese's normal state.) This "divine look" occurs occasionally in other visions, too (e.g., the vision of the Three Kings). At this, Simon abandons all resistance, and seizes the wood of the cross so powerfully that the Savior hardly has any load to support himself. Resl continues along the way of the cross, close to the Savior. She hears a loud noise towards the rear of the procession. It is the group around the "thieves".

39th [*sic*] *vision:* A woman comes up with a young girl who is carrying a jug of water. Resl knows the woman: it is the one who came up secretly behind the Savior and touched his clothing, thereby being healed from her hemorrhage (Veronica—Mt 9:18-26). The poor woman is consumed with pity when she sees the Savior's face, all disfigured and clotted with blood; she takes off her shoulder-cloth and hands it to him. He takes the cloth "with one hand; he could not let go with the other," wipes his face with it, and gives it back to her: the impression of his face is visible on the cloth.

40th vision: The procession comes to the city gate.

41st vision: Women with children are standing along the path. They are crying. Resl hears the Savior say *"Benáth Yerusaléma"*. (Daughters of Jerusalem). The "upright men" (soldiers) move the women out of the way.

42nd vision: Outside the city gates the path changes, becoming quite uneven. The Savior cannot get a good view of it;

he stumbles, one of his feet becomes entangled in one of the ropes by which they are leading him, and he falls headlong to the ground.

43rd vision: The policemen shout *"Kum"* (Get up) and seize the Savior by his shoulder in order to lift him up. They are afraid that he might die before they have crucified him. In a later vision, counting in her peculiar way, "once and once more, etc." Therese says that the Savior fell to his knees four times and fell down flat three times. The policemen always kept dragging him to his feet. After this heavy fall at the gate, where he was lying stretched out on the ground, the leader of the soldiers "severely scolded" the policemen for trying to drag the exhausted Savior back to his feet: "he had pity on him". Then the policemen lifted him up.

44th vision: The procession has arrived at the place of crucifixion, on the mountain of Calvary, which is not very high. It stops there. The Savior is led into an old and partially collapsed grave.

45th vision: The three beams of the cross are put together. The ends of the two hewn side-beams, formed into tenons, are driven into the corresponding holes cut into the long, unhewn piece of wood, and fixed into place with wooden wedges and pins.

46th vision: The Savior is forced to lie down to test the cross for length. They throw him down. They mark the position of his head, his hands, his heels, and his seat. Then he is lifted up again—"left to himself he could never have got up"—and led back into the grave. Resl sees him sitting there, still dressed, but trembling with cold. "Just think," she told me once in her normal state, "it was still pretty early in the year and besides that he certainly must have had a high fever from his many wounds".

After this vision, which usually ended around eleven o'clock in the morning, there was another lengthy pause, about an hour, during which time Therese recovered her strength in her state of elevated calm. During this time, as Therese told me in her normal state, in the summer of 1947, the cross was being put together in the following manner (she sees it lying there later at the beginning of the vision of the crucifixion proper): the unhewn stem piece is barked and planed down from the top down as far as the place marked for the heels. Three hollows have been hewn out, one for the crown of thorns, one for the middle of the body, and one for the heels, this last particularly deep. In addition to the hollowed area for the heels, a wedge of wood has also been nailed to the cross to support the feet. Two holes have already been bored in the places marked for the hands, and a third in the area hollowed out for the feet. Above the head, an area has been cut out to receive the title after the cross has been raised. A vertical hole has been dug into the rocky ground—Golgotha is made up largely of limestone—in order to receive the cross after it has been raised.

Around noon Therese suddenly abandons her weakened, prostrate position for an upright sitting position, with both hands held out in front of her. The great vision of the Crucifixion now begins and lasts until about a quarter to one. The Savior is brought out and they tear off the clothing which has now stuck to his body with the dried blood. All the wounds are reopened. The Savior stands there naked, and appears to be deeply disturbed by this shameful treatment. He keeps looking around for help. Then a courageous woman takes off her shoulder-cloth and hands it to him. With a look of gratitude he accepts it and wraps it around himself. The policemen then throw the Savior down onto the cross and bind him tightly around the hips. Then they tie his right arm tightly against the crossbeam, close to the wrist, and drive a nail through his right hand into the prepared hole. When they come to the left hand, they find that the hole had been bored too far out. They tie a rope around his wrist, and while one of them kneels on his right arm, the others pull until his hand reaches the hole. In performing this operation they wrench his arm out of the shoulder socket. Then this arm too is tied tight to the wood and the nail is driven through the hand. Therese can hear the individual blows of the hammer. Every time the nail bites into the hand, she jerks her knees up under the covers. From the wounds and the marks of the stigma fresh blood flows. Her fingers, curved inward over her palms, are moving convulsively throughout the vision.

Author's note: As a result of the support prepared for the heels and the seat, and the ropes holding the arms to the cross, there was much less weight supported by the hands than there would have been if the entire body had been fastened to the smooth wood by only three nails. This consideration greatly weakens the anatomical argument that the palms of the hands would have been ripped out if the nails had been driven directly into them. Dr. Hynek, of Prague, originally thought, basing his conclusions on an illustration of the Sacred Shroud of Turin, a study which had appeared in 1936, that the nailing of Jesus' hands had taken place through the wrists. Father Naber, however, informs me that after the Second World War, Hynek had seen the bleeding from the stigmata in Konnersreuth and established that the blood flowing from the stigmata in the hands regularly flowed as far as the wrists and then dried into a clot there. When he had heard of the various supports and the binding ropes, he revised his opinion and conceded that the great clot of blood which formed along Jesus' wrists, by chemical reaction with the myrrh and aloes with which the body was anointed, would have been able to leave a stronger impression on the linen cloth than the wounds left by the original nailing itself. His thoughts on the likelihood of the hands being ripped out by the nails were now proved to be invalid by the fact that the body was otherwise supported, especially by the ropes tying the wrists to the crossbeams.

This is not an attempt to make any unqualified claims for the fidelity of the description of Jesus' wounds as exemplified in the stigmata at Konnersreuth. Charismatic stigmata frequently deviate from the original. St. Francis, in contemporary illustrations, is always portrayed with the stigmata on the back of his hand or on the palm of his hand, and never on his wrists.

Professor Mayr, the best informed of the living witnesses to Konnersreuth, in a letter of April 22, 1972, says: "First of all we must establish the fact that the wounds of all stigmatics do not need to be faithful reproductions of the original wounds of the Savior. They are merely signs of the intimate union between the stigmatic and the suffering Christ. In the case of Therese Neumann, the position of the wound over the heart as well as the form and variations in the stigmata on the hands are a clear indication of this fact. Fr. Ulrich Weh, O.F.M., Cap., is of the opinion that Resl would have been too much impeded in the use of her hands and suffered too much pain had the stigmata occurred in the wrist. In a certain sense, too, the stigmata are perhaps simply an ornament for the person so favored. We feel, accordingly, it is very possible indeed that, despite the situation as described by Therese Neumann, the Savior had wounds on his wrists. Dr. Mittendorfer, at all events, thinks that the ropes supporting the hands were so strong that they could easily have supported the weight in question."

We might point out that, on the back of her hands, Therese has large stigmata marks while on the inner surface of her hand she has only small incision-like marks, whereas the representations of Christ on the cross usually represent the nailing of the hands as beginning on the inner side, so that the palms have at least as large a stigma mark as the back of the hands. But if we evaluate the need to avoid extreme physical inability, and the desire to provide a recognizable stamp of special grace and favor, then we can well understand the position of Therese's stigmata, which, according to her own testimony, did indeed go all the way through her hands and feet and thus involved painful physical disabilities for her, and did not simply lie on the surface.

The nailing of the feet was described by Therese as follows: first the knees are tied together. Then the executioners hold the right foot against the footrest, and drive a nail through it about the length of the nails used for the hands. This nail is later withdrawn and cast aside (later it was collected together with the other nails used in the Crucifixion and preserved as a precious memorial of Christ's Passion). The only purpose of this nail was to hold the foot and keep it from slipping until both feet were secured. Then the right foot is crossed over the left and a long nail is driven through the right foot, which the other nail has bored in advance, and, with a powerful blow followed by a series of further blows, it is driven through the left foot as well, into the hole in the wood.

7

The policemen put the title made by Pilate into place, raise the cross with the aid of a few beams, and then let it fall into the hole dug out in the stone. From Resl's sudden jerking movements and the expression on her face it is easy to see what a terrible suffering this sudden shock caused the body of the Savior. Therese sees the Savior lapse into unconsciousness for a short time; his head falls forward. The cross did not penetrate deep enough into the ground; it does not have sufficient footing. The policemen pick it up again, dig the hole deeper, and pull the bits of stone out of it. Then they put the cross back into place, somewhat more carefully than the first time.

At first it is not perfectly vertical; the weight of the body pulls it a little forward. It seems that they were prepared for this difficulty: perhaps they had experience from other crucifixions. On both sides of the smooth surface of the stem piece, somewhat towards the rear and rather high off the ground (information from the tape recordings) two rings were already attached, with cords hanging down from them. The cross was now drawn backwards by these cords, which were stretched tightly and fastened to two pegs off on the corners. Then stones were put into the hole that held the cross and wooden wedges were hammered in. When she was asked in what direction the Savior was looking, Therese said that, standing directly in front of the Savior, she could see the Temple. The Savior must, accordingly, have been crucified with his back to the city. The crosses of the two thieves, she said, were somewhat in front and off at an angle, so that "the Savior had them both in sight".

From time to time, Therese also describes the crucifixion of the thieves, which, according to her vision, was much different from that of the Savior (source: tape recording): First the crosses were set up and anchored solidly in the ground. They consisted of a vertical stock and a "board at right angles across it". On both sides of the vertical stock, starting from the bottom to a height of about two feet, there were a few short pegs, alternating on the right and the left. A ladder was leaning against it from the back. The thieves were then girded with a loop of rope, the knot to their back, and raised up by a man who climbed the ladder behind the cross, while they, with their back facing the stock of the cross, had to help climb the cross by using the little pegs. Then their arms were forced back around the cross-piece, so that "you'd think they were going to break", and then they were bound very tight around the arms, the chest, and the legs. They were not nailed.

From now on in the vision, Therese's gaze is upwards. She hears the mockers and the words of Jesus, praying for the mockers and executioners, and forgiving them. She turns her head to the two thieves who have meantime been fastened to their crosses. She senses the content of their speech and looks indignantly at the one on the left, while she gives a friendly look to the one on the right. She hears the Savior cry *"Amen, amen, amárna lach te émmi bardésa"* (Truly, truly, today you will be with me in Paradise).

Meantime, rivulets of blood have been flowing from the stigma on the inner and outer surface of her hands, coming together in the vicinity of the wrists and drying there. She hears the Savior's words again, this time speaking to someone beneath him: Mary and John have meantime come up and are standing under the cross. Once or twice, Therese looks tenderly and sympathetically, first up and then down, from Jesus to Mary and John, and the words she remembers are *"char emmách"* (Behold your mother). When Jesus speaks these words, John goes over to the Mother and steadies her. Therese also sees Mary Magdalene; "the maiden is there, very close to the cross, and covered with blood."

Darkness descends. Darkness comes down upon the soul of the Savior, too, struggling in the agony of death, and wrenches from him the words that Resl remembers: *"Éloi, éloi, láma sabak-táni"* (My God, my God, why have you forsaken me!). The most difficult, the most solemn moment in his entire life has arrived. Darkness rules in the world of nature, a lowering and gloomy light. It is "aweful." Therese hears the birds making terrible, frightening noises.

She says (tape recording): "the Savior felt as if the Father didn't want to have anything to do with him any more, and I felt as if the Savior didn't want to have anything to do with me". His burning fever forces him to say "*Aes-che*" (I am thirsty).* They hand him a sponge with vinegar. The Savior sucks on it, finds further strength, and cries out "*Salém kuléchi*" (It is consummated). And, after a while, "*Ábba, beyadách áfkedh ruchí*" (Father, into your hands I commend my spirit). Resl sees rocks bursting open. The Savior bows his head and gives up the spirit. At that same moment, Resl too sinks back onto her pillows like a dead person. Her lower jaw settles somewhat, like that of a corpse, and her mouth is open a little, her face turns ashen and pallid, her nose looks more pointed, and one would certainly think that she were dead.

At this point, as a rule, the Passion visions come to an end. On Passion Friday and Good Friday, however, there are a few other visions that follow after a brief interval:

1. The thieves' bones are shattered. Therese turns away with a shudder and can hardly manage to look up at the Savior, because she fears he will suffer the same fate. Then a soldier comes along with a lance and pierces the dead Savior's side.

2. The Mother Mary is standing under the cross. They take out the nails, untie the Savior, and, with the aid of a long cloth, let the body down from the cross. Therese already knows the people who are helping. They were with the Savior during the night (Joseph of Arimathea, and Nicodemus). The ladder did not look like the kind of ladder we are used to seeing: it was a strong pole with pegs set into it, slanting somewhat upward, alternating on right and left.

3. The Mother of Jesus is sitting on a carpet and resting against a stone. Her dead son is laid on her lap. Resl sits quite still and watches, deeply moved.

*When these words were first recorded, Professor Wutz could not believe it. He had expected something quite different—*sachena*—and he pronounced the word for Resl. But she would change her story: she had heard the word *aes-che*. Then Wutz consulted some specialized research volumes and found that there is such a word meaning "I am thirsty." As far as he could determine, it is a Modern Hebrew word. Modern Hebrew seems to stand midway between Ancient Hebrew and Aramaic. This obviates any attempt to explain these phenomena on the basis of suggestion.

4. Resl sniffs the air. Her nostrils distend. She smells something sweet, the fragrance of the ointment with which Mary Magdalene, her clothing still sprinkled with blood, is spreading the
long linen cloth—perhaps the cloth used to take Jesus down
from the cross—which is going to be wrapped around the Savior.
Therese lays one hand over the other to show how Jesus' hands
were arranged. Then the dead body, wrapped as described above,
is further bound with swatches of cloth. Therese moves her hand
suggesting the manner in which the body is being wrapped, while
she watches it in vision. She also sees them carrying the corpse
away; "the one who pierced the Savior with his lance" and another soldier are helping with this work. The body is laid into
the tomb, which is not far from the hill of crucifixion. In a
further vision she sees the priests and Pharisees very ceremoni-
ously sealing the tomb. She falls back onto her pillows and sinks
into a death-like sleep.

This is the general course of the visions of the Passion, the
Friday visions. They were not always divided in precisely this
manner, from one vision to the other. In terms of content, they
were always the same; that is, Therese never saw anything different
from what she had seen in another Friday vision, even though
the total material included in her visions did vary in the course
of her life, sometimes developing somewhat and at other times
somewhat abridged.

In a conversation with Therese, in 1947, when she was in
her normal waking state, I received the following bits of information about the Passion visions: "When the Savior was hanging
on the cross, you could see a little empty space between his arms
and the crossbeams, not as much as in our pictures where the
crosspieces are horizontal, with the crosspieces above and the
arms underneath, but just the opposite. One of the crossbeams
was set lower (on the stock piece) than the other."

A further note: "Longinus was not the captain who said
'Truly, this was the son of God.' This captain sprang from his
horse at the death of the Savior, surrendered his position of command, and promoted his immediate inferior in rank. This was
Longinus, who then pierced the body with his lance. Both of

them were baptized on Pentecost. Pilate's wife was also there, for the Pentecost baptism. In fact, she was even allowed to be present at the Savior's Ascension into heaven."

The tape recordings also contain the following interesting addition to our information: when the soldiers had divided the clothing and cast lots for the tunic (not with dice, but with little pieces of wood), the "old man who was with the Savior at night" (Nicodemus) came up to them and offered them money for the clothing and the tunic. They were happy to sell them to him. "They were happy that they had got some money for the bloodstained clothing; and the other man was even happier, but he didn't let them know it." Presuming the historical veracity of this vision, Jesus' clothing would thus, from the very beginning, have been preserved by his followers, so that some survival down to our own day—for example, the sacred tunic at Trier—gains considerable credibility.

By way of conclusion to the great Passion vision, allow me to quote from an entry in Father Naber's journal under date of March 6, 1930. The death of this very saintly man will certainly vindicate me of any charge of indiscretion: "Therèse has her Friday Passion ecstasy. During the crucifixion ecstasy, it happened that, while the visitors were passing in and out of the room, I was alone with Therese and was sympathetically contemplating in her the person of the dying Savior. Then she opened her eyes and gave me a very melancholy look. In her state of prepossession afterward she said: 'I saw you, too, under the Savior's cross; you looked at the Savior with sympathy and the Savior looked graciously upon you.' "

I believe that Father Naber's experience has shown us a path in which everyone can follow him. Those whom we address in prayer do not remain aloof when we pray. Often we are aware of this. Therese quoted the following little verse in order to cheer me up. The verse is known in many forms, but in simple translation: "Everywhere you look in nature you see some evidence of the great God. But if you want to see it more so, stand beneath a cross."

Within the framework of the Passion visions we must also

include the visions on two special feast days of the Church, the feast of the Seven Sorrows of the Blessed Virgin Mary, and the feast of the Precious Blood of Jesus.

Seven Sorrows
Friday before Palm Sunday (Passion Friday) and September 15

This day, on which the Church commemorates not only the Passion of Our Lord but, in a special manner, also the psychic agonies which his mother suffered when she witnessed his Passion and death, has been celebrated in a very special sense in some areas since 1423 and, in 1727, was introduced as a feast for the universal Church (Benedict XII). Pope Pius VII established a special date for this commemoration, outside Lent, on September 15, the day after the feast of the recovery of the Cross. Father Naber describes Therese's experience of this feast day under date of March 30, 1928 (1, 5), and March 27, 1931 (2, 56; the two are combined): The Feast of the Seven Sorrows of the Blessed Virgin Mary; Friday Passion ecstasy as usual. Since it is the Feast of the Seven Sorrows, Therese is able to come closer to Mary after the words "Behold your mother" and witness, in addition to the Savior's death, also the piercing of his heart, the taking down from the cross, and the burial.

On the feast of the Seven Sorrows of the Blessed Virgin Mary, Saturday, September 15, 1962, after seeing (on the day before) the last recorded vision of her life, the triumph of the cross, the exaltation of the Holy Cross, while she was sitting up and dressing, Therese suffered a cardiac infarction which, three days later, on September 18, 1962, led to her death. In the interval lay the feast of the stigmatization of St. Francis. For thirty-six years Therese had lived without food or drink. Before her last Communion on September 18, at about 10:00, she asked for some water, her mouth was so dry. Father Naber, astonished at this request, accordingly offered her the Sacred Host on the tip of a spoon in which there were a few drops of water. According to the exact words of Father Naber to the Author, preserved on a tape recording, the Host entered into Therese's body in the form of a Mystic Communion, as it always had in such cases before, upon coming into contact with her mouth, without any swallowing motion (and disappeared). Father Naber was then called to the confessional and the housekeeper, Resl's sister Marie, went into the kitchen to prepare dinner. Therese was left all by herself. Perhaps she experienced the "I am thirsty" of the Savior on the cross, and his terrible sense of abandonment. At the very hour at which she regularly saw the agony and death of Christ in her vision, she made her departure. The vigorous shaking of her little bell was still summoning the members of the household.

Father Naber, in his conversation with this Author on the subject of Therese's death, was of the opinion that it was Therese's Guardian Angel who had rung the bell. Therese herself, he said, was lying absolutely helpless in her bed; because of her heart condition and the indescribable pain it caused her, she had to lie supported by several pillows, and turned away from the wall, and she was so weak that, when she experienced her Mystical Communion in her ecstatic state, she was not able to raise her head. He thus considered it quite impossible that she could have rung the bell herself. To do so, she would have had to turn completely around and then exert all her strength to raise her hand in order to reach the button. He feels that it was only by the extraordinary assistance which Therese frequently enjoyed from her Guardian Angel that he was able to assist her here as well.

There is, however, the possibility of another explanation. I had made photo copies of the journals that Father Naber had loaned me in 1962, and when I examined them once again for this book, I came across a sentence—apparently forgotten by Father Naber—which I must quote here. Under date of December 5, 1930, he writes (N2, 10): "On All Souls' Day of that year the Savior appeared to Therese. Immediately after that, the memory of the visions filled Therese with such great joy that the wound over her heart opened and the blood poured out, soaking a huge thick compress which Therese still had over the wound, because of an expiatory suffering she had recently undergone. Shortly after, Therese showed me the stain. It appeared to have been completely drenched in bright red blood. In her state of elevated calm she had once said that she would die one day of just such a welling up of love."

It is possible that, after experiencing the first abandonment of the hour of death, the final "It is consummated" was experienced in a great surge of love, a beatific vision, which gave her the strength to summon her family.

Feast of the Precious Blood; July 1
(Introduced by Pope Pius IX, 1848.)

Father Naber records, under date of July 1, 1928 (1, 24): After midnight Therese sees the Savior for the third time praying during his agony in the garden, and her heart begins to bleed. About 5:45 in the morning she sees the crucified Savior's heart being pierced by the soldier. Today her heart bleeding is particularly heavy, until about 9:00, when Therese receives Holy Communion and then sees the Savior in transfigured glory.

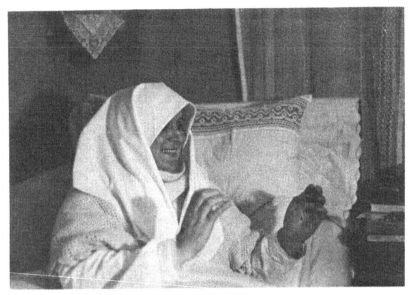

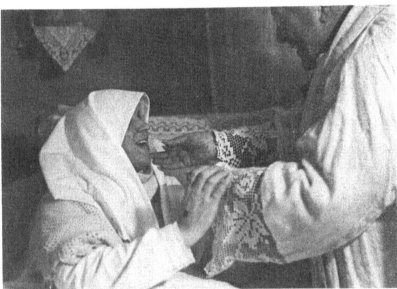

Ecstatic Communion, Easter Sunday, 1936. In place of the priest, Therese sees the Savior himself approaching with the Sacred Host.

CHAPTER TEN

BLEEDING FROM THE STIGMATA AND LACK OF NOURISHMENT

(Sources: Dr. Seidl; G1, 276ff.; Dr. F.X. Mayr, Bloody tears
and bleeding from the stigmata; deposition under oath
by Therese Neumann—Excerpts.)

The Passion visions were such a central factor in the events at Konnersreuth that we cannot permit ourselves to leave the subject without addressing the related problems. This problem is the impossibility, from the point of view of natural science, of such considerable expenditure of energy and substance without any natural recovery by food and drink. Both elements of this incongruity must be established by our testimony. For the frequency of the Passion visions—as already observed, they occurred about 700 times between Therese's stigmatization and her death—and her peculiar ability to involve not only the eye of the spirit, but her entire body, in sensing and experiencing details of her visions naturally aroused considerable interest throughout the world, and brought hundreds of thousands of visitors to Konnersreuth over the course of more than three decades.

It was widely discussed and published by newspapers throughout the world that Therese Neumann did not need any food or drink and it was observed that, in addition to the normal physiological discharges through respiration and the expenditure of calories involved in physical activity, she also lost a considerable quantity of blood on Friday Passions and her liquid level was appreciably diminished by onsets of perspiration during and between the Passion visions. This contrast between the expenditure of substance and the lack of any energy replacement was absolutely inexplicable in any natural terms, and thus the world of medicine was called in.

It was, after all, quite contrary to all laws of nature for someone who lost two or three pounds in every series of Passion visions because of the immense physical exertion and enormous loss of blood to regain her normal weight three or four days after this loss without any form of nourishment and particularly without any intake of liquids. In order to establish that the facts in this case seem to have no natural explanation, the Bishop's Office of Regensburg, with the consent of Therese herself and her parents, arranged for a vigorous observation (1927) for fifteen days by two doctors and four nurses, who were under oath. This observation took place on July 14-28, 1927.

It was established that during this time Therese actually took no food or drink, but that her weight, which was 121 pounds at the beginning of the observation and which dropped as the result of her two visions of the Passion which occurred during this period of observation, was, at the end of the examination, without benefit of any food or drink, once again 121 pounds. Medical and theological skeptics were unwilling to admit these facts and came to Konnersreuth to be convinced of the bleeding on the Friday Passions. Some of them had no opportunity to witness themselves the acute bleeding. They saw only the dried blood and based their accounts on these negative indications. This led others to take an even more extreme position, and Michael Waldmann, professor of theology at Regensburg, went so far as to make the slanderous accusation that Therese was prepared for her Friday visions by being smeared with menstrual blood. Since such statements also made their way into the literature on Konnersreuth, and were thus given considerable circulation, it would seem appropriate to cite some actual witnesses who did observe the stigmatic bleeding.

Dr. Otto Seidl, sanitarium director at Waldsassen, was officially charged with the observations of 1927. Dr. Ewald of Erlangen was also called in for final observations. His account comprises thirty-four typewritten pages. I reproduce here excerpts from his main chapter III on the results of the observation: Subchapters 1, nourishment intake, 3, maintenance of weight, and 7, ecstatic states and bleeding.

"*1. Nourishment intake*. The nourishment intake was the object of the greatest and most painstaking attention throughout the entire period of the observation. All the instructions, for washing, for water to rinse her mouth, etc., were most strictly adhered to. Despite this most painstaking observation, it was not once observed that Therese Neumann, who was never alone for a single second, ever ate anything or ever in any way attempted to eat anything. Not only was the patient's bed subjected to a rigorous examination at the start of the observation, but it was made fresh every day not by one of the staff, but by one of four nurses under oath. Neither I nor any of the sisters could possibly admit that any failure in observation could have occurred with respect to the nourishment intake. Throughout the period of observation, only the following elements entered Therese's body:

"a. At her daily Communion, she was given a small particle, about one eighth of a normal host. Even if one were to compute that, in the time from July 14-28, about three entire hosts were thus consumed, the total combined weight still would be only thirty-nine grams.

"b. In order to help her swallow the host, she was regularly given some water, in the measure of approximately three ccm; the combined volume of the water given to her from the morning of July 14 to the morning of July 28 would thus be about fifteen times three ccm—approximately forty-five ccm, or about the volume of three teaspoons full of water.

"c. As was carefully described in the instructions, whenever Therese wanted to rinse out her mouth, the nurse would give her a precisely measured volume of water; the water was afterward caught into a basin and carefully measured. The volume of water before and after was different only on two occasions: on July 16 (Gr. H. II W. 8) there was a deficit of five ccm. The nurse mentions that when Therese spat out the water "some of it spilled on the floor". On July 17, in the evening, there was another deficit of five ccm (Gr. 8. H. II W. 10). For all the other occasions, there was no measurable deficit observed.

"3. *Maintenance of weight*. Therese's weight, in order to avoid any possibility of error, was always taken without shoes and wearing the same clothing. On Wednesday, July 13, she weighed fifty-five kg, and on Saturday, July 16, her weight had gone down to fifty-one kg. The weighing on July 20 shows fifty-four kg; on Saturday, July 23, 52.5 kg; on Thursday, July 25, fifty-five kg. The original weight on the first day of observation had been reached again. This is the most surprising element in the entire observation. The fact that the weight on the Saturday weighings showed a loss of four kg. the first time and a loss of 1.5 kg. the second time is to be explained by the activities of the preceding Friday: the elimination of urine, blood, vomit, the extraordinarily intensive metabolism during the ecstatic states, and the extensive perspiration which followed the ecstatic states (Gr. H. I W. 6, Gr. H. 2 W 28). The fact, however, that Therese showed a gain in weight, three kg. in the first case and 2.5 kg. in the second case, without taking any nourishment or liquids, is to be explained by none of our physiological laws or experience.

"Now it is true, and clinical observations to this effect have been made available to me, that people who are starving often do not experience thirst, since when the albumen breaks down, enough water is released to support life. This would demand a considerable reduction in albumen, and this simply was not the case with Therese Neumann.

"Two objections will be made against the facts established by this observation. Some people have doubted that the controls enforced by the Catholic nurses were strict and foolproof enough to prevent Therese from possibly obtaining some nourishment or liquid. I must emphatically stress the fact that these nuns, as is obvious from the entries made in the continuous record at the beginning of each shift, were absolutely without any prejudice whatsoever, and, under the influence of the oath administered to them by the bishop, carefully saw to their duties, and that, further-more, after the time of observation, they expressly and repeatedly assured me that there could not have been any possible opportunity for Therese Neumann to have taken any nourishment during the period of observation.

"The second objection would be that the observation period was too short since it would certainly seem possible for a person whose metabolism was kept to a minimum to go fourteen days without eating and not show any appreciable loss of weight. The force of this objection would, under all circumstances, have to be admitted, even though one must not lose sight of the fact that, in the short period of observation, it was possible to establish a loss and gain of weight in each of the two weeks in question. The details of metabolism must certainly, under any circumstances, be subjected to a thorough examination. This would be easiest to achieve in a clinic or at least in a hospital. But if Therese's obstinate father, who apodictically stated that the current observation was the first and also the last official examination of his daughter, declares that he will under no circumstances permit such a procedure, then at least one must insist that all the patient's stools and urine be sent to me, in their full quantity, so that I could conduct the proper laboratory examinations."

Author's note: One might well inquire what justification there would be for the world of medicine to impose a sort of intensive quarantine on an innocent person who has never been found guilty of any deceit, after submitting her to a period of observation to which she and her family both agreed, an observation which established the full truth of her abstinence from all food and drink, with the exception of daily Holy Communion, or to submit her to further observations and experimentation such as artificial nourishment, etc., simply because the results of the just completed observations cannot be medically explained.

Prior to this clinical observation, it had been established on the basis of medical and biological data that a person could live without any nourishment, and especially without any liquids, for eleven days at the very most, and it was within reason that a fifteen days' period of observation was determined upon. Therese Neumann, who would have run the risk of death had she not been sure of herself, was just as fresh and healthy after these fifteen days as she was before. She had, accordingly, brilliantly passed the examination undertaken at the wish of the bishop's office.

If her "obstinate father" had given his consent for further experiment, then surely we would have experienced what Cardinal Prysing (Eichstätt and Berlin) foresaw when he warned so urgently, namely, that one clinic would refuse to credit the results of another and would demand one experiment after another. Suppose the experiment did not work out satisfactorily the second or third time? Perhaps the visions or the bleeding would have stopped, or perhaps Therese's strength would have broken, if, for example, they had experimented with refusing her daily Communion. The events of Konnersreuth must be viewed with something more than the eyes of natural science. It is enough to dwell on the imperious words from Therese's ecstatic state which Father Naber was once directed to address to a clergyman waiting with other visitors outside the door: "There is someone standing out there who wants to know something that has already been said. Go out and tell him he doesn't need to bother coming in, the Savior will not let himself be experimented with."

This clergyman was carrying some relics that another clergyman had already shown to Therese, asking her to distinguish which were genuine and which were not genuine. The priest now wanted to submit them to a second test, to determine whether the judgement would be the same. The same posture reflected in these words of Therese's ecstasy was taken by Jesus himself during his lifetime: when the Pharisees asked him for some sign to prove his Messianic mission, he refused them but those who follow him with perfect trust are privileged to see and experience his miracles. Father Naber, a very pious man, and a man whose faith in Konnersreuth could never be shaken, views the mystery of this lack of nourishment from a mystical point of view. He writes (2, 47): whenever she was asked what she lived on, Therese would say, quite simply, "On the Savior." She meant "on Holy Communion." Her life was a literal fulfillment of the Lord's words: "My flesh is meat indeed and my blood is drink indeed."

"7. *Ecstatic states, bleeding.* Even though the nuns were primarily concerned with observing Therese's nourishment intake, throughout the time of the observation, they were also concerned, on the Fridays during this period, when the bleeding began, with the possibility of some, even unconscious, self-inflicted wound, and the course of Therese's ecstatic states occupied the full interest of their attention. The ecstatic states begin in the night of Thursday-Friday, and last until Friday noon. They are of unequal duration and are interrupted by periods of rest, also of unequal duration. Therese's physical and psychic involvement in the objects of her visions is clearly evident by her facial expressions and her bodily movements, stretching out her arms, wringing her hands, etc. The tableaux of her ecstatic visions are concerned with scenes in the Garden of Olives, the scourging, the crowning, various scenes along the way of the cross, and finally the crucifixion. She seems to be completely carried away from the world during these ecstatic states, and insensitive to anything that goes on around her. Even during the periods of respite, she is not entirely awake, only alert enough to understand questions asked of her which she usually answers abruptly and in a manner reminiscent of a child. Usually it is not until late Friday evening that she comes completely to herself.

"The individual observations made by me and the nurses during the Fridays concerned can be summed up as follows.

"a. Thursday, July 14, to Friday, July 15.

"Since about 11:00 Therese has been engaged in lively conversation about her childhood and her family. Suddenly, at 11:17, her body suddenly jerks upright in the bed, into a sitting position, her hands outstretched, her eyes half open, half closed. Duration: fourteen minutes. There is no sign of any bleeding. Immediately after this experience I arrived in Konnersreuth by auto.

"11:43, ecstasy: From the left eye, all of a sudden, there is a spontaneous flux of blood which is immediately used for a blood test. Immediately after that, blood flows from the right eye.

"12:10, ecstasy; there is an increased flow of blood from both eyes. Duration: 2 minutes.

"12:32, ecstasy. The wound over her heart also begins to bleed. About one finger's width from the left side of the breast bone, and about the level of the fourth rib, one can see an approximately three cm. stripe, not quite as wide as one's finger, slanting from right to left, edematose, and slightly raised from the surface of the surrounding skin. It looks as if the outermost layer of the epidermis were laid bare. Examining with a magnifying glass, one notes a watery fluid, similar to small drops of perspiration, emptying from the wound, and turning a blood color as they flow from the wound.

"A blood test was immediately made from the blood flowing from the wound over her heart.

"From 11:17 until 2:13 there were eighteen ecstasies; the first lasted fourteen minutes, the others from two to five minutes.

"From 3:05 to 6:45 there were twenty-one ecstasies, each of them lasting three or four minutes.

"From 7:00 to 12:02 there were twenty-one ecstasies, lasting each from three to eight minutes. Around 8:00, at the vision of the crowning with thorns, blood appeared in the general pattern of a crown from the part of her head covered with hair. About 7:30, photographs were taken.

"From 12:02 until 12:06, the great ecstasy, which lasted fifty-four minutes. Around 12:56 Therese sank back on her pillows. A short time afterward she experienced a strong outburst of perspiration. In the course of the afternoon Therese presented a very exhausted impression. The total number of ecstatic states which appeared on this Friday were fifty-two.

"b. Thursday, July 21 to Friday, July 22. 11:17. Once again, quite suddenly, during an ecstasy, the first bleeding from the eyes.

"11:27, ecstasy; duration three minutes. Bleeding begins from the heart wound.

"12:15, ecstasy; duration three minutes. The bleeding from the left and right eye becomes stronger.

"From 7:00 until 11:48 there were twenty-five ecstasies (lasting from two to five minutes). Around 8:00, bleeding from the part of her head covered with hair; around 11:00 photographs taken.

"The total number of ecstatic states observed on this Friday was twenty-three. The Passion ecstasy displayed, in general, the same course as before, the same convulsive jerk at the beginning of the ecstasy, sitting posture in bed during the ecstasy, the same play of expressions on her face, stretching out her arms, wringing her hands."

On the occasion of this official observation, accordingly, not only Therese's lack of nourishment intake, but also her acute stigmata bleedings were definitely established by the physician in charge and the four nurses who were working under oath. A second unexceptionable witness is provided by a man who had thorough training as an historian, a man employed in a responsible position in the state archives, at this time active as editor-in-chief of the "Müncher Neuste Nachrichte," the biggest newspaper in southern Germany, Dr. Fritz Gerlich. He gives an explicit account (I, 276ff.) of the stigmata bleeding on Holy Thursday and Good Friday, 1928 (excerpts).

"On Holy Thursday, at 10:27 PM, Therese experienced her first vision. This lasted until 10:31. The stigmata were raised and had a wrinkled appearance. She saw Christ on the street with ten apostles; Peter and John had been sent ahead. . . .

"In the twelfth vision, from 11:40 to 11:43, she saw Christ's second prayer (in the Garden). Her eyeballs began to bleed. The upper eyelids forced the blood down on her lower lid. After 11:43, at the end of the vision, Therese Neumann fell back onto the pillows. A drop of blood lodged in the corner of her right eye; from the corner of her left eye a drop of blood began to run down her face.

"In the thirteenth vision, 7:49 to 11:52, a drop of watery blood came from her right eye, from the inner corner of the eye.

"Around 11:50 the bloody tears had grown so numerous that the first drops of blood were falling from her face onto her bed-jacket. A second stream of blood came from her left eye. Suddenly she said: 'What's that on my neck?' Blood was dropping onto her neck.

"This conversation was interrupted by the fourteenth vision, 12:04 to 12:05, during which the bleeding of her eyes increased. She saw the policemen coming with Judas.

"Around 12:07 the surface of the stigma on her left hand

was still dry, as determined by an examination with the aid of her electric night lamp.

"For the sixteenth vision, 12:18 to 12:20, I did not ask any questions. My whole attention was taken up observing that the surface of the stigma on the back of her left hand, which was turned toward me, suddenly showed a rupture.

"In the seventeenth vision, 12:26 to 12:27, during which Therese saw Christ being led away by the policemen, as she explained when questioned in her state of prepossession, the stigma of her left hand began to bleed. The edge of the surface closest to her wrist began to rupture. In the bleeding part something like an air bubble was visible. The blood was dark red.

"12:37 to 12:38 Therese had her eighteenth vision. The stigma on her right hand began to bleed, and the stigmata on the top of her feet also began to bleed.

"During the nineteenth vision, 12:41 to 12:43, she made a powerful attempt to grasp something with her hands. Asked about this in the ensuing state of prepossession, she explained: 'One of them struck the Savior for no reason at all. The Savior said something sharp.' The stigma on the back of her left hand had, during this time, become quite swollen, and, when examined from the top, the surface was smooth and of a dark blood color. It had been ruptured by the first bleeding, and then it was completely open, with bright red blood flowing out over the back of her hand. For some time she groaned at the pain from the wound over her heart. 'It hurts so much.'

"In the ensuing state of prepossession she appeared very exhausted and oppressed with the heat. She wanted to take off her smock, and asked me to leave the room. I did not want to break off my observations, however, and thought that I might be able to create the impression I had left the room by simply turning my head for a moment and speaking out into the room. The attempted deception did not succeed.

"The twenty-first vision lasted from 1:05 to 1:08, on Good Friday morning. Christ was being led before Caiphas, as she explained from her ensuing state of prepossession.

"During this state, she kept crying out in pain: 'Savior, I just can't.' During this time the stigmata on her hands began to bleed again. One could observe that the surface of these wounds sank somewhat when the blood began to flow.

"At 1:37 Therese experienced her state of elevated calm. She spoke with her customary energy and explained that the Savior was now comforting and strengthening her. During this conversation she referred to my above-mentioned attempts to deceive her, and severely reprimanded me, telling me to make no further such attempts. I should realize that I would see everything there was to see. 'Look,' she said, 'The Savior has said it all. If you would gain the entire world with a lie, what profit would you have? What is the world worth?'

"Then she advised us to get some rest. We were too tired from the journey, she said to me. We should come back around 7:00. Thereupon, we left her room. There was no denying our weariness following the more than eight hours spent in the car and the three hours of most intense observation, with no intervening rest since our arrival in Konnersreuth; I was glad to follow her advice.

"Next morning, around 7:00, I was in Therese's room. I stayed there until 8:25.

"I found her in her state of elevated calm. From her eyes and hands fresh blood was flowing strongly. The stigmata in her hands also showed fresh blood. Around the stigma itself was a dried crown of blood.

"On Good Friday morning, in her state of elevated calm, Therese offered her left hand, when I asked her, for a more exact observation. I informed those present, that is, the pastor and Professor Wutz, of what I was about to do and explained to them that a rather superficial examination might lead to the impression that there was a thin layer of skin right under the surface of the blood. But if one examined more closely, one could note what I thought I had seen the previous night: a little layer of skin extending from the outer edge of the blood which had overflowed and dried down in the rupture as far as the stigma itself. In the continuation of this rupture towards the inner core of the stigma itself, one could see only red blood, deep in the wound. Now, as Therese held her hand out quietly, so that we could turn it toward daylight, there was no longer any doubt that I had made a correct judgment the night before. My two companions confirmed my observation. I could not refrain from saying that the little piece of skin, stretched smooth around the area of the stigma, appeared to be the epithelium, the little piece of skin underneath the scab of the stigma, observed from the other side.

"During this period of observation and during our conversations, Therese lay there in her state of elevated calm, silent, eyes closed, with a gentle smile on her face. She let us move her left hand and do everything required to achieve the best conditions for observation, and even allowed me to examine it several times. When I expressed the above opinion, she suddenly began to speak, and told me that I had seen it correctly. What I had observed, she said, Dr. Seidl had identified as newly formed epithelium under the scab of the stigma. Later, Therese explained that the same thing could be perceived in the wound over her heart. I had not previously asked to see the wound over her heart. Since there were many visitors on this Good Friday, there was no opportunity in the morning for the form of observation that I had been able to pursue the night before.

"At 1:51 on this Friday afternoon, Therese's great vision of the death on the cross was over. The blood from the stigmata on the inner surface of her hands had joined with the bleeding from the stigmata on the back of her hands to form streams of blood which ran together under the ball of the thumb, on the side of the little finger. The stigmata on the back of her hands were dry and contained many ruptures; in the most pronounced of these the skin was once again visible, extending from the uppermost edge of the crown of dried blood to the edge of the stigma proper. Beyond that the blood was dark, and of the same color as the stigma itself. The observations made at different times were thus in complete agreement.

"After the vision of Christ's death on the cross I did not observe any further bleeding from the stigma. The quantity of blood flowing from the stigma was so considerable that the sleeve ends of her white bed jacket, decorated with small ruffles, were drenched in blood. I do not know if there was any blood elsewhere."

These two statements, made by the observers who could hardly be surpassed for exactness and detail, should certainly have prevented any later visitors, who for one reason or another were unable to observe the acute bleeding themselves, from spreading the above-mentioned calumnies to the effect that during the intervals between her visions, Therese was smeared with her own or someone else's blood in order to impress the visitors.

These accusations were properly and unequivocally answered by Franz X. Mayr, professor of biology at the philosophical and theological high school in Eichstatt, in the lengthy statement "Bloody Tears and Stigmata Bleeding in the Case of Therese Neumann of Konnersreuth, an Argument against Hilda Graef." The following is an excerpt:

In the book of Hilda Graef, *The Case of Therese Neumann* (Cork, 1950), much attention is given to an account written by Professor Paul Martini in the year 1928 for the bishop's office in Regensburg. The situation and the essential content of this statement are, in brief, as follows.

On Thursday, March 22, 1928, Bishop Michael Buchberger of Regensburg, who had been enthroned only ten days previously, on March 12, the consecrating Bishop Heirl of Regensburg, Dr. Killermann, professor of biology, and Dr. Stockl, professor of physics, both of these last at the philosophical and theological high school at Regensburg, as well as Professor Martini all came to Konnersreuth.

Immediately upon their arrival in Konnersreuth, on Thursday afternoon, they visited Therese and her parents for a short time and then immediately went to their lodging. During the night they came back, in order to observe the beginning of the bleeding. Unfortunately, according to Martini's statement, Therese's eyes were already "filled with blood" when the visitors arrived.

Between the visions Therese complained of the great heat and said she needed some relief, something to cool her off. Thereupon, as Martini describes it, "she lifted up her covers, three times, so that we could no longer see anything of her head".

It is remarkable that Martini observed fresh blood on Therese's face and on her wound only when she had tried to cool off in the manner described above, or when they had just left the room. "The fact," he writes, "that the observers were asked to leave two or three times, at the precise moments when a new stream of blood apparently covered the wounds, necessarily arouses the suspicion that during these times something happened that was being concealed from observation." He concludes his observations:

"I was not in any position to find a proof for the spontaneous flux of blood from the skin, and 2. I was struck by a whole series of facts which make it obligatory for me to maintain a very critical attitude toward these phenomena."

Furthermore: "My reflections on the subject require me to make it clear that one cannot absolutely exclude the possibility of a 'pious deception based on psychological grounds' ".

The "pious deception" which Martini regards as possible could only consist in the fact that Therese or her mother either initiated or aggravated the bleeding in some way, in order to present an edifying spectacle and promote the reputation of their own family.

Hilda Graef paints a more precise picture of how we are to imagine this "pious deception". Professor Martini reports that, around 11:30, Professor Killermann received permission from Therese's parents to keep some of the blood on a little piece of cotton wadding. Hilda Graef (p. 64) adds the following remark as a footnote: "Commentary by Professor Waldmann, in a letter addressed to me, February 27, 1949:

"The observations of Professor Martini, together with Monsignor Buchberger, Bishop Hierl, Dr. Killermann, and the other visitors, were and are, in my opinion, of the greatest importance for the historians of Konnersreuth. It seems certain to me that Therese's mother aided in this "bleeding". Not simply on account of the observations made by Professor Martini and Professor Killermann, but also because Killermann was able to examine the blood which he took as a sample, and thereby determine that it was not normal blood, but menstrual blood."

One needs to read these lines more than once to realize that Professor Michael Waldmann of Regensburg is here, in perfect earnest, claiming that the blood which Professor Killermann took from Therese Neumann during her Friday passion of March 23, 1928, is not normal blood, but menstrual blood. There are only two possibilities here: either the claim is true or it is false. If it is true, we are faced with an act of incredible deception. It would mean that Therese and her mother were using menstrual blood to simulate a true bleeding from the stigmata. This would be a shameless mockery of the Passion of Christ, of which genuine stigmatization is an image and a copy. Could God possibly give a person who was guilty of initiating or allowing such a monumental deceit the special grace of genuine visions, mystical union, lack of physical nourishment, etc.? This would mean that all the other extraordinary phenomena of Konnersreuth were an illusion and an imposture, and had been for many years.

If this were really the case, and Professor Waldmann is truly convinced of the truth of his claim, then why did he not make it known earlier, why did he not issue a public warning against this imposture? Why does Hilda Graef conceal this important discovery from her readers in a footnote, as if ashamed of it? We must only conclude that both parties are not so terribly convinced of the truth of their claim. And if what they say is not the truth, if the blood in Therese's Friday passion is genuine blood from the stigmata, then their claim involves a most irresponsible slander. There are grounds for examining the truth of the situation with the most painstaking attention.

Professor Killermann was gracious enough to give a precise description of his examination of this blood in a letter addressed to Dr. (M.D.) J. Mittendorfer, of Munich, dated July 27. He had received the blood samples from Father Naber, he said, but since these were already dried, he solicited Therese's parents' permission to take some fresh blood, with a bit of cotton wadding, from the area around her eyes. Under microscopic examination he was struck by the fact that there were no red corpuscles to be found. He thereupon had the "fresh" sample sent by his friend Professor Birkner, an anthropologist from Munich, to Professor Merkel, at the forensic medicine institute at the University of Munich, without identifying the source of the blood sample.

According to Killermann, Professor Merkel's verdict, dated March 16, 1928, is:

"The sample is blood, and, moreover, human blood; the lack of traceable corpuscles is peculiar. Human blood without traceable corpuscles is menstrual blood, which, however, generally contains ephithelium cells containing glycogen from the vagina. No such cells could be found in the sample studied. The lack of corpuscles seems to me to be an interesting peculiarity; it is not normal."

Obviously, then, the sample proves to be blood, remarkable for two peculiarities: 1. It had showed a most peculiar lack of traceable corpuscles. In this, according to Professor Merkel, it was similar to menstrual blood; 2. The blood examined did not have any epithelium cells containing glycogen from the vagina, as menstrual blood regularly does. What, then, is the final verdict?

The blood sample was taken around 11:30. During this time, Therese undoubtedly was not experiencing a vision, but was rather in her so-called state of child-like prepossession, during which time the stigmata never bleed. The blood which was taken from under the eye can, accordingly, have come only from the preceding vision. It has been our experience that the blood which flows from Therese's eyes and from her stigmata is possessed of a full and normal coagulation faculty. Thus, the blood under the eyes could well have coagulated already to a considerable degree, and during this procedure, as is well known, the corpuscles would be held fast by the fibrin fibers as they began to segregate. What Professor Killermann gathered as a sample on his cotton wadding was certainly nothing more than red colored blood serum.

Professor Merkel is perfectly correct in stressing the fact that the blood of this kind is not normal. Neither are bloody tears normal; in fact, they are much less normal than menstrual blood.

It is a shame that Professor Waldmann did not inquire into the possible sources of such a great quantity of menstrual blood as was necessary for each Friday Passion. As we see in Gerlich (II, 132), since the summer of 1918, Therese did not experience any menstruation (with the exception of one time, somewhat later, which was the result of medication). As for Therese's mother, who died in 1949, her family are witness to the fact that she stopped experiencing menstrual periods immediately after the birth of her youngest son already in 1912. From whom did this blood come? Even if the quantity of blood lost during one Friday Passion amounts to only approximately one liter, still, this is an enormous loss of blood and this can be substantiated by the experience of washing the blood-drenched towels and linens which Therese used during every Friday Passion. Now the quantity of blood lost at each menstruation is only thirty to fifty ccm. Anyone can figure out what a tremendous number of young women would have had to participate in what Waldmann calls the "swindle at Konnersreuth". One must also remember that stigmata bleeding took place not only once a month, but almost every week.

Now for the statement of Martini. As we have observed above, he is writing about the possibility of "a pious deception". If, like Waldmann, he is referring to the alleged use of menstrual blood, then the arguments against Waldmann are valid here. According to the examinations made by Professor Merkel and others, there was absolutely no possibility of using animal blood to deceive people. The only possible maneuver that could have accomplished the deceit would be the use of human blood coming from a wound. Are we to understand that this blood came from some other person, who repeatedly kept wounding himself in order to supply the requisite blood, or was it artificially prepared blood, perhaps blood used for transfusions, quantities of which are always on hand in our large hospitals? Nobody could seriously believe such a suggestion.

If there is still supposed to be some element of deceit, the only possibility is that Therese's wounds were not spontaneous, that they did not bleed of their own accord, but that she had wounded herself, or that during her Friday Passions she would regularly irritate the surface of her own already existing wounds so that the desired blood would appear. Such conduct would be entirely at variance with the widely known character of Therese, and such deception would long since have been unmasked, given the constant controls and observations to which Therese was subject, especially during the Friday Passions. Moreover, wounds which are artificially induced or aggravated or kept open never remain so unchanged in appearance year after year. On the contrary, they would have a tendency to heal, to become infected, or to change in some other way. Even in the case of very serious hysteria, artificial wounds behave much differently than Therese's.

We see that Professor Martini also gave too little reflection to what he wrote. A few simple considerations such as those mentioned above would certainly have told him that in Therese's case the bloody tears and the stigmata were really genuine.

By way of conclusion, let us quote Professor Ewald, M.D., a teacher at the University clinic of Erlangen. Toward the end of the official observation of Therese Neumann (July 13, 1927, 8:00 P.M. to July 28, 1927, 11:00 A.M.), he came to Konnersreuth in order to assist Dr. Seidl in performing a careful final examination. One might note, anticipating the eventual objection that the observation was carried on too exclusively under Catholic auspices, that Dr. Ewald was a Lutheran. Dr. Ewald published a report—without the consent of the person involved, thereby losing the trust originally accorded him—in the *Munchner Medicinische Wochenschrift* (Munich Medical Weekly), no. 46, 1927 (pp. 1981ff.), describing the details of the supervision and investigation. With respect to the bleeding he writes:

"I shall sum up the considerations which lead me to consider that, in the case of the stigmatic under question, every deception can be considered excluded:

1. Microscopic investigation has definitely established the fact that Therese Neumann's case involves genuine blood-flow.

2. The spontaneous onset of this bleeding has been observed by several doctors, sometimes with the magnifying glass.

3. The quantity of bleeding is such that it could not very well result from any artificially induced wound, without resulting in some identifiable scar, for example, in the *conjunctiva tunica* of the eyes, given such a frequent repetition of the bleeding.

4. In the case of the heart wound, what is involved is not a discharge of pure blood, but rather a blood-serous fluid, such as could hardly be induced by an artificial wound.*

5. There was no tendency to infection or festering, which could certainly not have been avoided if the bleeding had been artificially induced.

6. The alterations in the stigmata on the hands, at the termination of the ecstasy, speak for a spontaneous alteration of somatic condition in these areas.

7. One might also cite that the controlled observation of this patient for a period of fourteen days was so thorough that it seems most improbable that there could have been any artificially induced wounds that went unnoticed by her attendants."

*In connection with the point made by Ewald in this paragraph, the peculiar fact that it was not pure blood which came from the heart, but a blood-serous fluid, we might point to the Gospel of St. John (19, 33-34): "But when they came to Jesus and saw that he was already dead, they did not break his legs. But one of the soldiers pierced his side with a spear, and at once there came out blood and water." That is, coagulated blood and serum, because Jesus was already dead when he was pierced with the lance, and his blood had already broken down.

Testimony given under oath, part of it earlier but most of it accumulated more recently (1971), make it unequivocally clear that Therese Neumann's lack of nourishment intake, established as a fact in 1927, lasted until her death (from 1926 until 1962). Professor Carl Sträter, S.J., of Regensburg, was commissioned by Bishop Rudolf Graber to determine whether or not an informative process should be opened regarding Therese Neumann, to assemble all relevant material and to interrogate all living persons who had any close connection with Therese, and to make an official record of their statements after explaining to them the significance of an oath they were asked to take.

In execution of this commission, Father Sträter spent a few days in Konnersreuth in June of 1971. He addressed a request to the population of Konnersreuth and vicinity, which was published in Konnersreuth in the form of a public notice. It was also preached from the pulpit, and made known through the local press, that anyone who had information about Therese Neumann, be it against her stigmatization, her lack of nourishment intake, or, in general, against her moral behavior, should appear and make a statement. No one appeared.

Many people did, however, appear to recount benefits or help that they had received from Therese. During these days, Father Sträter visited all the living sisters and relatives of Therese Neumann and received statements from all of them, under oath, without exception, that they had not given Therese anything to eat or drink from the year 1926 to the time of her death, that they had never seen her eat or drink anything, that they had never observed anything which would point to any kind of discharge from bowel or bladder. Almost identically worded statements, taken under oath, were also made by her parents before their death, regarding the time from 1926 to the date of their signature: these are available at Regensburg.

Therese herself has left us a statement, made under oath, before the ecclesiastical commission in January of 1953, answering questions referring to chapter four, her lack of nourishment intake: "I have been living absolutely without nourishment, and without any need for food or drink, since Christmas of 1926; in the period from Christmas 1926 to September 1927, I regularly received the Sacred Species at Communion with a spoonful of water. Since that time, I have no longer done so; since August 6, 1926 I have felt a strong repugnance and nausea towards it. According to my conviction and knowledge, I am living from the sacramental Savior, who remains within me, according to eye-witness accounts and my own experience, until shortly before the next Communion. After the dissolution of the Sacramental Species, I am seized with a feeling of weakness and a strong physical and psychological longing for Holy Communion." This statement from the stigmatic herself, made under oath, is a fitting conclusion.

CHAPTER ELEVEN

THE BURIAL OF CHRIST

During Therese Neumann's life, and even during the last years of her life, it was customary for the celebration of the liturgy for Holy Thursday and Good Friday to be held in the morning, and for the Easter Vigil liturgy to be held on Holy Saturday morning. The faithful could receive Holy Communion on Holy Thursday, not on Good Friday, but once again on Holy Saturday. This I mention for the sake of the younger generation who are unfamiliar with the older forms of the liturgical usage.

Despite the intimate connection between the visions and other phenomena of Konnersreuth and the celebration of the liturgy, in this particular case the bond appeared to be broken, more or less in anticipation of the present-day liturgical usage, which corresponds more accurately to the actual course of Jesus' death and resurrection. On Holy Saturday Therese would generally sleep for the entire day, until Easter Sunday morning. Only with great difficulty could she be aroused, for her bath.

Still, towards evening, she usually had a very interesting vision. The content of this vision is recorded on tape, in the form of an extended conversation. I present an abridged form: Therese is speaking in her state of prepossession:

In the night a man, the one who went to "I can't make up my mind" (Pilate), the one who owns the garden and the tomb in which they have laid the Savior—meantime, Therese has given an explicit description of the appearance of the beautiful tomb with its marble facing—goes out onto the street. He is met by men who were around the Savior and they ask him a lot of questions. You can recognize the man and the other people only when they stop under the burning firepots, the ones on the fork-like posts; it is so dark already. Then all of a sudden some people come from the Temple district, and they have an argument with the other people. You can see at once that they have nothing good in mind. All of them who can run fast run away. "In fact, you can say they really run away fast." Only this older man could not run so fast, and he's the one the other people wanted particularly to find. And so he is caught.

They lead him then to the wall and through a gate and then along the wall to a tower. They put him in and bar the entrance. "What they are planning is that he won't ever come out. He looks so tired, and he must be hungry too; he didn't have time to eat anything, and he's probably very frightened. He makes me very sad." Then he gets up and prays and stretches his hands up to heaven. "What else can you do but pray when you are in a situation like that?"

All of a sudden there is a luminous man standing on the circular wall of the open tower, and calling to him: "Arimathai," or something like that. He says nothing else to him and extends a long cloth down to the astonished man. He ties it around himself, following the directions he has received, and holds onto it tight with both hands. He held it with his feet against the wall, which seems to be made of rather coarse stonework, while the luminous man lifts him up. And so he comes to the top which is not very much higher than the broad wall, built for walking on, and he climbs down. Then the luminous man together with his cloth disappears.

Joseph of Arimathaea—obviously, the hero of this story— now looks around in order to orient himself in the darkness and to be sure that there will be no further unwelcome encounters. Then he walks along the wall moving from one section to another, until he comes to a point where he knows there is a way down, "in the vicinity of the house in which the Savior washed their feet". Presuming that Jesus' followers are up there, he goes up and knocks on the door. After considerable hesitation on the part of those inside, and only when they have determined who this nocturnal guest might be, he is admitted into the house and everyone rejoices at his deliverance. "It all worked out just fine." End of the vision.

In her description of a later vision, Therese mentions that the capture and freeing of Joseph of Arimathaea took place not on the Passover feast (Saturday), but on the night before, that is, Friday night.

Gerlich (1, 232) records the following for Holy Saturday, April 7, 1928: Since about 10:00, Friday evening, Therese has been in a deep sleep which—so far as Father Naber knows—has been interrupted only for a brief interval, in the morning, by her elevated state of calm. Because of the duration of her sleep, she did not receive Communion today at all. She had told us in advance that the Savior would remain sacramentally within her from Thursday until Easter Sunday.

Father Naber records the following in his journal (N2, 57) for the Holy Triduum, April 2-4, 1931: At her Communion on Holy Thursday Therese receives an entire Host, although she was not privileged to have a vision of the Savior before Communion —this was normal for her during Lent. The Host entered her body without any swallowing motion. On Good Friday and Holy Saturday she did not receive Communion. The sacramental presence of the Savior within her lasted until Easter Sunday. The visions of the eating of the Paschal Lamb up to the burial; deep sleep during the Savior's rest in the sepulchre, as before.

Apropos of the exceptional events of Holy Saturday, April 4, 1942, as described above, Professor Mayr says the following: On Holy Saturday, Father Naber, Father Kraus from the Cathedral of Eichstätt, and I were visiting Therese about 8:00. We found her sitting in bed complaining of an attack of vomiting. From time to time she would be seized with a fit of coughing and bring up a little foamy viscous discharge, as well as gall, as she described it, into a small cloth which she held in her hands.

While we chatted with her and observed her, she suddenly had a vision. She saw Joseph of Arimathaea being held captive in a tower and being freed by an angel. When the vision and the ensuing state of childlike prepossession had passed, she was once again seized with a fit of vomiting, which had terminated during the ecstasy. Suddenly, when her choking was particularly pronounced, she cried out in fright and held the hand with the cloth in front of her mouth, which was half open. As well as she was able without closing her mouth she said "The Savior, the Savior" in a tone of mourning. Then she put out her tongue to show us what had happened. On her tongue lay a white object of the form and size of a small host, but swollen and pliant.

There could be no doubt that this was the host which Therese had received on Holy Thursday morning in Holy Communion. It had remained undissolved for three days and two nights, and now her attack of vomiting had brought it into her mouth. Therese was totally at a loss as to how she could handle what was for her a most painful situation. Strangely enough, she did not make the least attempt to swallow, but made motions as to take hold of the host with her fingers, whereupon Father Naber took her hands as a precaution, and held them fast. Then he tried to calm her and told her to ask the Savior to enter her soul once again. Therese immediately complied with his advice and began praying with childlike gestures, holding her hands up.

Suddenly she was quiet, her mouth closed, although for only a short time, her hands were crossed over her breast and her face took on a peaceful and happy expression, as it always does when she enters her state of elevated calm. When she opened her mouth again, one could see that it had disappeared. None of us had noticed even the slightest swallowing motion. The Host had again entered Therese's body in the same way it always did on the occasion of her ecstatic Communion. Her state of elevated calm lasted for some time, during which the pastor was informed that this violent attack of vomiting would not continue, and this was actually the case. The choking and vomiting seemed to have been connected with a suffering of reparation.

We were able to make a precise observation of the Host as it lay upon her tongue. During the time, Therese's brother Ferdinand came into the room and made the same observation.

(This account was prepared by me during the Easter vacation in 1942, read to Father Naber, and guaranteed to be fully correct).

CHAPTER TWELVE

THE EASTER VISIONS

(Sources: N1, 8; 2, 58; G1, 234ff.; Witt 2, 27; Tape*
conversation between Therese Neumann and the Author.)
[*The dialect phrases, with one or two identified exceptions,
have been transposed into High German, preserving as faithfully
as possible Therese's own form of expression.]

The Resurrection

Beginning of the vision: Easter Sunday, 5:00 A.M., Therese,
after sleeping more or less continuously since Good Friday, is
transported before the Holy Sepulchre in Jerusalem. Roman
soldiers are keeping watch in front of the tomb, obviously very
weary. A radiant morning is dawning; the sun is just about to
rise. Therese is terrified, looks up, and—is radiant with joy.
What has happened is this: While the earth was trembling, the
Savior, with a glorified body, comes out of the wall of stone.
The stone in front of the tomb falls to one side, pushed by a
"luminous man" (angel); a second luminous man hovers over
the tomb, while the first sits on the stone.

The soldiers on guard "keel over" flat on their faces; only
one of them manages to "act hold of himself" and stand up
again; he is the one who pierced the Savior's side. Therese sees
the Savior gliding through the air to the place of crucifixion.
His mother, in obedience to an impulse, had gone there earlier
that morning (according to Father Naber, this detail was added
in a state of elevated calm). In her state of prepossession Therese
says that she did not see this, it is only her opinion, as she puts

it: "She probably went with the other women and then said, 'Go ahead, let me alone for a while.'" Therese, in her vision, follows the Savior ("It wasn't very far"), and observed his meeting with his mother who sees the glorified Savior in the midst of her sorrow. He says a few words to his astonished mother and then disappears.

Therese's description of the details of this vision, prompted by Father Naber's questions, is indeed moving. He says: Resl, tell us everything, all in order. Didn't the luminous men come first and roll away the stone and then the Savior came out? *Therese*: You can't say it in any order. The earthquake, the Savior comes out through the stone wall, the luminous men come, the stone is gone—it was all at once. *Naber*: But then didn't the Savior come out of the doorway of the tomb? *Therese*: He would have had to stoop, but he didn't have to do that. He came out above through the rock wall, standing perfectly straight. *Naber*: Then you must have looked up. *Therese*: Yes, I did. And how radiant the Savior was. He was like living light, and yet you could tell that he is flesh and blood and his wounds were particularly brilliant. Each of them had a "brightness" of its own. And his garments were like light too; they didn't fall in a straight line to his feet, but were sort of tied in the middle. *Naber*: Then you also saw the wound over the heart, even though he was wearing something over it? *Therese*: Yes, indeed I did: His clothing was not "the kind of material our father (he was a tailor) used for making a suit; it was all luminous, like nothing in this world, and the wounds over his heart shone brilliantly through it. Oh, how beautiful it was." The luminous man "moved the stone, and there he is like something out of this world". What a magnificent picture it is.

The Women at the Empty Tomb

Second vision: Therese is once again in front of the tomb; the men are still lying about on the ground, except for the one who still has a puzzled expression on his face. Then comes the "maid" (Magdalene) and the three women. They are frightened by the spectacle. It all looks very terrifying, "the men all lying around on the ground" and the tomb open. (The luminous man who was sitting on the stone was no longer there.) The women hesitate to come closer. But Magdalene and one of the others, the "tall one," take courage from the silence all around and cautiously make their way past the guards. They are carrying some vessels,and Magdalene is shielding a small light under her shawl. (The other two women stay outside.)

With considerable exertion they push open the inner door, which was still closed, and looked into the tomb. This inner door to the tomb was made of metal (in her Good Friday visions, describing the burial of Jesus, Therese says it is "red, like it was made of copper." The efforts of two women are sufficient to open it. It was still closed even though the Savior has already risen, the heavy stone, which they would not have been able to move by themselves, has already been pushed aside). Magdalene takes a few steps into the tomb, but does not see the Savior. She sees a luminous man who speaks a few words to her.

She runs back out in her excitement, calls to the women outside, and then runs up the mountain as fast as she can, and through the entire city to the house in which the men of the Savior (Apostles and disciples) have locked themselves. Therese follows her (in her vision). Magdalene pounds hard upon the door, and shouts several times. Finally a "young man" (John) and the man who "wept when the Savior looked at him" (Peter) opened the door. She quickly tells them what she has seen, but the Apostles do not believe her. Then Peter and John hurry along the road to the tomb.

Peter and John at the Tomb

Third Vision: Therese is once again in front of the tomb. The man who pierced the Savior's side with his lance and afterwards helped carry his body to the tomb (Longinus) goes into the tomb. He does not see the luminous man, but is quite surprised to find the tomb empty. He touches the cloths, then goes out and admits the other women. They see the luminous men standing at the head and foot of the place where the Savior had been laid. The angels speak with them briefly, then the women run back out, apparently still quite frightened.

Shortly after this, John, who could run faster than Peter, arrived at the tomb. The guards are still lying around like corpses; Longinus is no longer mentioned. John looked in the empty tomb, but does not go in. Therese, in her state of prepossession, wonders why he was unwilling to enter. Father Naber tells her that he was waiting for the elder Peter, to let him go in first. *Therese*: "That's probably it." As soon as Peter arrived just outside the garden, the Savior suddenly appears to him; he looks at him just for a moment, without saying a word. This encounter obviously makes a deep impression on Peter, especially after he had denied knowing him in the courtyard.

John runs out to meet him and leads him by the arm through the garden gate and up to the tomb. There John lets him go first and then follows him into the tomb. Peter touches the cloths and is convinced that they are empty. They are lying there "just as if something had crawled out of them." Not unfolded, not balled together, but simply fallen in a heap; only the cloths that had been bound around his head were lying apart. Peter takes the cloths and puts them under his cloak. The luminous men are nowhere to be seen. John (whom Peter has probably told about his vision) now goes into the garden and looks all around, trying to see the Savior somewhere. Then they all rush back to the other Apostles, not through the large city gate, but through a smaller one. Longinus then also leaves; later, apparently, the other guards also leave when they come to their senses. During the next vision they are nowhere to be seen.

Jesus Appears to Magdalene and the Women

Fourth vision: Magdalene, who had probably been informing the other people of the events (perhaps she had been looking for the mother, Therese thinks) comes back, weeps, and looks into the tomb once again. Suddenly she sees the luminous men once more, and one of them speaks to her. She goes out into the garden very sad, weeps and starts looking. Then, in the sunshine, she sees a man coming to her dressed in a brilliant garment. Magdalene does not know him (neither does Therese), but she speaks to him in a questioning tone and, weeping, puts her hands over her face. Then—"all of a sudden the man turns into the Savior," radiant and beautiful, just as he was when he came out of the tomb, and says 'Miriam' ". Magdalene falls to her knees and cries "Rabboni". She wants to come up to the Savior, but he raises his hands in gentle refusal and points to heaven with the other hand, saying a few very kindly words to her. Therese recognized one of them, "Abba". Immediately after these words he "went away" (disappeared). Magdalene runs back to the women, who are still in the garden, once again looks to the tomb, and then "kept running and running," back to the big city. Where she went Therese could no longer see.

Fifth vision: The other three women now search all around the garden, inside and out. All of a sudden the Savior is there, not standing on the ground, but "higher" (hovering in the air). The women fall down and try to embrace his feet, but the Savior holds them back. "He went like this with his hands"—Therese raises her hand with the palm outwards—" he said something kindly to the women and then is gone again. Later the women went to the tomb and wept for joy. Now they were no longer frightened, because the upright men (soldiers) weren't there.

Therese comes back to the Savior and describes how beautiful he was. All the wounds from Good Friday were healed, she said, and could no longer be seen, only the marks of the wounds on his hands and feet and over his heart were brilliantly shining, as described above. Therese wonders whether we ourselves would ever appear so beautiful, and then decided that the closer we get to the Savior the more we will be filled with the light that emanates from him, and the more we will be radiant together with him. And certainly everyone who wants to come to the Savior can do so; if only he really wants to. Then she explains that her stigmata "don't hurt at all" today. This was true throughout Easter week, every year. Once (in 1928) in her state of prepossession, she asked the pastor to say only one thing in his sermon for that day: "The Savior is good, the Savior is good," even though the parishioners might consider it foolish. Thus far the visions for Easter morning.

I have a very precise recollection of a visit with Therese in the pilgrimage chapel at Kapel, close to Konnersreuth. This church is dedicated to the Holy Trinity and, as a result of its unusual plan, in the form of a cloverleaf, has three semi-circular sanctuaries, one of which is dedicated to God the Father, a second to God the Son, a third to God the Holy Spirit. The fresco in the first cupola represents the religious and secular states giving homage to God the Father, the fresco to the left shows the Resurrection of Christ, and the one on the right portrays the effect of the Holy Spirit and his gift of grace. While looking at the painting of the Resurrection, Therese said "My God, how unreal that is. These are just miserable colors. If you could really see how the Savior came out of the tomb, just radiant with living light, and his wounds shining brighter than the rest of him, then you couldn't ever look at a picture like this again."

At noon on Easter Sunday Therese generally had a vision that took her to Rome where she saw the ceremony of the papal blessing *urbi et orbi*. This will be described in a later section.

In describing this vision, however, Therese always returns to the vision of Easter morning, commenting on how beautiful they were and what a beautiful day the Savior had chosen for himself. And how "the maid and the young man ran so fast that the other man couldn't catch up with them."

The Emmaus Vision

The young man and a considerably older man are coming out of the big city (Jerusalem). They keep walking for some time, and are very sad. Therese has seen them earlier, with the Savior (disciples). While they are on their way, talking sadly to each other, another man comes up from the side, someone they do not know, and after greeting him continue to walk with him in the middle. (Therese does not know him either.) In their conversation with this stranger they are quite lively and tell him things and are surprised at what the man says. ("The Savior must have smiled at all this," Therese said after the vision.) They pass a neat little "village" and go into a rather tall house that is isolated from the rest. They stop there and prepare to enter.

But the stranger is ready to say goodbye and go his way. "Then they begged him to stay. They had to beg for quite a while." After that he goes in with them. *Naber*: "Did you beg him too?" *Resl*: "No, I didn't beg him, but I was happy to see that he was going in with them." It was already towards evening time. Inside the house they speak with the man who brings them something to eat and drink. You can tell that they are hungry: it was a long journey, and they had been "moving right along". The food set before them was bread in the form of flat oval cakes, rather light in color, "grooved" cross-wise on the top, and fish. With curved yellowish knives (brass?) the guests cut off pieces of the fish, which they then eat with their hands, just like bread. Finally their host offers them honeycomb. The stranger does not eat very much, though he does take something.

After a while he gets up—Therese still does not recognize him—holds his hands over the bread, looks up to heaven, picks up the bread, blesses it, and says something over it. Then he breaks it and gives it to them. "And at that moment they recognize—and so did I—that it was the Savior. He became so beautiful, just as when he came out of the tomb, and all of a sudden you could see his wounds shining brightly. Before that they could not be seen. He became just as beautiful as when he came out of the tomb and made his way, hovering in the air, to his Mother. On the road he also wore a white tunic, not a brown one; but it looked just as fine and white as the one he had there. At this moment, however, his clothing was all made of light again, more brilliant than snow in the sunshine. Then the Savior immediately rose off the floor and disappeared."

Therese felt sorry for the disciples left behind: "They would certainly have liked to keep talking with him. Do you know when the whole thing dawned on them? When they took the Savior into themselves. The Savior did it just as he did that night; he gave them Communion himself" (she refers to the Communion of the Apostles on Holy Thursday).

According to this vision, when Jesus took, blessed, broke, and distributed the bread to the disciples of Emmaus it was a true second Communion, and Jesus himself administered it. At the very moment of Communion the disciples were able to recognize him. And this is certainly the way we are to understand the Gospel of St. Luke, when he says: "He took the bread, blessed it, and broke it, and gave it to them. Then their eyes were opened . . ." (Lk 24:30), and somewhat later, "then they recognized him in the breaking of the bread" (24:35). For at the time in which Luke was writing his Gospel the expression "breaking of bread" was already the established usage of the early Christian community for the preparation and administration of the Blessed Sacrament. In her further conversations, Therese Neumann returns to this point: "It was just as when we receive the Savior in Church; and at the very moment that they took him into their souls he let himself be recognized. That was beautiful; I envied those men."

The vision continues: The disciples are so impressed and so happy and excited by their experience that they immediately call the inn-keeper and settle their account with him. The elder of the two has a purse tied to his belt; they pay their bill, put on their cloaks, and immediately set out upon a trip back to Jerusalem. Their weariness seems to be forgotten. Therese sees them walking for a while, and then the vision is over.

Jesus Appears in the Upper Room

Vision: After the two disciples have walked for some time, they come to the big city (Jerusalem) and to the very house in which the Apostles are staying (in the upper room). The Apostles were still keeping themselves locked in, because, as Therese says, they thought they would be imprisoned, "just like the man who was just locked into the tower" (Joseph of Arimathaea), after the burial of Christ, cf. the visions of Holy Saturday. The disciples kept pounding and pounding on the door, shouting out

who they were. Then Peter and John came out and let them in.
Then they locked up again. The atmosphere of the room was a
serious and troubled one. They had prayed and read from the
scrolls and would not believe what some individuals had told
them.

Then these two men came, and filled with joy and enthusiasm,
described their experience. "That is the first thing, to want to tell
something like this immediately; that is why they turned right
around and hurried back as fast as they could. Now, the others
didn't believe them. That's terrible. Why didn't they believe them?
Certainly you ought to believe somebody when he tells you
something." Peter was confused. Why, Therese asks. Did he not
really believe what he had seen himself? The two men tell their
story full of enthusiasm and the others laugh at them and think
that it was all their imagination.

"And while I see them arguing with each other, all of a
sudden the Savior is there. Now you must pay attention to how
I said this. All of a sudden the Savior is there. I didn't say that
he came, he is there. Not on the floor, a little bit higher." *"Shelám
lachón aná latéro."* (Peace be with you, it is I)—This is Therese's
pronunciation of his greeting. What astonishment. What joy. And
still there is some doubt. Is this perhaps not a ghost? They
hardly dare to speak to him. Then they bring up a "little lounge
chair" for him and invite him to sit down. He does in fact sit
down. But they still are not quite willing to believe. "They
thought that something wasn't right," and so they bring him
something to eat. And the Savior takes it and eats it, so that
they will see that he can eat. Not that he was hungry. Then he
speaks with them for some time, very seriously.

"All of a sudden he gets up, rises somewhat above the floor,
and says something, something powerful," and then he goes like
this:—and here Therese breathes heavily—"He breathed on them,
looked up to heaven, said something else, and then spread his
hands out over all of them. Then something tremendous happened, I could feel it (institution of the Sacrament of Penance—
A.). After this he says something else to them, something different from the rest, something not so powerful, I could feel it

(perhaps some words of farewell—A.). And then he disappeared; he didn't leave, he was just gone. When I talked about the other two, I said that they went away; but when I talk about the Savior I say he was just gone. That was beautiful, much more beautiful than when these two were walking along the road so sadly and then they brought on (literal expression) the Savior. Something beautiful follows something bad. That is the way it always is."

Father Naber asks how many of the Apostles there were in the upper room, if she could recall precisely. Therese counts in her usual manner, "One and one more and one more," etc., up to ten; it is obvious that she is attempting to recall the number she had seen, passing from one face to another. The pastor asked her again and once more she counted ten. When she was asked if there were not one more present, she answered: "That's all I can bring back." Father Naber laid particular stress upon this question, because the Gospel according to St. Luke (24:33) says: "They (the disciples from Emmaus) found the eleven together." According to John (20:24ff.), Thomas was not there for this first apparition in the Upper Room. Asked about this in her state of elevated calm, Therese later gave this answer: Copyists had introduced the reference to "the eleven". Perhaps, and this is the author's opinion, it later became the normal usage to refer to the "college of Apostles," after Judas' departure and before the election of Mathias, simply as "the eleven" without implying any more precise reference to the number actually present at any given occasion.

Jesus Appears to His Mother and St. John

Just as surprising and moving as Jesus' appearance to his Mother on Easter Sunday, because it too is recorded in none of our Gospels, is the following vision from Easter week: Therese sees Jesus' Mother with John, in Jerusalem, walking along the route that Jesus followed on his way to the crucifixion. They follow the way of the cross in a spirit of sad recollection, speaking now and then of what happened at a particular point along the way: they are, as it were, praying the first "stations of the cross". "With deepest compassion they kiss the ground, particularly in the place where the Savior fell for the third time" (N2, 58). Then suddenly the Savior appears to them, once again in the full glory of his Resurrection, looks at them lovingly, and speaks to them. Great joy is mirrored in Mary's face, and in St. John's—and for the observer, in Therese's face too, just as one could also observe the deep sense of sympathy that preceded it.

Jesus and Thomas
(Sources: N1, 10; A.)

This second apparition of Jesus in the upper room, Therese would see sometimes on the First Monday after Easter, a date suggested by St. John in the section from his Gospel read on that day (20:24-29), "Eight days later the disciples were all together in the house and Thomas was with them." Thomas had been missing on the occasion of Jesus' first apparition on the evening of the day of his Resurrection. When he returned and the other Apostles told him about Jesus' apparition, he spoke the famous words which stamped him as the greatest doubter of all time, and prompted Therese to refer to him, in her state of prepossession, by the name *"der Netglaubenwollerer"* (the man who didn't want to believe): "Unless I see in his hands the print of the nails, and place my finger in the mark of the nails, and place my hand in his side, I will not believe." In the selection from St. John's Gospel, which is faithfully followed by the course of Therese's vision, Jesus announces his constant omnipresence, even though he is not visible, by immediately inviting Thomas to touch his wounds; he makes his invitation immediately after his salutation, without any other exchange of information relative to Thomas' statement made during Jesus' (material) absence.

Content of the vision: Therese finds herself once again in the Upper Room, where she sees eleven Apostles. They are still keeping the doors locked, when suddenly she sees the Savior in their midst. Once again she says "He was there, not that he came." Once again she hears his greeting: *"Shelám lachón"*

(Peace be with you), whereupon the Savior immediately turns to Thomas. His gestures, as he points first to one hand and then the other and then to the wound over his heart, clearly indicate the meaning of his words. Thomas then falls on his knees and says a few words with an expression begging for pardon ("My Lord and my God"), whereupon the Savior speaks some more serious words to him.

Jesus Appears Bilocationally
Third Sunday after Easter
(Sources: N1, 11, recorded on April 29, 1928.)

The content of this vision is not described in the Gospels. St. Paul does indeed, in his first letter to the Corinthians (15, 5-8), refer to some apparitions of Jesus, among them one to "more than five hundred brethren," after the Resurrection, visions which are not recorded in the Gospels; but the apparitions seen by Therese in the course of this vision are not to be found among those described by Paul either. Perhaps one of the reasons they particularly strike our attention is the fact that the Savior appears almost simultaneously in two different places. Therese sees the following (as recorded by Father Naber): In the evening, around 9:00, the risen Savior once again appears in the upper room, where ten apostles (John is missing) and about forty disciples are sitting at table, eating fish and honeycomb; the Savior joins them.

The vision then continues with a different scene: The Savior appeared to his mother, John, Magdalene, the other Mary, and Salome at the city gate where Jesus had spoken to the mourning women. After the apparition they all run to the upper room, where both parties, in joyous excitement, tell each other what they had just experienced. These apparitions took place about twenty days after the Resurrection.

Apparitions at Lake Tiberias, and on Mountain in Galilee

After the apparitions which took place in the vision just described, the Apostles must have made their way into Galilee, presumably following instructions they received at the Resurrection. At all events, this would be only for a short time, since forty days after the Resurrection, for Jesus' Ascension, they are once again in Jerusalem. Galilee, however, is the setting for the apparitions recorded by John (21:1ff.) and Matthew (28:16ff.).

Therese sees both events on the days on which the corresponding sections of the Gospel are read, the apparition at the Lake of Tiberias on Wednesday after Easter, and the apparition on the mountain on Friday after Easter.

Tiberias: Seven men ("The earlobe cutter—Peter; the man who wouldn't believe—Thomas; the tall man—Bartholomew, also called Nathanael, the young man—John, and one more and one more and one more") fishing, without catching anything. They discover a man on the shore whom they do not know (Therese does not know him either) but when he instructs them to row back out, they do what he says, apparently with a sort of presentiment of who it is, and take a great quantity of fish. Then they recognize Jesus, who thereupon offers them bread and broiled fish. Therese sees more than what is described in the Gospels. Jesus asks Peter something three times and he answers him. (The three-fold question, "Do you love me?", whereupon the office of chief pastor is entrusted to Peter to "Feed my sheep" and, in conclusion, reference is made to his death). N1, 8; 2, 60.

The mountain in Galilee: Therese sees the eleven Apostles on the mountain ("In Galilee where Jesus had told them to go," Mt 28:16). The Savior is suddenly there, the Apostles fall to their knees, radiant with joy, and stretch out their arms as if in worship. A few of them are somewhat hesitant and watch the proceedings rather diffidently, until the Savior comes into their midst with his greeting of peace. He speaks some mighty words to them and holds out his hands over them: "All authority in heaven and on earth has been given to me. Go, therefore, and make disciples of all nations, baptizing them in the name of the Father and of the Son and of the Holy Spirit, teaching them to observe all that I have commanded you; and lo, I am with you always, to the close of the age" (Mt 28:18-20).

CHAPTER THIRTEEN

THE ASCENSION

(Sources: N1, 14; 2, 63; G1, 248; W2, 34;
Kaspar op. cit., p. 104; tape; A.)

"Most beautiful of all was the way the Savior took leave of his Mother. She was the last one he spoke to." This is how Therese, still weeping, describes this vision, after passing from her visionary state into her state of prepossession. Only with some difficulty could she be eventually led to describe the details in some sort of sequence. (The vision is here reproduced in abridged form, in the literary language, although with some quotations from the original dialect version—A). Her brother Ferdinand, who is trying to make a tape recording, keeps interrupting her with individual questions of details, which she refuses to answer, saying that he is too curious. Father Naber tries to calm her: "Resl, that is not curiosity, that is interest." Resl, speaking in the direction of her brother, who is still asking her to stick to the story and not jump around so much, answers: "You are so dense you need the Enlightener" (Therese's expression for the Holy Spirit). Ferdinand: "Yes, that would be a good idea."

First vision: Very early in the morning, around 4:00, the Apostles and Jesus' Mother are together in the big house in which the Last Supper was held. There are other men and women in the house as well, but in other rooms. They are having breakfast, and the beaked lamps are still burning. Suddenly the Savior is among them, even though the doors are closed. At first they are frightened. He says (phonetic transcription according to the tape recorder): *"Salém cho(n) aná latéro* (or: *latéru*)."* They offer him a cushioned chair and give him something to eat, and he takes a little of it. Then he speaks to them for some time. Perhaps, in addition to the instructions and promises he is giving them (cf. Ac 1) he is also telling them that he must now finally leave them, in his human form, because the Apostles are apparently informing a whole group of persons who thereupon join the subsequent activity (author's conjecture).

Second vision: Therese sees the Savior, together with all the people from the house and others who have joined them, going out, crossing the brook, and then continuing in the direction of the house of Lazarus (towards Bethany). "But only in that direction, not up to the house itself." After a while they turn off to the left, climbing up the mountain. The Savior is wearing a radiant white tunic. They are all barefoot. The Savior is walking, not gliding; and he is speaking with everyone.

Third vision: On top of the mountain the Savior first speaks to everybody once again, then to the Apostles, and finally to his Mother, whom he looks at with an expression of particular love. Then he holds his hands half raised and begins to rise up towards the rear, to the east. "Behind his back the sun had just risen. That was a beautiful picture: the wounds were brilliantly lighted and his clothing glistened like snow. The wound over his heart could clearly be seen shining through his clothing. And behind him the sun, all red and fiery, oh that was beautiful. And then he gave me a good long look, too. He rose very slowly, and then began to hold his hands downward. Then a beautiful white cloud came and then I didn't see anything more." Resl, who had wept during this vision, also weeps in recounting it. "Suddenly there were two luminous men (angels) there and they said something friendly to everybody. And then they were gone too."

At the end, Therese also sees the veneration of the footprints: John the Apostle looks reverently at the place on the ground from which the Savior was lifted into the air. Something on the stone strikes his attention and he points it out to everyone else: the prints of the Savior's feet have been left behind on the stone.

When asked if it was not rather Magdalene who had first seen the footprints, Therese clearly answered that it was "the young man," that is, John. "Then the mother comes up and the maid, and then all the rest of them, and they kiss the footprints. The one foot had pressed more deeply than the other."

In further conversation about the subject of his departure, Therese repeats that the Savior first "spoke to everybody, then to those who were always around (Apostles) and finally to the mother. Then the mother cried" (At the sight of this, Therese too had tears in her eyes, during the vision). "Oh if only the Savior had remained. We wouldn't have needed the hole" (the impression in the stone; Therese's expression in her state of childlike prepossession).

Among those present, besides the Virgin Mary and Magdalene who accompanied her, besides the Apostles and some of the disciples, she had also noticed a whole group of persons already known to her. First she mentions someone who is new to her. "The woman who wanted to help the Savior and sent her husband that shiny thing (Pilate's wife, cf. Passion visions); also the one who came back to life (Lazarus) and the one who pierced the Savior (Longinus) were there and the three who wrapped him up." Her description of the Ascension visions ends with a repeated reference to the magnificent tableau: The glorified Savior rising against the early morning sun (cf. Mk 16:19-20; Lk 24: 49-53; Ac 1:4-14).

Scenes from the Pentecost Visions. Above: Therese listens with rapt attention to St. Peter's Pentecost Sermon (the Pentecost miracle repeated!). Below: her expression reflects joy at the many baptisms.

CHAPTER FOURTEEN

PENTECOST

(Sources: N1, 15, G1, 248; W2, 35; Mayr; tapes.)

The first description of the Pentecost visions is a brief statement by Gerlich in the year 1927. In the lengthy record of Father Naber, for the year 1928, they are described as fully as they are in Witt's account—where they are given a pastoral interpretation. Father Naber, who refrains from any commentary, records under date of May 27, 1928: "May 27 (Pentecost Sunday). At about 8:30 Therese sees the twelve Apostles (she recognizes Matthias as a new addition) together with Mary and a great number of other people assembled in the Upper Room praying. Suddenly a powerful storm wind arises, a great tongue of fire appears in the air near the ceiling of the hall, from where it breaks down into thirteen smaller tongues which then appear over the heads of Mary and the Apostles. Then Therese hears the Apostles speaking in various languages, and finally she hears Peter standing outside in front of the hall, delivering a powerful sermon to the congregated people, in the German language.

"Then she sees the Apostles, outside of the city, near a pond which is surrounded by a wall, baptizing and laying on hands. Around 10:30, 12:00, and 1:30 she sees them still baptizing. Around 3:00 she sees that the baptisms are drawing to a close and Peter and John are on their way to the Temple. In her visions she sees the man born lame being cured at the Beautiful Temple gate; she sees him then rejoicing in the Temple with the two Apostles, while the enemies of Christ's cause are furious and finally have the two Apostles bound and cast into prison.

The cured lame man spent the entire night in front of the prison. Twice during the night Therese sees the Apostles in their prison. They are praying."

In the tape recordings, made some twenty-five years after, there is mention of many other interesting details, which are abridged in the following excerpts. On the evening of Pentecost Sunday, on the occasion of her final vision for that day, several persons were gathered around Therese, and in answer to their questions she recounted the content of various Pentecost visions. She begins:

"Now that didn't work out very well, after it started so beautifully."—She had just seen the imprisonment of Peter and John. "Early in the morning light and fire came down into this house and then the men inside spoke so courageously, and then they baptized all day long, and now these two are locked up."

We shall now arrange the events of this day, which Therese saw in six visions, into proper temporal sequence and reproduce them in Therese's manner of expression, but not in her native dialect. Many of the details have been added to her original description upon later questioning by her audience.

About 8:30 in the morning Therese sees the Savior and the twelve Apostles—one of them she had previously seen among the disciples; this is the newly chosen Apostle Matthias. They are in one of the rooms of the house where the Last Supper was eaten. There are some other women there too, but in a different room. There are also disciples in the house. But only the Mother is with the Apostles. All of them have been praying. Then, suddenly, with a frighteningly violent storm wind and a noise like that of thunder, brilliant light and fire come down from above into the room in which the Apostles and the Mother are gathered. The fire divides into thirteen flames, which burn brightly over their heads, but do not burn anything. "The big fire in the middle turned into smaller fires, which you could see burning for a while over their heads, in oblong flames, flickering at the top. The storm wind and the fire were all one." The Apostles could look at the flames over each other's heads, but they do not appear frightened, or sad, anymore; they are filled with energy and courage.

Since the sound of the violent wind could be heard throughout the whole city, but subsided precisely at this house, a multitude of people quickly gathered. Therese asks if it might be some festival day, since she sees so many foreign-looking and foreign-dressed people in the crowd. Father Naber confirms her conjecture. (It is the Feast of Pentecost, an eight-day festival, occurring fifty days after the Passover. It was the commemoration of the Law given in the Old Testament on Mt. Sinai). As more and more people gathered, Peter went out and spoke to the crowd with a mighty voice. Therese hears his words in the German language—the miracle of Penttecost, "each man heard in his own native tongue," is repeated here after 2,000 years—and his words are reproduced on the tape recording. These words were recorded by Therese not on the occasion of her first hearing them, but only afterward, in her state of prepossession, drawn from her memory, so that one might logically expect some gaps in her memory or some alterations in the words. She recites the sermon of Peter in High German, whereas her parenthetical remarks are in her own dialect.

"You men of Judea, and all you who dwell in Jerusalem, hear my words. We are not drunk, it is only the third hour. This is the fulfillment of the word of Joel, 'In the last days,' says God, 'I will pour out my spirit upon all flesh, and your children will prophesy, and they will see visions, and your old men will have dream visions, even upon my men servants and maid servants will I pour out my spirit in those days and they will prophesy. I will perform wonders in heaven above and on the earth below, the sun shall be turned into dark and the moon into blood before the exalted and great day comes. But all who call upon my name will be saved.'" Then the people started talking and were excited. He spoke very loud. Once or twice he had to brush aside the hair which the wind kept blowing into his face.

He started again—"You men of Israel, God gives witness for Jesus of Nazareth through the many mighty works, signs, and wonders which he has done among us. According to the plan of God and his foreknowledge, Jesus was delivered up and you tortured him through the hands of the godless, nailing him to the cross and killing him."— Some of them were really struck when he said that.—"But God brought him back to life. Death could not hold him in its power. David had already said of him: 'The Lord I have always before my eyes, he stands at my right hand, that I may not be shaken.' "

That's what he said, but I don't know what it all means. In fact, I couldn't catch everything. Then he continued—"My brothers, let me speak freely and openly of our patriarch David. He died and his mortal frame can be found among us up to this very day. His prophetic spirit and the well-known promise that God gave him under oath that he would raise up his posterity upon his throne allowed him to have a vision of the resurrection of Jesus. This is the one who is not destined to abide in death nor his spirit to look upon corruption."

Then he waited a while again and then he spoke powerfully—"After he was exalted and God gave him the promised spirit, he poured this spirit out, as you see and hear. And we are witnesses that God has made Jesus of Nazareth, crucified by you, Lord and Messiah." There were other things in between, and at the end there was something, too, but I don't remember it accurately. Then he said, "Let each and every one of you have himself baptized and thus receive the gift of the Holy Spirit." He talked a while longer, but in such a way that I could not grasp what was being said. (She could no longer hear him in German.)

Then they went out, Peter and all the others with him. Then the one who said *"Ganapa magera"* (one of the Apostles who had called Judas "villain" when Jesus was taken prisoner in the Garden) had some water and something white like salt, but not in a powder form; it was "all stuck together" (probably rock salt). When they came outside, he held his hands over the pool, poured the fluid into it, and threw in the white fragments. *Question*: Was the pool far away? *Answer*: Not far; you go down over the mountain on which the house is standing, then off to the side a ways, then down a little bit further, and the pool is built in such a way that you can climb up to it, on steps, just like the place where the Savior was baptized; there were steps like that there too. And when the other man had put the water and the white stuff into the pool and had held his hands out over it, Peter began speaking again, but I could not understand anything more. On one side of the pool and on the other side there are large halls.

And what is in these halls? "Nothing but white clothing with black bands around the neck and the arms, and around the bottom of the hem. They are something like little shirts. They are white, really more like yellow wool, and hemmed with black. All of those who were baptized received this kind of dress. It lasted for a long time. That way you could tell exactly who was baptized and who was not. The baptized people came out wearing the clothes. *Question*: Who distributed the clothes? *Answer*: Those who were not always with the Savior (disciples). The others upon whom the fire came down were not baptized, they did the baptizing. Not only Peter, but all of those who got the fire. The disciples were baptized first. There were shells already there, and when the people were immersed in the pool water was poured over them at the same time.

Around noon, it was very hot there. Peter spoke once again, but in his own language. He was always by the pool and they were all baptizing all the time. *Question*: Did you recognize any of them? *Answer*: Yes, several. The man who came back to life (Lazarus) and those from his house, the tall dark girl (Martha), the maid from the tomb (Magdalene) and one other woman who was sort of different, not stupid, but a little peculiar, and another man who sort of helped her (servant). Then there was the lady who offered the cloth to the Savior along the road (Veronica) with two maids, and there was the woman who wanted to help the Savior during the night, the one who sent something sparkling (Pilate's wife), she was present already at the Ascension. Then the man who jumped down from his horse and cried out "Amen, amen," and something else ("Truly, truly, this was the son of God," the captain who gave up his commision in the Roman army) and the man who pierced the Savior's side (Longinus) and some of the soldiers who were keeping order, many of them.

Both old and young were baptized, even children.

Question: Where did they get all these white clothes? *Answer*: I don't know; they were in the hall, and they were not new. Once before, for a festival, the people wore these white clothes. Morning and afternoon there was no opposition to the baptizing. But there was towards evening. Peter and John had gone to the Temple during the afternoon, while the other Apostles continued baptizing. There were round steps leading up, and there was a beautiful door with shining plates on it, magnificent. There are people sitting there begging. There was one man there who couldn't help himself. He was begging too, and one "particularly smug Pharisee" spat in his cup.

As Peter and John were going by, Peter says something to him. He looks at Peter, then Peter looked up to heaven and said a prayer, and all of a sudden the beggar felt strong and jumped to his feet. Everybody was amazed and the beggar threw down his hat, or whatever it was, with all the money in it, and didn't worry about himself anymore; he went into the Temple with Peter. He went right straight in, and then they went through the many tall columns and into a beautiful long corridor with a beautiful ceiling of carved wood. There were a lot of people there wearing white robes with the black hems, people who were just baptized today. There were other people standing around the columns too, also wearing white clothing, and they followed after Peter. Then John said something, but primarily it was Peter who spoke, powerfully. But he spoke in his own native language, and I could understand nothing.

The Pharisees and scribes were in a perfect rage, because all the people were on the Apostles' side. Then they got together with the other people (Temple guards?) and tied the Apostles up and carried them out, terrible. Then the "robe-cutter" (Caiphas) made some arrangements and had them locked up. Answer to the question: Not individually, but together in the same cell; they could talk to each other. They were not afraid. The man they had just cured stuck close to them in the Temple, and then I saw him in front of their prison.

Meantime, the other Apostles were still by the pool, baptizing. Then some people came up and started arguing with them. But these people who keep order in the Temple had no rights outside the Temple. Only inside could they arrest Peter and John. Therese laments once again that the day had begun so beautifully and now came to such a sorry end: "What is going to happen to them; they will never let them out." We tried to comfort her and tell her that "the Enlightener" was with them, and that he would soon help them.

Afterward, Therese returned to the subject of Peter's sermon and asked: "Who is Joel?" They answered her: "A prophet from the Old Testament." "And what does patriarch David mean?" *Answer*: "That is King David." "Why patriarch? Tell me clear and simple what Patriarch David means. And what does this mean: His mortal frame is to be found among us up to this very day?" *Answer*: "His body or his bones, just as we have relics." "I see, and what about his prophetic spirit and the promise God made to him under oath?" *Answer*: (Father Sollner): "He had a vision of the future Savior, centuries before his coming, and saw that death would have no part of him."

The discussion then turned back to the white garments and Resl remarked that she had already brought many of them to baptisms, and that, in the future, she would also "have black bands sewn around the edges of the white baptismal robes." (I never heard, however, that she actually did this in any of the many cases in which she was selected as godmother for one of the children in her large family relationship or for some convert—A.). The conversation also turned to the Apostles' prayer before Pentecost. When we mentioned the fact that there are nine days between the Ascension and Pentecost Sunday, and that these nine days of preparation are probably the origin of the novena devotions, Therese mentioned that she regularly observes such novena devotions, one right after the other, and frequently one overlapping the other, depending on the order of the feast days. At that particular time, she said, she had just begun a novena in honor of "the Enlightener" (Holy Spirit).

Pentecost Monday
(Sources: N1, 17.)

May 28, 1928. At 6:00 in the morning Therese sees Peter and John and the cripple they had cured standing before the Sanhedrin. The case concludes with the acquittal of two Apostles, who immediately make their way back towards the Upper Room, followed at a short distance by the cured cripple. There they are warmly greeted by the other ten Apostles. Then they all pray, whereupon they once more hear the storm wind. Then they celebrate the Last Supper, just as they did on Holy Thursday, except that Peter plays the role of the Savior, and the Apostles are much more aware and reverent. Finally they hold the communal meal.

Pentecost Tuesday
(Sources: N1, 17; 2, 74.)

May 29, 1928. At around 8:30 in the morning Therese sees the account described in the Epistle for Pentecost Monday: Peter is in a house belonging to a pagan (the house of the captain Cornelius, who had begged him to visit him) : He is speaking to the members of the family and some guests. His six companions are there too. While he is still speaking, he notices that they are all filled with the Holy Spirit, the pagans as well as his Jewish companions. He acquiesces to their wishes and has his host's entire family baptized, as well as the guests he had invited (cf. Ac 10).

In his entry for Pentecost Tuesday, May 26, 1931, Father Naber records the visions of Peter and John going to Samaria. Peter and John laid their hands on the baptized people, and the Holy Spirit comes down upon them. Simon Magus offers them money (he wants to buy their priestly power), but is sharply refused by Peter (cf. Ac 8:5-25; one excerpt from this story is read in the Epistle for Pentecost Tuesday).

Feast of the Blessed Trinity; First Sunday after Pentecost
(Sources: N2, 75.)

May 31, 1931. Therese sees the Gospel for this feast (which

is partly the same as that for the Friday after Easter, Mt 28: 18-20, A.): Jesus appears to the Apostles on the mountain in Galilee and gives them their formal mission and command to baptize "in the name of the Father and of the Son and of the Holy Spirit."

Corpus Christi
(Sources: N1, 18; 2, 75.)
Recorded by Father Naber:

On the Feast of Corpus Christi, June 7, 1928, at 6:00 in the morning, Therese has a vision of the institution of the Blessed Eucharist, preceded by the washing of the feet and the high-priestly prayer of the Savior.

During the Mass, she sees the Savior, at consecration time, coming down to earth from a multitude of singing angels, hovering on white clouds, and remaining before her eyes until Communion.

Therese has already finished one novena, and is in the middle of a second, praying for the grace to make a proper genuflection before the Blessed Sacrament; on account of the wound in her foot, she was unable. But today she received the grace of making a proper genuflection once again.

Corpus Christi, May 4, 1931: Therese has a vision of the washing of the feet and the institution of the Holy Eucharist. She notes particularly that the Savior spoke most kindly to Judas when he washed their feet.

CHAPTER FIFTEEN

ASSUMPTION OF THE BLESSED VIRGIN MARY

(Sources: N1, 35; G1, 262; W2, 40; Tapes: A.)

Preliminary Note: The following notes are based on observation and questioning of Therese in her room in her parents' home at Konnersreuth, during and after the visions of August 15, 1947. The notes were read to Father Naber and Therese in September of 1950 and corrected by both of them on many points. The following presentation is based, as a preliminary report, on other visions for other feasts of the liturgical year and on statements made in the state of elevated calm, and also draws heavily upon the notes of Dr. Fritz Gerlich, August 15, 1928 (I, 262-3).

The unlikely a priori assumption of Witt that two angels had opened the door to the tomb, escorted Mary out, and then left the tomb open, is contradicted by all the other sources, and by the author's personal questioning of Therese herself. How could a glorified body be circumscribed by any material limits, when even a body not yet glorified, like that of St. Peter, can be struck free of its chains by the touch of an angel and escorted through closed gates without any notice on the part of the doubled guard outside (Ac 12: 1-19)!

It must be noted that these visions do not begin with the promulgation of the dogma, "Mary bodily assumed into heaven," which took place in 1950, but already occur at the very beginning of Therese's visions, more than twenty years earlier.

Ephesus and Jerusalem

Mary, the mother of Jesus, had spent a few years with St.

John in Jerusalem after Jesus' Ascension: John was working in and around the city. Then they both moved to Ephesus. A few years later, during which time the primitive Church kept spreading, they were given a beautiful house, a few hundred yards southwest of the city, and they lived there for several years.*

Mary now receives a revelation to the effect that she has not much longer to live and expresses a desire to journey to Jerusalem to see and venerate the places where Jesus worked and suffered, one last time. John happily agrees in this desire and he accompanies her on the journey. In Jerusalem they are surprised to meet with all the other Apostles who had come together there.

Perhaps (mere conjecture on the part of the Author) the Apostles had convened, from their areas of activity in and around Jerusalem, for the Apostolic Council, which took place around 49-50. Perhaps, too, they were already working in widely scattered areas and, like John and Mary, had been guided to Jerusalem by some special impulse of the Holy Spirit. It is Father Naber's opinion that, in his loving kindness, the Savior had wanted to give all the Apostles one final opportunity to see his Mother and to experience both her death and the fact of her special distinction, her preeminence above all other human beings.

---

*This presentation obviously contradicts the account of St Epiphanius (403), and the Church tradition which has always maintained that Mary did not leave Palestine after Jesus' death. She had been committed to St. John's care by her dying Son. Given to him as a mother, she was received and acknowledged with great love and respect; why should she have any reason to part from him? Nor are there grounds, on the basis of contemporary research, for putting off St. John's apostolic work in Ephesus until after the Blessed Mother's death. We merely report Therese's visions as precisely as possible, and leave everything else to the subsequent judgement of the Church.

Mary's Death

First Vision: Therese sees Mary and the Apostles gathered in a large hall, which she recognizes from her earlier visions as the room outside the Last Supper room, the room in which the holy women were waiting during the Last Supper and preparing for the Passover by prayer and meditation. The Apostles have grown much older, but Therese still recognizes all of them. She does miss James (he had already been beheaded by Herod around the year 44 - Author) and Thomas. But then the number is increased by the presence of the temperamental Paul, whom Therese also knows from her other visions, and another man, whom all the Apostles treat as an equal, but whom she does not recognize and has never seen in any other visions. In Father Naber's opinion, this must have been St. Barnabas (cf. Ac 9:27; 11:22-30; 13:1-2; 15). The Apostles are reclining, as was the custom in those days, around the Blessed Mother. They are resting on upholstered couches. Therese also notices some earlier disciples and some women she does not know, "but they were sitting farther to the outside." None of the women were known to her. And there were no women sitting among the Apostles.

They are talking about Jesus, and while the Blessed Mother is moved with great longing and love for him, she suddenly grows very weak and pale and sinks back. John catches her and she dies with her head resting on the breast of her "second son," lying in his arms. At the same moment Therese sees her soul rising up from her body, a living but incorporeal luminous shape. The Savior appears with a tender smile on his face, radiating in the bright light, and takes her soul; then the luminous shape disappears from view. The Apostles stand sorrowfully around the dead body. John closes the Blessed Mother's eyes and mouth and kisses her on the forehead, the right cheek, and the mouth. Then all of the Apostles and women do the same. Therese takes a lively part in their grief, and during the vision tears stream down her cheeks. When she tells the story later in a state of pre-possession, she goes back into the state of visionary contemplation and the second vision follows, the burial of the Virgin Mary's body.

Her Burial

Second Vision: The body is prepared for burial by the women, anointed and wrapped in winding cloths, with pungent herbs bound into the bandages. Peter and James (the Younger) go out into the valley of the Cedron and look after a tomb for the Blessed Mother's body. It is hewn out of the rock that rises up from the valley floor, in such a way that the entrance is not vertical (as in Christ's tomb) nor horizontal (as in Lazarus'), but rises at an angle. First you go up a few stairs (there were more stairs in Lazarus' tomb, none in Christ's), and then the burial chamber narrows into a horizontal tunnel. There is no antechamber, as in the Savior's tomb, only a slanted gate lying right before the entrance. On that same day, a Saturday, the body was laid to rest and the sepulchre was sealed. The fact that it was a Saturday does not come from Therese's first telling of the story: it was a note she added upon being questioned in a state of elevated calm. The other indications of the day of the week involved in each vision all originate from a like source. The Blessed Mother's death occurred on the same day, but rather early in the morning. Therese recognized that it was morning by the position of the sun and the angle of the shadow, because she had seen this same hall at other times of the day as well (dinner time).

The Assumption

The following third vision is the most beautiful and moving, the principal vision of the Assumption. Therese sees herself transported before the Blessed Mother's tomb. It is early morning (Sunday); no one is to be seen far and wide. Suddenly there comes a light from heaven. Two angels come hovering down with the luminous substance of Mary's soul. Therese recognizes one of them; it is the angel of the Annunciation, Gabriel; the other she does not recognize (later, in a state of elevated calm, she mentioned that it was the Blessed Mother's Guardian Angel). The three luminous shapes make their way into the sepulchre without being hindered by the closed door. They come back out immediately, but Mary is no longer a transparent luminous form; she comes out with her living and transfigured body, radiant, and wearing a garment of light. It is indescribable; the closest description would be to say that it was as radiant as fresh new snow in the sunlight. But even that is not enough. Her head and hands are free, and only a little of her feet can be seen. The glory and joy of the apparition is shared by the visionary, and even those present can share something of it, since they are privileged to see a radiant human countenance, more brilliant than ever before.

The angels are escorting the Blessed Mother, supporting her with one hand under her arm and the other on her back; they are carrying her up into the air. This carrying is to be considered as an honorary gesture rather than a necessity; there is no longer anything material or heavy about the glorified body of the Blessed Mother (it had passed through the closed door of the tomb).*

Therese's eyes follow the figures and the expression of joy in her face suddenly mounts to its fullest possible measure. Christ appears from above, radiant in unspeakable glory, together with all the heavenly court, countless angels and saints. The Savior moves towards the Blessed Mother, St. Joseph at his side, incorporeal but still recognizable. When they meet in heaven, St. Joseph and the Savior take the place of the angels who were escorting the Blessed Mother, in order to lead her solemnly into heaven as Queen of heaven and earth, amid the jubilation of the blessed choirs of angels—since it was she who first joined together heaven and earth.

---

*The Latin names for *Ascension* and *Assumption* imply the essential difference between the manner in which Christ went up into heaven, of his volition and by his own power, and the way in which the Blessed Mother was taken up, not of her own power

With a genuine enthusiasm that far surpassed anything observable on the occasion of any other visions, Therese was able to share this glorious and joyful event. She cried "Take me along!" and raised her hand out towards the luminous figures hovering overhead, standing on the very tips of her toes, so that you had to look to see whether she was still standing on the floor or not. Actually, a group of absolutely trustworthy witnesses, among them priests, declared that on the occasion of the same vision in 1938 at the cloister in Steyler in Tirschenreuth, she was actually raised a little bit from the floor and hovered in the air for a while. On September 24, 1950, in Konnersreuth, I met an eyewitness to this event, Mr. Dost from Hildersheim, who vouched for its truth. Therese was lifted about a foot off the floor and stayed for a while in this position, hovering freely in the air.

Another experience must be recounted in connection with this vision: On July 1, 1940, when Therese was on her way back from the First Mass celebration of her convert priest friend Paul Lütten —formerly Lutheran, a high-school teacher in Hamburg—she had suffered a stroke. It attacked the left side of her brain in three distinct seizures (on July 7, 10 and 13) and made the whole right side of her body lame, witnessed by the attending physician, Dr. Josef Mittendorfer, of Munich. Her right leg was lame, the arm hung down. Her right eye could not coordinate with the left but stared straight ahead, resulting in squinting and great difficulty in seeing. The right side of her mouth was paralyzed, her tongue was impeded so that she could make herself understood only with difficulty. For nine days she lay in a sort of coma, her consciousness more or less impaired. On the occasion of the vision of the Assumption in 1940, the following occurred, in Therese's own words:

"When the Blessed Mother was taken away from the tomb by the angels, she smiled at me, then moved slowly towards me and held her right hand over my head. Then, although I otherwise never feel anything from without in the course of my visions, I suddenly felt a very strong electric shock in the right side of my body. I raised my hand to grasp our Blessed Mother's hand." Father Naber adds: "For all of us it was a very moving sight.

Therese suddenly shuddered during the vision and then with joy in her face she raised her formerly lame right arm towards the left side of her head. Her eye also straightened out at once and she could speak normally once more. Her eye kept moving throughout the rest of the vision and she could stand up and walk. We all experienced great joy." After the vision Therese was able to go into the church unassisted.

This even was also substantiated (in personal conversation) by the doctor who had been attending Therese immediately after the stroke for eleven days. He was also present for the sudden cure. There were other witnesses too, religious among them, including the Cathedral Preacher from Regensburg, Father Leo Ort, who had already related the whole experience to the Author.

It was fortunate indeed that Ferdinand Neumann was able to be present with his tape recorder when Therese had this vision in 1940, the year of her sudden cure. Resl also said: "The pain in my right hand has come back again (from the stigma): I hadn't felt that at all before." It is a most moving experience to listen to the tape recording and hear how everyone, especially Father Naber, are both laughing and weeping for sheer joy, and how their weeping for joy and laughing for joy alternate and overlap.

The visions did not close with this third apparition. In the midst of her joyous announcement of the cure she had just experienced, Therese suddenly sits up again. Her hands rise to shoulder height and she witnesses the following fourth vision.

The Apostles at the Empty Tomb

Thomas, who was missing at the Blessed Mother's death, (she refers to him as the "Netglaumwöllerer,"—"the man who wouldn't believe") has meantime arrived in Jerusalem (Monday). He is much disturbed at having come too late, but he does want to see the Blessed Mother once more, even in her grave. So all the Apostles agree to go to the tomb again, together. Therese sees them coming to the tomb and testing the unbroken seal (early Tuesday morning). They unseal and open the door to the tomb and look around in astonishment. They cannot find the body anywhere. The wrappings which had been used to prepare the Blessed Mother for burial are still in their place, and just as if they were still wrapped around a body. Therese smilingly tapped with her index finger twice. Later, when she recounted the story of the vision in her state of prepossession, she said that she was imitating one of the Apostles who tapped on the winding cloths with his fingers in two places in order to convince himself and the others that they were empty.

The wrappings had probably been stuck together by the ointments and propped up by the herbs that were wrapped together with the dead body of the Blessed Mother: this kept them from collapsing, apart from any outside influence. The departure of the Blessed Mother's body cannot be regarded as such an outside influence: her body was no longer subject to the laws of matter and thus would not be impeded by the wrapping cloths any more than by the rock walls and the door.

The Apostles all remark at the presence of an unearthly fragrance in the burial chamber. Therese shows that she can smell the same aroma by the way she draws in her breath strongly and gently dilates her nostrils. Her hand gestures and her expressions keep pointing upwards, where the Apostles are also looking intently.

After some time spent in lively discussion, the Apostles leave the burial chamber, obviously convinced that under the circumstances (sealed tomb, undisturbed wrapping cloths, unearthly aroma), the Blessed Mother's body must have been taken up into heaven, even though they did not witness the event themselves.

Author's note: They pass on this conviction to the Church, which in turn faithfully preserves it across the centuries, finally sealing it with official inclusion in the Marian dogmas during the Holy Year of 1950.

EPILOGUE

The limitations of this present volume force the Author to interrupt the presentation of Therese Neumann's visions at this point, and to incorporate the later visions in a second volume. Particularly in view of the fact that during 1972 many unscrupulous attacks have been leveled against the events of Konnersreuth, the Author does not wish to further delay the publication of a book which might serve as some defense. Inclusion of all the other visions in this one volume would involve such an unwelcome delay. The preparation of this volume involved not only the current year, 1972 (when the text was actually written and corrected), but also builds on many years of preparation and gathering of materials. A second volume will also require considerable time, since the Author must find time for this project in the midst of his many professional duties. Hopefully this companion volume should be realized in two or three years.

—Johannes Steiner

CPSIA information can be obtained at www.ICGtesting.com
Printed in the USA
LVOW01s1840250515

439755LV00041B/2182/P